Mummy

**Results of Interdisciplinary
Examination of the Egyptian
Mummy of Aset-iri-khet-es from
the Archaeological Museum
in Cracow**

Thadeo Smoleński in memoriam

Polish Academy of Arts and Sciences

Mummy

Results of Interdisciplinary Examination of the Egyptian Mummy of Aset-iri-khet-es from the Archaeological Museum in Cracow

Cracow 2001

Publication financed by the Committee for Scientific Research

Editors
Hanna Szymańska, Krzysztof Babraj

Executive editor
Elżbieta Fiałek

Design
Władysław Pluta

Cover photograph
Tomasz Kalarus

DTP
Inter Line SC
Piotr Hrehorowicz, Małgorzata Punzet
ul. Mogilska 43/204, 31-545 Kraków
tel./fax (48 12) 413 02 48
e-mail: biuro@interline.krakow.pl

ISBN 83-88857-25-8

Distributed by
Polska Akademia Umiejętności
ul. Sławkowska 17, 31-016 Kraków , Poland
tel. (48 12) 424 02 12, fax (48 12) 422 54 22
e-mail: office@pau.krakow.pl

Printed in Poland

Contents

Contents

Krzysztof Babraj
Hanna Szymańska

Introduction

The present volume contains a collection of articles written by specialists from various fields involved in research conducted on the mummy of a priestess of Isis named Aset-iri-khet-es,[1] who lived in Egypt during the Ptolemaic period (late 4th - 1st centuries B.C.).

In 1994, at the initiative of employees of the Division of Mediterranean Archaeology at the Archaeological Museum in Cracow, interdisciplinary studies were commenced on this mummy, which comes from the Ptolemaic necropolis at el-Gamhud, where excavations were performed in 1907 by Tadeusz Smoleński (cf. H. Szymańska). The very poor state of preservation of this mummy, which had been plundered in antiquity, and the necessity to empty the sarcophagus prior to conservation, led to the decision to conduct the research described in the present volume. The result constitutes an important contribution to our knowledge of mummification methods in Ancient Egypt, as yet not fully understood, and of various factors associated with burials in the declining years of Egyptian civilization.

The preservation of the human body after death was an essential precondition for prolonging that person's existence. According to Egyptian mythology, the first mummy was made by the goddess Isis, who assembled the dismembered limbs of her divine husband Osiris, after he had been quartered by his brother, Set. Every deceased person before being laid in the grave was identified with Osiris and subjected to complicated embalment operations, which were accompanied by specific religious rituals. Despite a great deal of information preserved in ancient sources regarding the methods of mummification, the process has never been recreated in a fully satisfactory form. Since the early 20th century,[2] scholars have attempted to verify the information given by such classical authors as Herodotus (II. 86-88) in the

[1] The name of this priestess was originally read as Iset-iri-hetes. Thus several of the publications cited here use this name. The change results from a later revision of the decipherment of her name; cf. A. Niwiński (in present volume, note 6).

[2] A. Lucas, *Ancient Egyptian Materials and Industries*, 4th edition revised and enlarged by J. R. Harris, London 1962, 270-326.

fifth century B.C., or Diodorus Siculus (I.91-92) in the first century B.C. The fragments of two papyri from the first half of the first century (papyrus no. 3 from Bulak and papyrus no. 5158 from the Louvre), copies of originals from the New Kingdom, are a much more valuable source; but although they provide us with many valuable indications regarding the embalming process, they cover only its final stages. At present it is necessary to verify all this information using the research apparatus that is available to us today.

The use of modern research techniques, the application of specialized analyses from various ancillary disciplines, and finally the unwrapping of the mummy brought extraordinarily interesting results. With due regard for the complex ethical factors involved in research on human remains, we were fully aware of the necessity to bring the mummy to a state that would make it possible to return it safely to the sarcophagus, its place of final rest. The decision was made to wrap the mummy in ancient bandages, with some additional modern bandaging added (cf. K. Babraj).

An Egyptological analysis of the sarcophagus and the cartonnage that lay directly on the mummy, as well as an extraordinarily painstaking interpretation of the highly unusual amulets found under the bandages, is presented by A. Niwiński in his article. During the autopsy a great deal of valuable information was obtained regarding the method of bandaging and the type of fabric used to wrap the mummy (cf. K. Tempczyk).

The first test performed on the mummy was spiral computer tomography, thanks to which it was possible to identify the bone elements, the remains of soft tissues, and the arrangement of bandages, which proved to be essential during the later autopsy (cf. A. Urbanik).

The anthropological analysis of the mummified remains, which made it possible to specify the age and height of Aset-iri-khet-es at the moment of her death, as well as the pathological changes in the bones and teeth of the skeleton, constituted an extraordinarily important part of the project. These examinations also produced her lifetime appearance, obtained thanks to a computer program (cf. M. Kaczmarek).

Physical, chemical, serological and histopathological examinations were performed on samples taken from the mummified remains. The results indicate that pine resin (*Pinus pinea*, *Pinus pinaster*) was used to mummify the Egyptian priestess from Cracow, while no traces were found of the bitumin universally used in the Ptolemaic period (cf. M. Kłys et al., *A chemical...*).

Serological tests performed on a sample of muscle tissue taken from the mummy made it possible to confirm the presence of human protein, which is testimony to the effectiveness of the mummification process. It was also possible to identify the blood type of the priestess (cf. M. Kłys et al., *A serological...*).

A skin sample taken from the scalp of Aset-iri-khet-es was used to clone a fragment of the genetic code (DNA) (cf. A. Sutkowska). Attempts to isolate ancient human DNA were first undertaken in the early 1980s. The goal of this research is to explore the mechanisms underlying evolutionary changes taking place in our species. In the present volume we have also included another article on DNA research, in which various procedures are presented to isolate ancient genetic material (cf. T. Grzybowski et al.). The experience gained during the genetic analysis of the Egyptian mummy turned out to be very useful in the routine casework of the Institute, particularly in the project of genetic identification of victims from mass graves in the former Yugoslavia, run by the International Commission of Missing Persons (ICMP).

During the autopsy a certain amount of plant and insect remains were also extracted. Thanks to microscopic and comparative paleobotanical analysis we know that underneath the cartonnage, between the first layers of the bandage, there were fragments of grain ears, leaves, and blades of grass (cf. M. Lityńska-Zając). On the basis of their morphological characteristics it was possible to specify the season of the year in which the priestess' funeral took place. An entomological analysis of the insect fragments indicated that only a few of them are of ancient origin. The extensive article by B. Gerisch includes an exhaustive listing of the insect remains found in Ancient Egyptian mummies from various historical periods.

Three further articles are devoted to the conservation work involved in securing the sarcophagus (cf. M. Paciorek) and cartonnage (cf. B. Aleksiejew-Wantuch), which had undergone significant destruction caused both by ancient graverobbers and by the unsuitable conditions in which the mummy was preserved. These articles are supplemented, in a sense, by a paper presenting the results of mineralogical and chemical tests of the pigments used in the polychrome ornamentation of the cartonnage (cf. J. Trąbska).

The volume is rounded out by two articles which, though not directly connected with this particular mummy, make an essential contribution to our understanding both of the process of mummification and of the preservation of mummies in museums. In the first of these articles, the author (M. Gomaa) attempts to prove empirically how natrite was used to dehydrate the remains during the embalment of Egyptian mummies. In the second article, the same author attempts to isolate the microorganisms found in the Egyptian mummies held in selected museums in Egypt.

It should be emphasized at this point that the interdisciplinary research on the mummy from el-Gamhud has engaged great interest and support from the curators of the Kunsthistorisches Museum in Vienna and the Szépmúvészeti Múzeum in Budapest, where some of the sarcophagi from this site are housed.

The sarcophagus of Aset-iri-khet-es, along with its mummy and cartonnage, are currently on permanent display at the Archaeological Museum in Cracow.

The publication of the present volume was made possible by the good will and support of the authorities of the Polish Academy of Arts and Sciences, especially its Secretary General, Prof. Jerzy Wyrozumski, and Prof. Janusz K. Kozłowski, and constitutes the crowning achievement of the excavations performed by Tadeusz Smoleński, whose stay in Egypt was supported by the Academy in 1907.

In conclusion, we would like to express our sincere gratitude to the institutions of the Jagiellonian University's Collegium Medicum; thanks to their understanding and good will it was possible to perform this research. Particular mention should be made of the late Prof. Józef Kuśmiderski, head of the Department of Radiology; Prof. Jacek Pietrzyk, head of the Department of Medical Genetics at the Polish-American Institute of Pediatrics; Prof. Bożena Turowska, head of the Department of Forensic Medicine, and Alexander Głazek, Director of the Institute of Forensic Experts.

We would also like to express our undying gratitude to our colleagues and co-workers, who, in their fascination with the topic, and heedless of the mounting difficulties, spared no effort or expense to perform the tasks entrusted to them in a faultless manner. Special words of thanks are owed to Iwona Woźniak, the data processing expert from the Archaeological Museum in Cracow, who with genuine devotion helped us both in performing the research and in publishing the present volume. We are deeply indebted to Anna Prokopowicz, head of the Textiles Conservation Studio of the National Museum in Cracow. Her excellent professional training and extensive experience were instrumental in preserving the remains of Aset-iri-khet-es according to state-of-the-art principles.

Krzysztof Babraj

The ethics of research on mummified human remains

Not once during the turbulent wake of events that followed their discovery were the four coffins from the excavations in the settlement of el-Gamhud treated by conservators.[1] All of them underwent successive conservation and restoration in the past five years with an eye to the coming permanent display of Ancient Egyptian art that was planned to open at the Archaeological Museum in Cracow. In one of the coffins there was a mummy much degraded by not so much the passage of time as the doings of ancient tomb robbers.

Despite the deeply ingrained religious belief of the Ancient Egyptians that mummification was intended as a means of preserving the body for eternity, the ancient burials in Egypt have mostly been disturbed. There is evidence for the procedure taking place already in the mummification ateliers or soon after interment. Papyrus sources bring information about the trials of tomb robbers, who were tortured and sentenced to the impalement (Papyrus Leopold II-Amherst).[2] Indeed, the persistence of tomb robberies was so trying that in the times of the Twenty First Dynasty the priests had the royal mummies carried off together with the tomb equipment to a specially prepared rock cache (TT 320), near Deir el-Bahari. Robberies were the first acts of corpse defilement, which took on an extreme form in modern times, when unwrapping mummies became commonplace and the remains were hardly ever treated as actually human.

[1] Cf. H. Szymańska, *Tadeusz Smoleński. Excavations at el-Gamhud* (in the present volume).

[2] S. Ikram, A. Dodson, *The Mummy in Ancient Egypt. Equipping the Dead for Eternity,* Cairo 1998, 63.

[3] Cf. B. Aleksiejew-Wantuch, *Conservation of a cartonnage piece of the mummy of Aset-iri-khet-es* and M. Paciorek, *Conservation of a wooden painted coffin from Ancient Egypt in the collection of the Archaeological Museum in Cracow* (both in the present volume).

[4] The commission included Prof. Kazimierz Radwański, then Director of the Archaeological Museum in Cracow (he headed the commission), Prof. Karol Myśliwiec, Dr. Zbigniew Szafrański, Prof. Andrzej Niwiński, Dr. Hanna Szymańska, Mr. Krzysztof Babraj and Prof. Maria Kaczmarek.

[5] In some cases, X-ray and computer tomography examinations should be followed by an autopsy to verify the results. The important symbolism of cloth amulet substitutes discovered in the mummy of Aset-iri-khet-es eluded us in radiological research, cf. A. Niwiński, *Coffin, cartonnage and mummy of Aset-iri-khet-es in the light of Egyptological research* (in the present volume). Also, without unwrapping the mummy it would have been impossible to take skin samples for determining the blood group and isolating DNA sequences. Radiological research in itself cannot determine the material used to make objects that can be seen under the bandages (e.g. papyrus, amulets, plant remains and insects). An opportunity for this has been provided by a series of studies of human and animal mummies and accompanying objects carried out by a team headed by Dr. A. Urbanik, cf. A. Urbanik et al., *Badania radiologiczne mumii egipskich – doświadczenia własne*, Polski Przegląd Radiologii 1 (2001), 79-83; A. Urbanik, *Comprehensive radiological examination* (in the present volume).

[6] The team participating in the project and analyzing the results included Egyptologists, a radiologist, anthropologist, paleobotanist, palinologist, entomologist, chemists, a histopathologist, IT specialist, textile conservation specialist, molecular geneticist.

[7] Keeping in mind that the wrapping of the bandages would have to be recreated at a later stage, the entire unwrapping process was filmed, while particular sections of the bandages were numbered and photographed, cf. K. Tempczyk, *The mummy's wrappings* (in the present volume).

In the case of the mummy in question, the chest and pelvis areas and the head had suffered the biggest damages, the bandages having been torn and the bones disturbed. The openwork cartonnage that covered the mummy was also seriously damaged. After being removed from the body, it was handed over for conservation.[3] An essential condition of effective treatment was removing the mummified remains. The issue was whether the body should be returned to the coffin after the latter's conservation, a step that seemed impossible due to the extent of the damages suffered by the mummy. Under the upper part of the body there was a thick layer of dust mingled with the remains of the cartonnage mask, which the robbers had destroyed practically completely, as well as single bones and pulverized substances that had been used in the embalming process. It was then that the idea formed for carrying out egyptological and other examinations of the mummy.

With the scientific importance of this project in mind, a commission was convened in August 1994.[4] The decision was that the mummy should become the object of investigations, including examination by autopsy,[5] after which it should be reconstructed. A team of specialists was called together[6] and in July 1995 the operation of unwrapping the Cracow mummy began.[7] Mindful of the respect due the dead woman and the need for the scholars to concentrate on their work, the organizers kept the presence of the press, radio and television to a minimum, admitting representatives only at the very beginning of the process and once it was concluded. The Ambassador of Egypt in Poland added to the importance of the event with his presence.

It was at this point that the organizers were faced with an ethical problem that has yet to be solved: is it appropriate in such instances to invite the public at large. Weighing human curiosity and the demands of science against respect for the bodily remains of a human individual is a difficult matter indeed. As a matter of fact, in our cultural sphere Ancient Egyptian mummies exemplify the evolution that has taken place in human consciousness regarding the moral principles of treating human remains. The civilization of Ancient Egypt has always been a fascination for people of other cultures, starting with the pyramids, hieroglyphs and the mummies, which were destroyed at first and later became an "object for display" to be treated in commercial terms.

Already in the 11th century the Arabs were destroying thousands of mummies to obtain bitumen, then a highly valued remedy used for a variety of ailments everywhere in the civilized world. The 12th-century Arab writer Abd el-Latif described a mountain in Persia, down which ran *mum/mumia* (mineral pitch). Dissolved in water, this substance had healing properties during inhalation treatment, as well as when administered orally.[8] The word, understood as a drug, appears in medical treatises, like that of the Greek physician and pharmacologist Pedanios Dioscurides (40-90).[9] It was much easier, instead of having the substance brought from Persia, to obtain it from embalmed corpses found in Egypt. Bitumen was either scraped off the bones or else parts of mummies were ground to powder. The conviction about the healing properties of mummy powder was so deeply rooted that it continued to be used even in the 19th century, although already in medieval times, Avicenna (Ibn Sina), the biggest authority in the field of medicine, who lived in 980-1037, warned against misusing the substance. Special expeditions, like that of André Thevet, chaplain of Catherine de Medici, who visited Saqqara in 1549, were organized to Egypt to collect mummies for medical purposes. King Francis I of France used to carry with him a purse containing mummy powder mixed with dried rhubarb.[10]

Forgeries were also commonplace, the object being to make false mummies that were later used to produce the healing powder, for which there was such a demand. The first to detect this procedure was Guy de la Fontaine, who visited Alexandria, then a known center of the mummy trade, in 1564. To meet the demand the corpses of criminals and unknown persons were embalmed using appropriate substances and buried in a mass grave for several years to produce in effect mummies. The procedure was stopped only in the 18th century with the high taxes that were then imposed.

Not everyone believed in the healing properties of the medicament. In his *Discours contre la momie*, Ambroise Paré questioned its effectiveness. Even so, as late as 1924 a respected German pharmaceutical company had on its price list a drug called *Mumia vera Aegiptiaca* (Photos 1 and 2a),[11] which was sold at 12 marks in gold per kilogram.[12]

In 1666 Sir Thomas Browne wrote that mummies had become goods; he expressed sadness that "Pharaoh is used for balsam," as this has led to mummies being destroyed on a vast scale, something that even the Persian

[8] Ikram, Dodson, op. cit., 64-67.

[9] Dioscurides Triumphans, *Ein anonymer arabischer Kommentar (Ende 12.Jahrh. n. Chr.) zur Materia medica.* Arabischer Text nebst kommentierter deutscher Übersetzung Hrsg. von A. Dietrich. 2. Teil: Übersetzung und Kommentar. Abhandlungen der Akademie der Wissenschaften in Göttingen. Philologisch-Historische Klasse Dritte Folge Nr 173, Göttingen 1988, 120-121. The author mentions a few ways, in which this substance could have been created, for instance, from rotten meat brought to caves by predatory birds. These remains combined with water allegedly formed *mumiya*, which Dioscurides recommended as a remedy for broken bones.

[10] The medicine is often mixed with various herbs, like marjoram or thyme; it was even used as fish bait (cf. Ikram, Dodson, op. cit., 64).

[11] I owe this information to Mrs. Monika Urbanik, curator of the Pharmacy Museum, to whom I would like to express my sincere gratitude for making available the objects presented here.

[12] R. Germer et al., *Das Geheimnis der Mumien. Ewiges Leben am Nil,* München 1997, 95.

conqueror of Egypt, Cambyses, nor the passage of time had not done. Despite this his *Hydriotaphia, or Urn Burial* of 1658 gives detailed instructions on how to use *mumiya* as a cure for all ailments.

Browne was the first to treat mummies as objects for display. The trend quickly caught on, mummies being treated as curiosities and placed as such in private and public collections. In the Völkerkunde collection in Lübeck there is a mummy that in 1696 was in the possession of the town pharmacist.[13] Tourists came to Egypt in large numbers hoping to find objects for display in their rooms of curiosities. Mummies were collected, whole and in parts (Photo 2a). For example, Napoleon and his wife Josephine received as gifts a male and female head cut off mummies.

How scandalous the attitude toward mummified human remains was still in the end of the 19th century is evidenced by an anecdote told by Mark Twain. The writer quotes a stoker calling to his assistant: "These poor guys aren't worth a cent. Give me a king!" He was referring to a royal mummy, as mummified bodies were used as fuel in the steam machines of the time.[14]

It is important to understand what terrible destruction met the bodily remains of people who had once been mummified with such piety. The mummies of Ancient Egyptian rulers were subjected to great perils over the ages. One August Stanwood imported tons of bandages from mummies to his paper production plant in the United States, while Cook's travel office offered its clients attractive vacations together with discovering a tomb and unwrapping the mummy found inside.

Yet the 19th century also saw a more positive approach to the issue. The mummies brought to the Louvre by the Napoleonic expedition, which had succumbed to the humid Parisian climate, were not thrown away, but were buried in the palatial gardens on avenue Perrault. The bodies of those killed in the 1830 revolution were also buried there. After some time the latter were removed to be buried under the column standing on the square of the Bastille, perhaps together with the mummies.[15]

With time a new way of revealing the secrets of Ancient Egyptian mummies was invented, invariably causing a public shiver of emotion. Examination of mummies by autopsy became an increasingly popular public event. One of the first, if not the first unwrapping in history was apparently carried out in a pharmacy in

[13] Ibidem, passim.

[14] Ch. de Vartavan, *Ce patrimoine exceptionnel a failli disparaître*, Géo 200, Octobre 1995, 196.

[15] A similar worthy example of an ethical approach to human remains unearthed in archaeological research can be cited from more recent history. Upon the initiative of Prof. W. A. Daszewski and K. Polaczek, with the permission of the Primate of Poland, Cardinal Józef Glemp, twelve ecclesiastics from the Faras Cathedral, whose remains had been brought to Poland by the Polish Center of Archaeology of Warsaw University for anthropological examination, were buried in one of the cemeteries in Warsaw, in a sector intended for priests. An appropriate epitaph was mounted over the burial.

Wrocław on December 7, 1658.[16] German playwright and poet Anderas Gryphius had the opportunity to participate in this event thanks to his friend, Ch. Hoffmann von Hoffmannswaldau, whom he had gotten to know in Leiden while studying medical sciences among others. Two mummies were examined at this time and Gryphius left a detailed account of the process in his *Mumiae Wratislavienses*.[17] In this work the author uses the results of autopsies carried out on mummies to verify the reports of ancient authors concerning mummification,[18] and confirms the custom of using mummies as a cure as well as ways of their procurement, writing: "Et postremum quod attinet, fuére quibus pridem decretum rimari conditoria, noscere medicamen, cujus virtute imbuti functorum artus exsangues, tot post seculorum decursum, in hunc annum durant, evolvere lintea, feralium reliquiarum vulgare titulos, & ut sumus avaritiae promti mortales, postquam ab Arabia persuasio cepit, expugnandae valetudini adversae, haec sive conditorum membra, seu confusum tabe demortui unguentum praestare; usu commerciorum, permutatione &..."

The next 17th-century unwrapping of a mummy took place in September 1698 in Cairo. It was carried out by Benoit de Maillet, consul of Louis XIV, for a group of French travelers. Nothing about the mummy itself was recorded, except for the fact of finding amulets.[19]

In the 1830s public autopsies were organized, during which mummified remains were examined in full view of the audience. A surgeon Thomas J. Pettigrew achieved a reputation in this respect, carrying out one of such "operations" in 1833 at Charing Cross Hospital. Members of the royal family were said to have attended this show. It should be noted, however, that Pettigrew's approach was otherwise truly scientific. Drawing on Champollion's discoveries, he frequently read the name of the mummy he was examining. He is also the author of the first full history of embalming,[20] which greatly popularized these shows once it was published. Giovanni D'Athanasi, the organizer of one of Pettigrew's sessions, advertised it thus: "Giovanni D'Athanasi respectfully informs the public, that on the evening of Monday, the 10th of April next at seven o'clock, the Most interesting Mummy that has as yet been discovered in Egypt, will be unrolled in the Large Room at Exeter Hall, Strand. Tickets, as under, with a description of the Mummy, may be now had of Giovanni D'Athanasi

[16] A. Bok, *Anderas Gryphius. Zarys życia i twórczości*, Głogów 1997², 37.

[17] A. Gryphius, *Mumiae Wratislavienses*, Wratislaviae 1662 (published by Viti Jacobi Drescheri on 121 pages).

[18] Ibidem, e.g. 7, 11, 12, 13, 16, 17, 18, 20 (at this point he describes a way to distinguish real mummies from ones that are false), 21.

[19] Ikram, Dodson, op. cit., 69. The authors believe this to have been the first recorded unwrapping of a mummy. What they presumably have in mind is the first autopsy of a mummy to be carried out in Egypt.

[20] T. J. Pettigrew, *A History of Egyptian Mummies and an Account of the Worship and Embalming of the Sacred Animals by The Egyptians; with Remarks on the Funeral Ceremonies of Different Nations, and Observations on the Mummies of the Canary Islands, of the Ancient Peruvian, Burman Priests, &c.*, London 1834.

at no. 3, Wellington Street, Strand. A limited number of Seats will be reserved, immediately around the Table on which the Mummy will be placed, at Six Shillings. Seats in the Balconica and Platform, Four Shillings. All the other Seats in the centre of the Hall and Gallery, Two Shillings and Sixpence."[21]

Unraveling the secrets of the mummies generated such popular interest that even scholars of the magnitude of Gaston Maspero, then Director of the Egyptian Museum in Cairo, succumbed to the excitement. A convenient opportunity for research came with the discovery of the cache of royal mummies (TT 320) in 1881. Five years later Maspero, under orders from the Egyptian Viceroy, unwrapped the mummy of Ramesses the Great. Attending were members of the government, physicians, archaeologists and artists. In his report Maspero assured that all accepted principles of science had been followed, yet the short time spent on the project (merely one day) suffices to question the reliability of the work done.[22] Most of the pharaonic mummies from the said cache were examined in 1905 by a physician, G. E. Smith, who restricted his interests, however, to recreating the facial features of the ancient rulers. Absolutely no attention was paid to evidence of the embalming process.[23]

The first truly scientific examination of mummified remains, during which an effort was made to avoid creating a sensation, was carried out relatively early – in 1828. A group of chemists conducted a professional, as far as the times are concerned, analysis of the so-called Leeds Mummy, which belonged to Nesamun (Twentieth Dynasty). The most extensive study in this field is that of the chemist Alfred Lucas,[24] written shortly after the discovery of the tomb of Tutankhamun. It treats on a broad range of subjects, including embalming.[25]

The first project to be carried out by an interdisciplinary team of scholars representing the sciences of anatomy, chemistry and the study of textiles, was the 1908 unwrapping of the mummies of the "two brothers" at the Museum of Manchester. Under the leadership of Dr. Margaret Murray, curator of the Egyptological department, the mummies were examined and for the first time lifetime portraits were attempted.

In the early 1970s a group of scholars representing different disciplines studied 21 human and 34 animal mummies from the same museum. An autopsy was carried out in only one case. The research objectives in this project

[21] B. Brier, *Egyptian Mummies. Unraveling the Secrets of an Ancient Art*, London 1996, 164.

[22] G. Maspero, *Les momies royales de Deir El-Bahari*, Paris 1889, 526.

[23] G. E. Smith, *The Royal Mummies,* Catalogue Général du Musée du Caire, Cairo 1912.

[24] A. Lucas, *Ancient Egyptian Materials and Industries*, revised and enlarged by J. R. Harris, London[4] 1962, 270-326.

[25] For the last results of multidisciplinary investigations on mummification process see A. R. David, *Mummification*, in: *Ancient Egyptian Materials and Technology*, ed. by P. T. Nicholson and I. Shaw, Cambridge 2000, 372-389 (with extensive references).

were twofold. Firstly, the authors of the project wished to verify current knowledge of the cult and burial practices, including the embalming process, and to identify diseases and possible causes of death. Secondly, their goal was to arrive at a methodology for future research of this type. The results of their work laid the groundwork for the *International Mummy Data Base*, operating from the Manchester Museum and collecting data concerning similar projects carried out around the world.

Mummy studies were undertaken practically simultaneously by the Philadelphia Art Museum (in 1973), where four mummies were examined, and the Royal Ontario Museum in Toronto (in 1974) where an interdisciplinary team conducted an autopsy on a single mummy.

An important project on a big scale was the investigation of the royal mummy of Ramesses II, carried out at the Musée de l'Homme in Paris in 1976-1977.[26] All the most modern methods of the time were applied in the research: radiological, endoscopic, bacteriological, mycological, paleobotanical, mineralogical; the hair was also studied, and the wood of the coffin was examined dendrologically and dated by radiocarbon means. One of the objectives of the project was to preserve the mummy of Ramesses II together with the coffin and prepare the objects for display. Although ethical issues were hardly an obstacle for the scholars in this case, it was veritably the first such case when an Egyptian mummy was treated not just as another object for study, but with all the respect due human bodily remains. Undoubtedly, the fact that it was the mummy of one of the greatest rulers of Ancient Egypt played a role here. At the airports in Cairo and Paris, the mummy of Ramesses the Great was met with all the honors due a head of state.

Taking advantage of the experience and results of these projects, the Institut für Anthropologie und Humangenetik in Munich prepared in 1982 a project for examining seven Egyptian mummies from the collection of the Staatliche Sammlung Ägyptischer Kunst in Munich. Another big project is underway at the Kunsthistorisches Museum in Vienna.[27] Here, the objective of studies on 48 Ancient Egyptian mummies from different periods is to collect data on pathogenic factors and information about Egyptian medicine. Only radiographic and computer tomography methods have been applied in this case. Of the projects executed in recent years, two interdisciplinary undertakings deserve attention in view of the application, similarly as in our case, of the most

[26] *La Momie de Ramsés II*, ed. L. Balout, C. Roubet, Ch. Desroches-Noblecourt, Paris 1985 (with abbreviated presentation of results in Arabic).

[27] *Mumien aus dem Alten Ägypten. Zur Mumienforschung im Kunsthistorischen Museum*, Hrsg. W. Seipel, Vienna 1998; for a review, cf. B. E. Borg, Antike Welt 30/1 (1999), 93.

modern scientific methods of examination. One of these was a project started in 1989 at the Kestner-Museum in Hanover, where the mummy of a woman from the 3rd century B.C. was studied; an extensive publication of the results followed.[28] The other project was carried out in 1995 at the Armenian monastery of S. Lazzaro, situated on an island near Venice. The mummy of an official from Diospolis, one Nemenket Amen, was examined (autopsy included) by a team of French experts representing different disciplines.[29]

Human intellectual development leads to broadly understood ethical transformation. The new possibilities offered by science mark out ever more distant goals, generating at the same time doubts of a moral nature. This aspect has long escaped the attention of both the scholars conducting experiments on Ancient Egyptian mummies and members of the general public taking part in such shows and visiting museum displays.

It was not until the early 1970s that the unsuitable behavior of visitors to the hall of the royal mummies at the Egyptian Museum in Cairo was remarked upon. Egyptian President Anwar Sadat had the room closed to the public. A few years ago a new display was opened, assuring a dignified and safe presentation of the bodily remains of the ancient rulers of Egypt. This part of the museum may be visited in absolute silence and a special fee ensures that there are no crowds here.

Of interest for the present discussion is the fact that the first cases of condemning the public display of prepared human remains date back to the late 18th century. One such case was the body of Angelo Soliman, a highly talented and educated African in the service of Prince Lobkovitz in Vienna. After Angelo's death, his body was put up for show at the Zoologisches Museum.[30] An official protest in this matter, drawing from the deepest springs of humanitarianism, was addressed to the Austrian government by a consistory of Vienna bishops: "It is the custom among civilized nations [...] not to display the nudity of a human body to the public eye, but to cloth it in life and allow the earth to cover it in death. An exception in this case may be constituted by important benefits for humanity resulting from the physician's ability to dismember a body and from anatomical experiments, but not to satisfy the greedy eyes and inquisitiveness, which arises from having the body of a black man shown publicly as a curiosity."[31] Sad to say, the protest did not bring about any positive results.

[28] *Mumie und Computer, ein multidisziplinäres Forschungsprojekt in Hannover,* Hrsg. R. Drenkhahn, R. Germer, Hanover 1991.

[29] J. C. Grenier, *Le savant strip-tease du mort de Venise,* Géo 200, Octobre 1995, 192-195.

[30] W. Seipel, *Mumien und Ethik im Museum,* in: *Mumien aus dem Alten Ägypten. Zur Mumienforschung im Kunsthistorischen Museum,* Vienna 1998, 7.

[31] Free translation from the original version.

Even in the nineties of our century the ethical aspect of treating human remains was still at stake. During the 1992 Olympic Games in Barcelona, a group of competitors from some African and Asiatic states threatened to boycott the games should the prepared bodily remains of an African continue to be displayed at a small museum near Barcelona.[32]

A tidal wave of ethical and moral doubts followed in the wake of the discovery of the so-called "Ice Man" in August 1991.[33] The body, initially believed to be of modern date, was found frozen in the Hauslabjoch glacier. Sensational information in the media, partly coming from the scholars themselves, bared the nature of the problem, namely, the difficulty in attempting a balance between reliable reporting of scientific research and reports aimed at cheap sensationalism. Images were shown worldwide and people learned how a man could be treated without due respect only because he had lived some 5000 years ago.

It must become part of Man's common consciousness that human remains, despite their age and civilizational affiliation, demand dignified treatment regardless of how important they are to science. This awareness should determine our ethical behavior. It is part of the duties of a modern museum holding in its collections objects of this type. The tasks of institutions devoted to this purpose is to make available to the public at large the results of scholarly examinations, preserving at the same time the peace and dignity of man after death. The problem has become a constant fixture of extensively planned projects for the study of Ancient Egyptian mummies at the Kunsthistorisches Museum in Vienna, as indicated by Wilfried Seipel's article on mummies and ethics in a modern museum, included in the publication of results.[34]

ICOM's ethical recommendations in this respect are as follows:

Article 2.6: "By definition, a museum is an institution in the service of society and of its development, and is generally open to the public (even though this may be a restricted public in the case of certain very specialized museums, such as certain academic or medical museums, for example)."

Article 2.8: "Subject to the primary duty of the museum to preserve unimpaired for the future the significant material that comprises the museum collections, it is the responsibility of the museum to use the collections for the creation and dissemination of new knowledge, through research, educationalwork, permanent displays, temporary exhibitions and

[32] Seipel, op. cit., 8.

[33] H. Rotter, *Ethische Aspekte zum Thema*, in: *Der Mann im Eis*, Bericht über das Internationale Symposium 1992 in Innsbruck, Veröffentlichungen der Universität Innsbruck 187, Innsbruck 1992, 24-28.

[34] Cf. note 30.

other special activities. These should be in accordance with the stated policy and educational purpose of the museum, and should not compromise either the quality or the proper care of the collections. The museum should seek to ensure that information in displays and exhibitions is honest and objective and does not perpetuate myths or stereotypes."

Article 6.7: "Where a museum maintains and/or is developing collections of human remains and sacred objects, these should be securely housed and carefully maintained as archival collections in scholarly institutions, and should always be available to qualified researchers and educators, but not to the morbidly curious. Research on such objects and their housing and care must be accomplished in a manner acceptable not only to fellow professionals but also to those of various beliefs, including particular members of the community, ethnic or religious groups concerned. Although it is occasionally necessary to use human remains and other sensitive material in interpretative exhibits, this must be done with tact and with respect for the feelings for human dignity held by all peoples."

Taking into account the ICOM ethics code, it remained for us to decide whether in our case it would be possible to return the woman's mummy to a condition, in which she could be returned safely to her coffin, her place of eternal rest. This was done on January 17, 1999, and after 48 hours of work, burdened by a lack of any previous experience, we finally managed to put together the skeleton of the Egyptian priestess and to re-wrap her bodily remains,[35] using an additional 30 m of modern bandages prepared in correspondence with the ancient ones,[36] Aset-iri-khet-es was laid to rest in her restored coffin, which was placed inside a glass case assuring appropriate climatic conditions, that is, a constant 60% humidity and light intensity not exceeding 50 lux. Optical fiber lighting was used for this purpose, bringing out all the aesthetic valor of the coffin, while guaranteeing that all the conservation requirements are met. The coffin lid has been lifted slightly to permit visitors a glimpse of the body of the priestess after the re-wrapping. Three optical fibers were introduced into the case to provide discreet lighting for the dead woman without disturbing her peace. The cartonnage of Aset-iri-khet-es, after conservation, has been placed in a separate case, in the immediate vicinity of the coffin.

On June 10, 2000, a permanent exhibition "The Gods of Ancient Egypt" was officially inaugurated at the

[35] Cf. Tempczyk, op. cit. (in the present volume).

[36] K. Babraj, H. Szymańska, *Eine Mumie unter dem Mikroskop. Die Untersuchungen an der ägyptischen Mumie in Archäologischen Museum zu Krakau*, Antike Welt 28/5 (1997), 369-374; iidem, *Kapłanka Izydy z Krakowa*, Archeologia Żywa 3/8 (1998), 4-10. On June 1, 1999, a seminar on the subject of this mummy was held at the Archaeological Museum in Cracow, cf. K. Babraj, *Die interdisziplinären Forschungen an der ägyptischen Mumie im Archäologischen Museum zu Krakau*, Kemet 8/4, (1999), 54-58; idem, *Examination of the mummy of Aset-iri-khet-es from the Archaeological Museum in Cracow*, in: K. Babraj, H. Szymańska, *The Gods of Ancient Egypt*, Catalogue of the Permanent Exhibition at the Archaeological Museum in Cracow, Cracow 2000, 17-26.

Archaeological Museum in Cracow. Part of the display is our priestess and the results of the examinations made of her mummy. As Seipel rightly observes in his article: "Immerhin gereichen menschenwürdige Behandlung und Respekt für die sterblichen Überreste unserer Vergangenheit auch den betreffenden Wissenschaften selbst zur Ehre. Ob nun Archäologie, Medizingeschichte, Urgeschichte oder Anthropologie: Am Ende finden sie einander alle in der gemeinsamen Suche nach Identität des Menschen, die nicht nur in den Errungenschaften von Kunst und Kultur, sondern auch in den physischen Resten der menschlichen Existenz ihre Spuren hinterlassen hat."[37]

[37] Seipel, op. cit., 10-11.

It is the responsibility of a museum not only to properly store, preserve and display objects and to interpret them, but also to present the results of scholarly studies on these objects made by specialists representing different disciplines of science. With regard to the latter task, the exhibition in the Archaeological Museum in Cracow has been furnished with glass cases holding information about the outcome of the mummy studies. The present volume of articles on the subject is also a way of delivering on this duty.

Photo 1.
Majolica vase with the inscription "Mumia Vera"
for mummy powder. Inv. no. 3628. Museum of
Pharmacy of the Collegium Medicum,
Jagiellonian University in Cracow

Photo 2.
Objects from the collection of the Museum of
Pharmacy of the Collegium Medicum,
Jagiellonian University in Cracow:
a – fragment of a mummy with the inscription
"Mumia aegypt". Inv. no. 7310;
b – wooden box with the inscription "Mumia", in
which a powdered mummy substance was kept.
Inv. no. 1864

Hanna Szymańska

Tadeusz Smoleński.
Excavations at el-Gamhud

The pioneer of Polish Egyptology, Tadeusz Smoleński was also the first Polish archaeologist to be active in Egypt. He was born in 1884 in the Silesian town of Jaworz, into a family with a background in historical studies and a strong tradition of scholarly achievement.[1] His father Stanisław was a physician specializing in hydrotherapy at Jagiellonian University; he published numerous works in his field, frequently taking into consideration the historical background of his specialty. Tadeusz's uncle, Władysław, was in turn one of the most prominent Polish historiographers. He took care of his nephew and after the latter's premature death he made every effort to gather together the young scholar's Egyptological and literary heritage. His aunt, Maria Babirecka, who was the official guardian of Tadeusz and his brother Jerzy Smoleński (1881-1940; professor of geography at the Jagiellonian University and corresponding member of the Academy of Arts and Sciences from 1935) after the death of their parents, was the wife of a recognized cartographer.

After graduating from the respected Sobieski Gymnasium in Cracow, Tadeusz enrolled at the Jagiellonian University, becoming a student of the Faculty of Philosophy, studying history and geography with prominent scholars, like Stanisław Krzyżanowski (1865-1917; historian and archivist, from 1898 a professor at the Jagiellonian University and corresponding member of the Academy of Arts and Sciences from 1902) and Wincenty Zakrzewski (1844-1918;

[1] T. Pilecki, *Działalność naukowo-badawcza w dziedzinie archeologii egipskiej*, Archeologia 10 (1958), 219-238; idem, *Tadeusz Smoleński – pionier egiptologii polskiej (1884-1909)*, Sprawozdania z posiedzeń Komisji Polskiej Akademii Nauk, Oddział w Krakowie, styczeń-czerwiec 1960, Kraków 1961, 67-70; idem, *Tadeusz Samuel Smoleński – pionnier de l'égyptologie polonaise (1884-1909)*, Folia Orientalia 2 (1961), 1-2, 321-248; idem, *Tadeusz Smoleński – pionier polskiej egiptologii (1884-1909)*, Przegląd Humanistyczny 5 (1961), 1, 147-160; K. Stachowska, *Wkład Akademii Umiejętności w początki polskich badań wykopaliskowych w Egipcie w latach 1906-1914*, Rocznik Biblioteki PAN w Krakowie 18 (1972), 93-148; eadem, *Z dziejów polskich badań archeologicznych na Bliskim Wschodzie*, ibidem 18 (1983), 171-200; eadem, *Studia uniwersyteckie Tadeusza Smoleńskiego w świetle jego listów do Władysława Smoleńskiego*, ibidem 29 (1984), 33-119; eadem, *Z listów Wincentego Zakrzewskiego do Tadeusza Smoleńskiego z lat 1905-1908*, ibidem 34 (1989), 126-142; eadem, *Zu den Anfängen des Interesses an Ägypten in Polen. Tadeusz Smoleński (1884-1909) und seine Nachfolger*, in: *Zur Geschichte der klassischen Altertumswissenschaft*, Jena-Budapest-Kraków (Wissenschaftliche Beiträge der Friedrich-Schiller-Universität), Jena 1990, 105-143; K. Grodziska, *Smoleński Tadeusz*, Polski Słownik Biograficzny 39/2 (1999), 274-276.

[2] *Skargiana, Z wieku Mikołaja Reja*, Warszawa 1905; *Wczesna młodość Stanisława Orzechowskiego (1513-1532)*, Przegląd Historyczny 12 (1906), 203-221, 352-361.

[3] K. Stachowska, *Listy Tadeusza Smoleńskiego do Mieczysława Geniusza z roku 1905. Pierwszy rok pobytu w Egipcie*, Rocznik Biblioteki PAN w Krakowie 37 (1992), 118-179; eadem, *Listy Tadeusza Smoleńskiego do Mieczysława Geniusza. Rok 1906*, ibidem 38 (1993), 105-184; eadem, *Listy Tadeusza Smoleńskiego do Mieczysława Geniusza z lat 1907-1908*, ibidem 39 (1994), 56-100.

[4] Stachowska, *Wkład Akademii...*, 96, note 9.

professor of history at the Jagiellonian University and member of the Academy of Arts and Sciences from 1881; head of publications in the Historical Commission of the Academy). A talented student, he began publishing his first source studies.[2] Collecting material for a history of geography in Poland, he even undertook to learn Arabic in order to be able to read the reports of medieval travelers.

After five semesters Smoleński was forced to break off his studies to treat a heavy case of lung disease that was still incurable at the time. In March 1905 he went to Egypt where he had been invited for a short stay at the home of Mieczysław Geniusz at Rassua on the Suez Canal. Geniusz, an engineer, was then director of the Suez Canal Sweet Water Company. A philosopher and occultist in his own right, Geniusz was to give the young scholar support, also financial, right until the Egyptologist's premature death. The letters between Smoleński and Geniusz, published by Krystyna Stachowska, draw a colorful picture of the two men and their mutual familiarity.[3]

Smoleński's historical interests, commenced during his studies in Cracow, focused on Poland's 16th-century history, which was to be the background of his Ph.D. dissertation. The young man changed his mind, however, under the influence of Jan Karol Kochanowski, chief editor of "Przegląd Historyczny" ("Historical Review"), who approached him with a proposition to write for the paper on egyptological subjects. "There is no one now who is dealing with this subject professionally," wrote Kochanowski. Thus we find in Smoleński's *Dzienniki* (*Diaries*) the proud words of a youth starting on a career: "So I will become the first Polish Egyptologist."[4] He would remain faithful to this task, which he also considered as his duty in the service of Polish science, until his premature death.

Not wanting to overstay his welcome in Geniusz's home and with this new goal in mind, equipped with recommendations from his host, Smoleński went to Cairo, where he was immediately extended the kindly protection of the chargé d'affaires of the Austrian diplomatic mission, Count Antoni Stadnicki. He was introduced to Gaston Maspero, the prominent French Egyptologist who was then the director of the Service des Antiquités (Antiquities Service) and the Egyptian Museum in Cairo. There followed a long and arduous period of intensive studies in the library of the Egyptian Museum. Thanks to Maspero's protection, Smoleński also had access to the museum's extensive collection.

Continuous financial difficulties forced him, however, to take up a position with one of the Cairo department stores where he worked as an accountant. After work, despite his illness, which was wearing him out, he spent his time learning hieroglyphs. Astounded by his quick progress, Maspero took a personal interest in the young man's study and started issuing him with semester reports. This, as it turned out, provided Smoleński with the opportunity to continue formal studies at the Jagiellonian University in the field of Ancient Oriental history. Not only could he study with the famous French scholar, but he was also given the chance to complete his Ph.D. in Cracow. At the same time, his protectors in Poland, professors Wincenty Zakrzewski and Bolesław Ulanowski (1860-1919; general secretary of the Academy of Arts and Sciences (1903-1919), professor of the history of Polish and canonical law at the Jagiellonian University) got him a subsidy of 600 crowns from the Cracow Academy. In return Smoleński was asked to present a lecture on excavations in Egypt in the preceding five years. This paper, which was excellently prepared based on data collected from the excavators themselves and from reports submitted to the Service, the young scholar read at a meeting of the Academy of Arts and Sciences in June 1906. A year later it was published.[5]

In the meantime Maspero was approached by the Budapest banker Philip Back with the request to grant a license for excavations in Egypt. Back's objective was to obtain from excavations new objects for display in the Budapest museum. When Smoleński returned to Egypt in October, Maspero asked him to head the Austro-Hungarian expedition, demonstrating his highest respect for the skills of the young Polish Egyptologist, who thus became one of the group of eminent scholars directing excavations in Egypt.

Smoleński started work in Middle Egypt, at a locality near Sharuna on the right bank of the Nile, in the ancient nome of Oxyrhynchos. The site was a necropolis of different historical periods, where excavations had been carried out on and off, but never completed. His first object of interest was a rock tomb of one Pepi-Ankh-Chua, a dignitary of the Sixth Dynasty, and his wife Merut. The attribution was Smoleński's undoubted success, as he managed to decipher the hieroglyphs on the tomb walls. These he published in 1908.[6] The interests of the young scholar are quite obvious in this work, as the epigraphic material is treated as a historical source of key importance.

[5] T. Smoleński, *O dzisiejszym stanie badań egiptologicznych*, Sprawozdania Akademii Umiejętności 11 (1906), no. 7, 9-20; idem, *Wykopaliska egipskie 1901-1906*, Kwartalnik Historyczny 21 (1907), 379-410.

[6] T. Smoleński, *Le tombeau d'un prince de la VIe dynastie à Charouna*, Annales du Service des Antiquité de l'Égypte (ASAE) 9 (1908), 149-153.

Investigations of the necropolis, which had been plundered already in Antiquity, did not bring the expected results, if one disregards some tomb equipment of the likes of Osiris figurines, offering tables, painted mummy masks and a few vessels. Soon, however, Smoleński decided to move the work to the nearby plateau of Kom el-Ahmar, encouraged by the stories told by the local *fellahin* about numerous finds of golden coins and fragments of sculptures found north of the necropolis. Almost immediately he hit on the ruins of houses built of limestone blocks taken from an ancient temple. On one of these blocks he read a cartouche of Ptolemy I Soter, establishing in this way the founder of the temple. An accidental discovery of the name of Philadelphos, Ptolemy's successor, carved on a stone fragment used in the walls of one of the Arabic houses, indicated how important this cult place had been for the Ptolemaic dynasty.[7]

Not much is known of the current location of the 18 reliefs that Smoleński discovered. Seven are held in the collections of the Fine Arts Museum in Budapest,[8] five at the Kunsthistorisches Museum in Vienna.[9] Two blocks, to judge by Smoleński's correspondence, were given to the Academy of Arts and Sciences in Cracow. No trace of these survives. The search investigated by Prof. Maria Ludwika Bernhard and Prof. Joachim Śliwa failed to yield any positive results. The fate of the remaining blocks remains unknown.

In February 1904 Smoleński, who was already slightly disappointed by the meager results of his work at Sharuna, learned from the local authorities that on the opposite bank of the Nile, in a place not penetrated as yet by archaeologists, the local *fellahin* were plundering "shaft graves with golden-faced sarcophagi and bodies covered with inscriptions."[10] Attempts to sell the objects at a nearby town led to the authorities alarming Smoleński, who immediately went to Cairo to request of Maspero a licence to excavate in the area.

Thus began Smoleński's excavations at el-Gamhud, a site at the edge of the Libyan dessert, some 150 km from Cairo. It was the necropolis of a locality established nearby in the Ptolemaic period. This cemetery, as a later excavator, Smoleński's successor, Ahmed bey Kamal, a curator at the Egyptian Museum in Cairo, told, was to be traced quite distinctly in the dessert sand. It formed a crescent-shaped earth mound 480 m long and 120 m wide. At either end there were shaft graves, most of which had two chambers at the bottom of the shaft. In the central part of the necropolis

[7] T. Smoleński, *Les vestiges d'un temple ptolémaïque à Kom-el-Ahmar, près de Charouna*, ASAE 9 (1908), 3-6; idem, *Nouveaux vestiges du temple de Kom-el-Ahmar, près de Charouna*, ibidem 10 (1909), 26-27. The exact location of this temple was established in 1986 by a team from the Ägyptologisches Institut of Tübingen University (J. Brinks, L. Gestermann, F. Gomaá, A. Israel, P. Jürgens. W. Schenkel, *Al-Kom al-Ahmar/ Šaruna 1986*, Göttinger Miszellen 93 (1986), 65-83).

[8] E. Varga, V. Wessetzky, *Egyiptomi Kiállitas, Vezetö* (Országos Szépmüvészeti Múzeum), Budapest 1955, 16-17; G. Wessetzky, *Les reliefs de Charouna et d'expedition de Philippe Back*, BullBaHong 30 (1967), 3-6.

[9] E. Komorzyński, *Das Erbe des alten Ägypten*, Vienna 1965, 167, 212, ill. 82.

[10] Smoleński's *Diaries*, February 18, 1907 (K. Stachowska, *Z egipskiego „Dziennika" Tadeusza Smoleńskiego (dwie kampanie wykopaliskowe)*, Rocznik Biblioteki PAN w Krakowie 33, 1988, 102).

the poorer burials were located; these, however, yielded an interesting archaeological assemblage, including cartonnages with Demotic inscriptions. These tombs that had partly been plundered in antiquity were not known to the Antiquities Service. In a letter addressed to Geniusz, Smoleński left a picturesque description of the excavated area: "Since the day before yesterday I am camping at the edge of the Libyan dessert, all alone, far from human houses, having only three tents before me and pure dessert, at one end of which I can see a rocky ridge and at the other a village. The cemetery is practically untouched: day after day I fish out Ptolemaic coffins with mummies, mostly nicely painted and inscribed, sometimes highly decorative and with gilded faces."[11]

Over a short period from March 4 to March 26, Smoleński excavated 47 sarcophagi, 20 canvas masks, including four gilded ones, a clay vessel sherd and a stele with Hieratic inscriptions, 70 masks belonging to painted wooden coffins, 11 caskets in the form of a naos with a vulture spreading its wings above it and four figurines of Osiris-Sokaris.[12]

The decoration of the wooden sarcophagi from el-Gamhud follows a generally uniform iconographic repertoire with the exception of one object, which aroused Smoleński's true enthusiasm. Here, above the embalming bed, on which the corpse was laid out, there is the image of a fish, which was the symbol of the nome of Oxyrhynchos, the district that included the cemetery where Smoleński was excavating.

His deteriorating health forced him to leave el-Gamhud. The work was continued by Ahmed Kamal, who discovered another 23 coffins, another stele with Hieratic inscription and a relatively insignificant set of other finds.[13]

Smoleński's *Diaries* and his letters reveal the extent of his struggle against his mortal illness and constant financial difficulties. He writes with determination: "But if necessary I will conquer this wretched body of mine."[14] He heroically suffers the hardships of excavations in the rainy season, as well as during the hot summer, worried that he would not be able to fulfill all his duties. When his exhausted body demands sleep and rest, Smoleński writes: "Sleep is healthy, but why so much of it and why does it rob me of time that I could use in a better way?"

In effect of a division of objects that transpired in Cairo after the excavations, 25 coffins were taken to the Museum in Budapest[15], and the rest to the Kunsthisto-risches Museum in Vienna (five pieces) and the Egyptian

[11] Letter dated March 7, 1907 (Stachowska, *Z egipskiego „Dziennika"...*, 106, note 201).

[12] The Archaeological Museum in Cracow has in its collection two figurines of Osiris-Sokaris that are typical of el-Hiba, a locality close to el-Gamhud (cf. K. Babraj, H. Szymańska, *The Gods of Ancient Egypt*, Catalogue of the Permanent Exhibition at the Archaeological Museum in Cracow, Cracow 2000, 11, 64-65, cat. 29). They may come from the excavations carried out by Smoleński, who anyhow visited the locality in 1908 (Stachowska, *Z egipskiego „Dziennika"...*, 132).

[13] A. Bey Kamal, *Fouilles à Gamhoud*, ASAE 9, 1908, 8-30, pls. I-III.

[14] Letter to Geniusz dated July 16, 1905 (Stachowska, *Listy [...] z roku 1905*, 129).

[15] This information I owe to Dr. Edith Varga, curator at the Museum of Fine Arts in Budapest.

[16] This is what Smoleński himself reported in his *Diaries* under the date of April 25 and May 6, 1907 (Stachowska, *Z egipskiego „Dziennika"...*, 116-117).

[17] The style of the three coffins in the collection of the Archaeological Museum in Cracow shows the typical characteristics of products coming from el-Gamhud; the fourth was made in all probability at el-Hiba (cf. note 16). Presumably this particular coffin was T. Koziebrodzki's gift. Cf. Babraj, Szymańska, *The Gods of Ancient Egypt*, 11, 78-81, cat. 39.

[18] Letter of March 5, 1907 (Stachowska, *Z egipskiego „Dziennika"...*, 106).

[19] T. Smoleński, *Recherches exécutées dans la Haute Egypte par la mission austro-hongroise en 1907*, Bulletin International de l'Académie des Sciences et des Lettres de Cracovie. Cl. D'Hist. et de Philos. 6/7 (1907), 104-106.

[20] T. Smoleński, *Le couvent copte de Saint-Samuel à Galamoun*, ASAE 9 (1908), 204-207; T. Partyka, *La contribution de Thadée Smolenski dans les recherches sur la topographie et l'archéologie de l'Egypte copte*, in: *Acts of the Second International Congress of Coptic Studies, Rome, 22-26 September 1980*, ed. Tito Orlandi and Frederik Wisse, Rome 1985, 257-259; Stachowska, *Z egipskiego „Dziennika"...*, 126-127.

Museum in Cairo (18 coffins).[16] Four objects were offered the Academy of Arts and Sciences in Cracow: three of these by Smoleński himself, one by T. Koziebrodzki, who received it from Phillip Back.[17]

The mummified remains of Aset-iri-khet-es lay in one of Smoleński three coffins. It is presumably about this coffin that Smoleński wrote in his *Diaries* under the date of March 5, 1907: "I have found a whole series of sarcophagi, some pretty, one splendid, huge, with golden face. Everything was left without removing the lids."[18] The Academy of Arts and Sciences had all of the coffins deposited with the National Museum in Cracow, where they met with a variety of circumstances, including being hidden during World War II in the boiler room of the Czapski Museum, a fact that was not without considerable detrimental influence on their condition. After the war, in 1952, they became part of the collection of Archaeological Museum, which took over all the objects from the Academy of Arts and Sciences.

Upon returning to Poland in June 1907, Smoleński reported on his research at the two sites in Egypt before a meeting of the Cracow Academy.[19] In October, despite deteriorating health, he was back in Egypt to start up excavations again in January of 1908. Philip Back continued to finance this expedition, which now dug at a Middle Kingdom necropolis at el-Gamhud and at the nearby Shinari, where there was a cemetery of the New Kingdom. The Coptic Christmas, which fell in early January, Smoleński spent at the nearby monastery of St. Samuel located already in the mountains. He went there with some Arabs. The trip made such an impression on the young Egyptologist that he even started reading Coptic inscriptions, promising himself to extend his knowledge of the language in the future. He even published a minor article on the monastery.[20]

At this point Smoleński was deep into planning a new expedition that would have been funded entirely from Polish resources. This would have been a team working under the aegis of the Academy of Arts and Sciences. The Academy had announced its readiness to cover the costs of his participation in the future expedition that was to be jointly organized by the Viennese and Cracow scholarly institutions. This plan took on shape in 1910, already after Smoleński's death, when Prof. Hermann Junker of Vienna and Prof. Piotr Bieńkowski from Jagiellonian University undertook research in Egypt and Lower Nubia. The archaeological data resulting from these explorations, published in part by Prof. Joachim Śliwa, is held now in the collection of the Archaeological Museum in Cracow.[21]

Named by Maspero secretary of the 2nd International Archaeological Congress, which was held in Cairo in April 1909, Smoleński took part in the highly exhausting work of organizing the Congress. He also had the honor of being the first Polish Egyptologist to attend the Congress as a representative of the Cracow Academy of Arts and Sciences.

In June 1909 he was back home for treatment. He died two months later at the age of 25. Shortly before his death he was still hoping to get quickly his Ph.D. degree at the Jagiellonian University[22] and return to Egypt where Maspero had offered him the position of secretary of the Antiquities Service.

It would be difficult to list here all of Smoleński's works, especially as his interests were more than just egyptological.[23] Suffice it to mention *Egipskie Norwidiana*[24] and countless studies in the fields of ancient and modern history, the history of science, translations from Greek, Latin and Egyptian literature,[25] as well as reviews published in domestic and foreign periodicals. He was associated with periodicals like „Głos Narodu" ("Voice of the Nation"), „Nowa Reforma" („New Reform"), acted as a regular correspondent for the paper „Słowo Polskie" („The Polish word"), where he published articles from Egypt, Palestine and Syria.[26] He left a rich collection of letters and some poetry. His wide scope of scholarly interests included also ethnographic and sociological research on the Egyptian population in the localities where he was conducting explorations.[27]

His achievements in the field of Polish Egyptology, of which he was founder and a pioneer, continue to be underestimated. Neither should the input of the Academy of Arts and Sciences for the development of this field of scholarly investigation be forgotten, as it was thanks to this institution that the Cracow collections grew to include priceless objects of Ancient Egyptian civilization and Poland, even though not yet an independent country, became one of the countries to conduct research in Egypt. Indeed, it is a mark of the importance accorded the role played by this young scholar that Gaston Maspero became an active foreign member of the Academy in 1908.

[21] J. Śliwa, *Pottery from Turah in the collection of the Archaeological Museum in Cracow*, in: *Ancient Pottery in Polish Collections*, Studia z Archeologii Śródziemnomorskiej 5 (1980), 7-24; idem, *Egyptian and Nubian pottery in the Cracow Collections*, ibidem 6 (1982), 11-42.

[22] Smoleński's Ph.D. dissertation was published after his death (*Północne ludy morskie za Ramzesa II i Minefty*, Rozprawy Akademii Umiejętności, Wydział Historyczno-Filozoficzny 55, Kraków 1912, 23-269).

[23] K. Stachowska put together a bibliography of Smoleński's works, counting some 260 items (*Studia uniwersyteckie...*, 36, note 17).

[24] Ateneum Polskie 2 (1908), 105-115. As part of his interests in *polonica* in Cairo Smoleński had searched for evidence of Jerzy Sułkowski, the tragically demised Napoleonic general, who thanks to his work on deciphering the Egyptian hieroglyphs had been enrolled in the Institut de l'Egypte.

[25] He translated into Polish the hieroglyphic text of a story from the Westcar papyrus, which appeared in Museion (3, 1 (1913), 43-53) under the title *At the court of King Cheops*, and a Demotic text from papyri in Strasbourg and Vienna, entitled *Seizing the armor* (unpublished).

[26] He was also associated with foreign periodicals, like the „Revue des Etudes Ethnographiques et Sociologiques", „Journal du Caire", „Le Bosphore" and „L'Etendard Egyptien".

[27] *Lud górno-egipski*, Lud 13 (1907), 267-281.

Andrzej Niwiński

Coffin, cartonnage and mummy of Aset-iri-khet-es in the light of Egyptological research

On the 5th March, 1907, in el-Gamhud, Tadeusz Smoleński wrote in his diary: "I have found a series of coffins, some of these nice, and one magnificent, huge, with gilded face."[1] This summary description may well fit for the coffin MAK/AS/2438, having quite a big size: 217 cm in length, 80 cm in width, and 52 cm in height, and gilded face (Photo 1).[2] The form of this anthropoid coffin represents a type, characteristic for the Late Period, with a flat bottom part (i.e. coffin case), being rather support for the mummy, and covered by a massif preponderant lid. This shape of the wooden coffin[3] was an imitation of the stone sarcophagi in the use from the Saitic times onwards, and particularly typical for the Ptolemaic Period.[4] Although a

[1] Translation from K. Stachowska, *Z egipskiego „Dziennika" Tadeusza Smoleńskiego (dwie kampanie wykopaliskowe)*, Rocznik Biblioteki PAN w Krakowie 33 (1988), 106; cf. also the foot-note 201 to the same article, where a fragment of Smoleński's letter to M. Geniusz, of 7th March 1907 is quoted: "day after day I fish a series of Ptolemaic coffins with mummies, most of which nicely painted and inscribed, sometimes very decorative ones, with gilded faces."

[2] The coffin was not mentioned in the publication by A. Kamal, *Fouilles à Gamhoud*, Annales du Service des Antiquités de l'Égypte (ASAE) 9 (1908), 8-27. Although several coffins described by him present, in some respect, analogies to Aset-iri-khet-es' one, this specific object is omitted, probably because it was already packed and prepared for transport to Cairo. In his diary, on the 24th March 1907 (i.e. three days before Kamal's arrival to Gamhud), Smoleński mentioned that "19 boxes were ready" (Stachowska, op. cit., 111). The objects previewed for the museum collections in Europe, including Aset-iri-khet-es' coffin, finally left Cairo on 8th May, 1907 (ibidem, 117).

[3] The type called "belly"-coffin in the typology outline by A. Niwiński, *Sarg NR-SpZt*, Lexicon der Ägyptologie V, Wiesbaden 1983, 455-456.

[4] M.-L. Buhl, *The Late Egyptian Anthropoid Stone Sarcophagi*, Copenhagen 1959.

Figure 1.
Original graphy of the name of the deceased from a legend on the coffin lid

[5] Among others, the coffins in Praha, Náprstkovo Museum, Inv. no P.622a, P.623a, P.624a (M. Verner, *Ältägyptische Särge in den Museen und Sammlungen der Tschechoslowakei*, Praha 1982, 281-299); Budapest, Szépmüvészeti Múzeum (E. Varga, *Szépmüvészeti Múzeum. Egyiptomi Kiállitás. Vezetö.*, Budapest 1976, 53, fig. 31); Vienna, Kunsthistorisches Museum, Inv. no 6688 and 6689 (unpublished); Liverpool, University School of Archaeology and Oriental Studies, Inv. no E.513 (unpublished); Cracow, Archaeological Museum, Inv. nos MAK/AS/2439 and MAK/AS/2440 (unpublished); cf. also A. Niwiński, *Zur Datierung und Herkunft der altägyptischen Särge*, Bibliotheca Orientalis 42 (1985), 491-508.

[6] Various inscriptions on the coffin and cartonnage offer the following versions of the name of the deceased:

The last-mentioned variant being the most complete seems to include the word *ḥt*, which allows the free translation of the name *'st-iri-ḥt.s* as "Isis making her offerings;" cf. Wörterbuch der ägyptischen Sprache (WB) I,124. The version: "Isis performing rituals," proposed so far (K. Babraj, H. Szymańska, *Eine Mumie unter dem Mikroskop. Die Untersuchungen an der ägyptischen Mumie im Archäologischen Museum zu Kraków*, Antike Welt 28/5 (1997), 371) seems to be less convincing, because of the lack of the sign that should precede the group in the word "ritual."

number of wooden coffins of this type is known from various museums,[5] the Cracow coffin of Aset-iri-khet-es[6] (Figure 1) is distinguished by the good quality of the paintings preserved, as well as by the freshness of colours. Unfortunately, the state of preservation of the figures is, in most instances, poor, as much of the original surface of the coffin is lost today, in consequence of humidity that affected it already in antiquity.

The only advantage of this is an insight into the joinery of the coffin. Both the lower part and the lid were produced of large single fragments of a trunk of sycamore tree, completed with several additional pieces of wood (Figure 2). The inside of both parts was adzed away, however very thick walls (about 10 cm of thickness) were left. The outside was sculptured in a way to get a rough appearance of mummy-shape. The joints, hollows and crevices were then camouflaged with Nile mud, and the exterior surface of the coffin was finally covered with a thin layer of plaster, on which figural decoration and hieroglyphic inscriptions were executed, with the use of yellow, blue, green, red, and black paints; the face, ears and a fragment of neck were gilded.

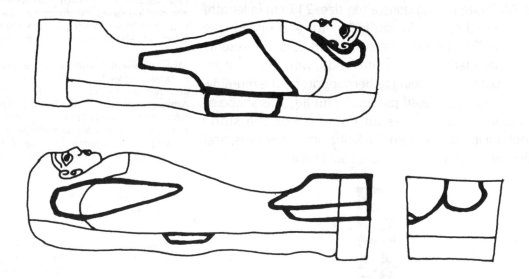

Figure 2.
Scheme of the joinery of the coffin, as observed from both sides of the coffin and from the foot-board

The deceased's head is represented as covered with monochrome (blue) wig. Large painted collar covers the lower part of the neck and the breast, reaching the level of abdomen. The collar is composed of parallel semi-circular ranges of various ornamental motifs (Figure 3), and is ended on both shoulders with large figures of sacred falcon's

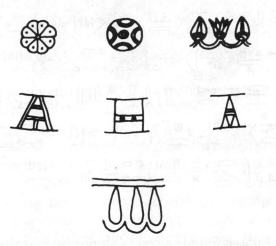

Figure 3.
Ornamental motifs from the collar painted on the coffin lid

head surmounted by solar disc (Photo 2). Beneath the collar two registers of figural representations, unfortunately only fragmentarily preserved, occupy the middle part of the lid. The upper register contains a figure of the winged goddess Nut, kneeling, with her arms and wings outspread in the gesture of protection; solar disc is represented over Nut's head. Several vertical columns of inscription once accompanied the figure; of these only four have survived, which contain the names of the deceased and her mother, as well as a prayer addressed to Nut:

"[Hathor] belonging to[7] Aset-iri-[khet-es], born of Ta-di-Usir [Tetosiris], justified; o Nut, her mother, spread out [?][8] over [her] in [your] name [...]"

In the second register, a middle part of a scene only remained, showing a mummy lying on the funeral bier, under which four canopic vases are depicted, with the characteristic lids in the form of four heads of the Sons of Horus. The mummy is accompanied by the legend saying: "Words spoken by Hathor belonging to Aset-iri-khet-es." Numerous analogous scenes on coffins indicate that the bier was originally bordered by figures of the kneeling weepers: Isis and Nephthys; only a small fragment of the figure on the left has still remained.

The frontal surface of the lower part of the lid is covered with a long inscription that was originally written in seven columns, of which the first one, and also a major part of the second, third and fifth ones are now destroyed; this makes the text rather little intelligible at first sight:

[7] The name of the goddess Hathor can occasionally precede that of female deceased, when replacing the usual appellation "Osiris;" cf. W. Spiegelberg, *Die Falkenbezeichnung des Verstorbenen in der Spätzeit*, Zeitschrift für ägyptische Sprache und Altertumskunde (ZÄS) 62(1926), 27; C. J. Bleeker, *Hathor and Thoth*, Leiden 1973, 45. The preposition appearing between the names of Hathor and Aset-iri-khet-es can probably be interpreted as the expression of the belief that the holy power of the goddess belongs to the deceased who plays the role of Hathor as a kind of her incarnation.

[8] The variant seems to be mistakenly written instead of *šsp*, "receive" (WB 4, 590-591) or *sšp* "shine" (ibidem, 282-283); in the prayer to Nut *sšp* usually the word *psš* "spread out" (with *ḥr* "over") appears (ibidem 1, 560-561), although without the sign (Gardiner's list 0.42).

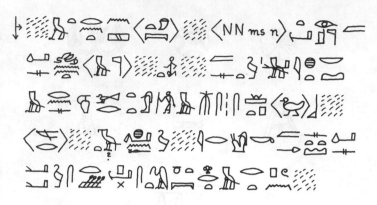

[9] Buhl, op. cit., 22, 29-32, sarcophagi: A.3 (Cairo, Egyptian Museum, Inv. no 18.11.14.15) belonging to Tja-en-hebu, from Saqqara; B.b.1 (Vienna, Kunsthistorisches Museum, Inv. no 3) from Saqqara, belonging to the wife of the King Nectanebos II; C.a.1 (Cairo Egyptian Museum, Inv. no J. 31566), from Kom Abu Yasin, belonging to the general Pa-di-sematawy (Potasimto) of the period of Psammetik II; C.a.2 (Cairo Egyptian Museum, Inv. no J. 34649), from Saqqara, belonging to a high official Psammetik.

[10] Among others: Berlin-Charlottenburg, Ägyptisches Museum, Inv. no 12/66A, coffin of Nes-pa-mai, from Akhmim (W. Kaiser, *Ägyptisches Museum Berlin*, Berlin 1967, no 868, 84-85); Bologna, Museo Civico, Inv. no 1963 (G. Kminek-Szedlo, *Catalogo di Antichità Egizie*, Torino 1895, 227-228); Florence, Museo Archaeologico, Inv. no 10582c, from El-Hibe (G. Botti, *Le casse di mummie e i sarcofagi da El Hibe nel Museo Egizio di Firenze*, Florence 1958, pl. 24); London, British Museum, Inv. no 6647, coffin used for the King Mycerinus (W. Budge, *British Museum. A Guide to the First, Second and Third Egyptian Rooms*, London 1924, 37-38, pl. I); London, British Museum, Inv. no 29776 (ibidem, 134-135, pl. XXIX); Montevideo, National History Museum, no inventory number: coffin of Aset-weret, daughter of Nes-pa-mai (owner of the coffin in Berlin?, J. J. Castillos, *A Late Egyptian Mummy at the National History Museum of Montevideo*, Toronto 1975, passim; reprinted in Revue d'Egyptologie 28 (1976), 50-60); Munich, Staatliche Sammlung Ägyptischer Kunst, Inv. no 1624 (unpublished); Stockholm, Medelhavsmuseet, Inv. no MME 1980:2 (B. George, *Ein anthropoider Sarg der Hapimen, Sohnes der Ptahirdis*, Medelhavsmuseet Bulletin 20 (1985), 42-52); also the coffins nos 11, 14 and 17 published by Kamal, op. cit., 17-21; for further references, cf. T. G. Allen, *Occurrences of Pyramid Texts,* Chicago 1950, 12-41.

[11] R. O. Faulkner, *The Ancient Egyptian Pyramid Texts translated into English,* Oxford 1969, 114, 121, 148.

[12] Cf. E. Naville, *Das aegyptische Todtenbuch der XVIII. bis XX. Dynastie*, Berlin 1886, Pl. CCII, lines 32-34; E. Hornung, *Das Totenbuch der Ägypter*, Zurich 1979, 377, lines 100-105.

[13] Principally based on Faulkner's translation proposed for the §§ 638-639 of the *Pyramid Texts* (Faulkner, op. cit., 121).

[14] Cf. WB 4, 551; originally the epithet *št-pt* was related to the name of Wadi Natrun: ibidem, 550; Faulkner op. cit., 7, n. 5.

[15] *Hnm-wrt*; WB 3, 382; K. Sethe, *Übersetzung und Kommentar zu den altägyptischen Pyramidentexten*, vol. III, Glückstadt 1939, 185 has proposed the translation of this appellation: "Great Sieve;" Faulkner prefers "Great Well" (Faulkner, op. cit., 121). However, an epithet "Nurse" encountered in Ptolemaic period in relation to various goddesses (WB 3, 381) seems better in the context of Nut's "motherhood" evoked several times in the text.

Parallels found on several stone sarcophagi[9] and also numerous wooden coffins[10] of the Saitic and post-Saitic periods make one, however, recognize in this inscription a variant of an old Nut-formula included in the corpus of the *Pyramid Texts* as the Utterance 368 (§§ 638-639, with some repetitions in the §§ 580 and 825).[11] This formula was also included in the *Book of the Dead*, as a fragment of the Chapter 178.[12]

The text on the Ptolemaic coffin of Aset-iri-khet-es presents an atypical version of the formula, since it seems to have been drawn up as a prayer pronounced by the deceased herself, i.e. composed in the first person instead of the second one, as it originally occurred in the *Pyramid Texts*. The reconstruction of the text is following:[13] "[Words spoken by Aset-iri-khet-es, born of Tetosiris. O my mother Nut, spread yourself over me] in your name «Mysterious sky»[14][...Aset-iri-khet-es born of] Tetosiris. She has caused me to be a god [without enemies, in my name «God». She will protect] me from all things evil in her name of «Great Nurse»,[15] for I am the oldest of her children. Geb [is gracious to me; he] has loved [me and] protected me [...] your companion justified in the necropolis. She gives her arms to receive you; o mother Nut, spread over me [in this your name...]."

The whole inscription was once bordered by a geometrical ornament consisting of white, blue and red squares.

The foot-board of the lid (cf. Paciorek in present volume, Photo 9) contains two representations of Anubis-jackal recumbent on his pylon-like chapel; these images are inverted in relation to the remaining decoration, and border the ending of the central column of the above – discussed text, that once descended to the tips of the feet. The whole scene was bordered with a geometrical ornament.

The rectangular front part of the cuboid socle is devoid of any trace of painting. From the decoration remaining on the other three sides it is, however, fair to deduce that it once resembled these and consisted of a green frame following the four edges of the wall, with a green rectangle painted inside. This configuration repeating the form of the hieroglyphic sign *š* evokes an idea of the primordial ocean, of which the new life emerges in the anthropoid shape of Aset-iri-khet-es' coffin.

The sides of the lid were decorated with mummiform figures of protective divine beings represented in three registers separated by geometrical ornaments and the signs of sky. On the left side (i.e. on the right side of the mummy imagined in the coffin) there are the following figures:

1. human-headed red painted mummy (Figure 4; cf. Paciorek in present volume, Photo 3) accompanied by the legend: "[Words spoken by Imset] making protection of Aset-iri-khet-es, justified;"

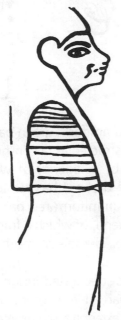

Figure 4.
Upper part of the figure of Amset, painted on the lid

2. traces of a green-painted mummy, and a fragment of the accompanying legend which can probably be reconstructed as jackal-headed figure of Duamutef described as "[Words spoken by Duamute]f making protection [of Aset-iri-khet-es, justified];"
3. serpent-headed red painted mummy (Figure 5) only traces of one hieroglyph ⌐ remained of the legend beginning with "Words spoken by..."

Figure 5.

Upper part of the serpent-headed figure represented on the lid

Figure 6.

Head of Hapi represented on the lid

On the right side the corresponding figures are:

1. ape-headed red painted mummy accompanied with the legend: "Words spoken by Hapi making protection of Hathor belonging to Aset-iri-khet-es, justified" (Figure 6);

2. a destroyed mummiform green painted figure; it can be safely reconstructed as falcon-headed Kebehsenuf, accompanied by a legend, of which only the last word: "Aset-iri-khet-es" has remained;

3. a destroyed mummiform red painted figure accompanied by a legend, of which a fragment of the name "Tetosiris" (Aset-iri-khet-es' mother) is still recognizable.

    The lid was not decorated inside.

    The bottom part of the coffin, undecorated inside, either, shows in its exterior a sculptured profile of human body (clear outline of heels, calves and buttocks), painted in yellow. The underside forms the protruding rectangular "dorsal pillar" decorated with a beautiful figure of Hathor/Isis standing on the hieroglyph š symbolising the primordial waters of Nu; the goddess makes with one hand the gesture of protection (cf. Paciorek in present volume, Photo 8).

    The beautiful coffin, one of the best of its period known from the Egyptological collections, can be understood as, originally, the outermost envelope of the Aset-iri-khet-es' mummy lying inside. This was wrapped in a number of layers of linen-bandages which is described in detail in the appendix below. Additionally, a cartonnage mask was put on the whole of the mummy's head, and multi-partite open-work cartonnage cover was laid upon the top of the body. Both the mask and the cover are richly painted and partially gilded.

The upper part of the mummy has been found badly destroyed in antiquity, probably in result of a robber's search for jewelry possibly deposited on Aset-iri-khet-es' head, neck and arms and hands. In consequence of the spoliation, also the upper part of the cartonnage were damaged, and had to be reconstructed of a number of small pieces found aside in the coffin.

The mask (cf. Paciorek in present volume, Photo 6) shows a full face, gilded, with the contours of the eyes, iris and eye-brows painted in black. The face is bordered by striped wig with lappets; over the front, from below of the wig, a row of black fringes appears. The back part of the mask, laid on the head's top and on the nape (Figure 7) is painted in blue, and its edge in red. The shoulders are decorated with a rhomboid ornament imitating a net of beads, painted in green and golden on the red ground.

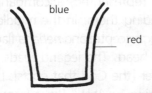

Figure 7.
Shape of the back portion of the cartonnage mask covering the mummy's nape

The upper part of the cartonnage cover (cf. Aleksiejew-Wantuch in present volume, Photos 2, 4) laying on the breast represents a large *usekh*-collar consisting of semicircular parallel bands of various ornamental motifs, painted in red, dark-green, pale-green, yellow and golden. The collar ends on both extremities with falcon's head surmounted with solar discs. Between these, winged scarab is depicted, with outspread wings, having between its posterior limbs a green circle being an echo of the hieroglyphic sign *šn* Ω (symbol of the eternal circuit).

The second (middle) part of the cartonnage cover which should be expected lying directly under the first, above-described part, was sewn on the edge of this, overlapping it by about 3 cm. Evidently, separately made parts of the cartonnage cover appeared too long in relation to the length of the mummy: it seems that such elements of the mummy-adornment were produced anonymous, and were inscribed only later, after having been adapted to a specific mummy. This part of the cover represents the winged goddess Nut kneeling, with her arms and wings outspread. The goddess has solar disc over the head, in both hands she holds the feathers of Maat – symbols of justification and divine order. Nut is kneeling on a rectangular support decorated with the repeated motifs of a gate. This resembles some box-shaped coffins encountered, with exceptions, throughout the Egyptian history. The figure of Nut is accompanied with a text composed in four columns that reads: "Words spoken by Nut the Great who bore all the gods: I make protection of Hathor-Osiris[16] belonging to Aset-iri-khet-es, born of Tetosiris."

The open-work part, crowned by the long sign of sky, is painted in golden, red, pale-green, dark-green, yellow and blue.

The third (lower) part of the cartonnage cover laying on the legs, was also sewn on the lower edge of the preceding cartonnage adornment part, overlapping it by 3 centimeters. This longest part (57 cm in length) shows, in its top a kind of rectangular pectoral bordered with geometrical ornament, and topped with an imitation of the hieroglyphic sign of sky. Inside, three standing figures of protective deities of the deceased are represented, accompanied by hieroglyphic legends preceding them: in the middle, Osiris is depicted, holding the *heqa*-sceptre and *nehaha* flagellum, with the *atef* crown on his head. The legend reads: "Words spoken by Osiris Wennefer [the God that exists]: I make protection of Osiris[17] belonging to Aset." Right from Osiris, mummiform jackal-headed Anubis is depicted, accompanied by the legend: "Words spoken by Anubis, the head of the Divine Hall: I make protection of Hathor belonging to Aset." Behind Osiris, Isis is standing, preceded by the legend: "Words spoken by Isis, great mother of the God: I make protection of Hathor."

Beneath the pectoral, four panels, each topped by the sky-sign contain four mummiform figures of the Sons of Horus: on the left: Amset and (underneath) Duamutef, on the right Hapi and Kebehsenuf. The figures face a long gilded band obviously intended to receive an inscription, that, however, remained empty.

On the soles of the mummy, another double cartonnage cover was fixed, reproducing the motifs of sandals-soles. The two feet-covers overlapping each other, were sewn on the

[16] The appellation of the deceased by the combined divine names of Hathor and Osiris is very seldom encountered on the objects of funerary character in the Late Period. It appears on the sarcophagus lid of lady Tadipekem of IV-III century B.C., in the Cairo Museum, Inv. no J. 43098 originated from Tuna el-Gebel near Hermopolis Magna, which hints at a possibility that this custom of naming the deceased Hathor-Osiris originated from middle Egypt. It is interesting to quote here G. Lefebvre's comment from *Un couvercle de sarcophage de Tounah*, ASAE 23 (1923), 239: "Le nom de la défunte n'est pas seulement précédé du mot 𓏏 (l'hatorienne Tatoupakem), selon un usage, d'ailleurs assez rare, de la basse époque (examples du Livre *Que mon nom fleurisse*, pl. I, IV, VII, XIII, XXXVIII, XXXIX, LXVII) mais encore de l'épithete générale des défunts les assimilant à Osiris. Je ne connais pas d'autre example de ce curieux composé 𓉠𓏏 ."

[17] Again, an analogy is given by the sarcophagus lid from Tuna, discussed in the preceding note; in several spots the deceased is called there "Osiris NN," beside of the aforementioned "Osiris-Hathor NN."

bandages. The ornament on the sandal-soles consisted of three vertical parallel thin bands painted in yellow.

The whole ensemble of the symbolic figures and motives represented on the coffin and cartonnage was undoubtedly believed as very efficient bearer of magical protective power. It is quite certain that some pieces of jewelry were put on the mummy (bracelets, ear-adornments, necklaces?) because this was object of precisely directed plundering by well-informed robbers; no traces of plundering have been found in the middle or lower parts of the mummy. It can be safely assumed that these objects of jewelry, lost today, also were shaped as, or decorated with symbolic figures of amuletic value.

In contrast, no amulets made of metal, stone, faience or wood have been discovered inside of the mummy. However, during the autopsy (Photo 3) some atypical objects have been found, all of them made of linen of the same kind as the bandages, shrouds and compresses used for mummy wrappings, and these can no doubt be understood as a kind of amulets, perhaps typical for the region.[18] Such objects (of linen) sandwiched between the linen envelops, are hardly detectable by radiograph methods of examination, even the most sophisticated ones, such as computer tomography, magnetic resonance etc.[19]

Objects made of linen have sometimes been found during the unwrapping examinations. As long ago as in 1827 in Florence Rosellini and Migliarini found on the wrists of a mummy, and also around the ankles "counterfeit bracelets made of gummed cloth to imitate, by the aid of colour and gilding, precious stones."[20] An imitation of the (leather) mummy-braces made of bandages is mentioned in the protocol of the unwrapping of a 21st Dynasty mummy in the Cairo Museum in 1903.[21] Finally sandals were imitated in linen on the Ptolemaic mummy ÄS 73b unwrapped in Munich in 1984.[22]

The common purpose of all these cloth replicas was to substitute other objects, similar in form but usually made of different materials. From the religious viewpoint such substitutes seem to have played the same role as the imitated originals, which might have been orally evoked in the texts recited simultaneously and accompanying the act of depositing an object upon the mummy. This rule can certainly be applied to five linen objects found among the wrappings of Aset-iri-khet-es' mummy.

[18] During an autopsy of a priest Amenhotep's mummy of the same period, originated from Thebes, in contrast, 55 amulets of stone, faience and gilded wood have been found, four balls made of earth, cartonnage hypocaephalus and remains of a funerary papyrus that once enveloped the mummy's legs. Cf. A. Niwiński, *Excavations in a Late Period priest's mummy at the National Museum Warsaw. Preliminary report*, in: *VI Congresso internazionale di egittologia. Atti.*, vol. 2, Turin 1993, 353-361, pl. 4.

[19] A major part of the text that follows was separately published as fragment of an article by A. Niwiński, *Some unusual amulets found on the Late Period mummies in Warsaw and Cracow*, in: *Egyptian Religion. The Last Thousand Years. Part I. Studies Dedicated to the Memory of Jan Quaegebeur*, Leuven 1998, 179-190.

[20] C. H. Cottrell, *Account of the Unrolling of a Mummy at Florence...*, Archaeologia 36 (1858), 166-167.

[21] G. Daressy, G. Elliot Smith, *Ouverture des momies provenant de la Seconde trouvaille de Deir el-Bahari*, ASAE 4 (1903),152.

[22] G. Ziegelmayer, *Münchner Mumien*, Munich 1985.

[23] E. A. Akmar, *Les bandelettes de momie du Musée Victoria à Uppsala,* Uppsala 1932-1939; C. Traunecker, *La bandelette de momie inscrite de la collection de l'Institut d'Egyptologie de Strassbourg,* Kemi 19 (1969), 71-78; R. Caminos, *Fragments of the Book of the Dead on linen and papyrus,* Journal of Egyptian Archaeology (JEA) 56 (1970), 117-131; S. Pernigotti, *Bande di mummia con il „Libro dei Morti" da Saqqara,* Egitto e vicino Oriente 3 (1980), 99-115; A. Gasse, *Les bandelettes de momie inscrites du Musée des Beaux-Arts de Besançon,* Bulletin de l'Institut Français d'Archéologie Orientale 82 (1982), 205-211.

[24] E. Tapp, *The unwrapping of 1770,* in: *Science in Egyptology,* Manchester 1986, 53.

[25] *Evidence Embalmed. Modern Medicine and the Mummies of Ancient Egypt,* Manchester 1984, 41.

[26] Tapp, op. cit., 53 and 56.

[27] A. Barsanti, *Fouilles autour de la pyramide d'Ounas (1900-1901). VIII. Tombeau de Péténéit,* ASAE 2 (1901), 102-104.

[28] In 1836 Thomas Pettigrew observed on a mummy of the 25th or 26th Dynasty at Hartwell House that "viscera had been removed and rolled up and placed between the legs," cf. W. Dawson, *Pettigrew's demonstrations upon mummies. A chapter in the history of Egyptology,* JEA 20 (1934), 176. The X-ray examinations of the mummies in the British Museum have shown several times "an opacity between the knees, probably a roll of linen," cf. W. Dawson, P. H. K. Gray, *Catalogue of Egyptian Antiquities in the British Museum. I. Mummies and Human Remains,* London 1968, 26-27.

[29] According to Pettigrew's description of an unwrapping of the mummy of the Royal College of Surgeons in 1834, "in removing the crumpled wadding between the thighs, a small clay model of an outer mummy-case rudely made and imperfectly if at all vitrified and now partly decomposed was found behind or beneath the scrotum;" cf. W. Dawson, *Pettigrew's demonstrations,* 174.

[30] G. Daressy, *Les cercueils des prêtres d'Ammon (Deuxième trouvaille de Deir el-Bahari),* ASAE 8 (1907), 34.

First of these is a small roll of bandage, about 4 cm long and about 5 cm in diameter, placed between the thighs just below the pelvis. When discovered during the CT scanning it initially looked like a papyrus scroll, often deposited in this place upon mummies. As the round-shaped object disappeared soon after from the CT-section picture, it became obvious that the object was rather too short when compared with the rolls of papyri; for a moment we thought it might be a roll of bandage inscribed with passages of the *Book of the Dead*. Although a number of such bandages exist in various museums,[23] hardly a single piece can be safely given an archaeological context; it is only repeated that the bandages originate from mummies.

During the unwrapping the object appeared to be a simple roll of bandage, uninscribed. A similar find was done in 1975 by the Manchester Museum Mummy Project team on mummy n° 1770 of the Greek or Roman period, and the authors interpreted it in a way that "...there was little doubt that this represented an artificial phallus."[24] This interpretation has never been reconsidered, in spite of the fact that the mummy finally turned out to belong to a girl, aged about 14 years at death[25] (two gilded nipple covers have been discovered upon the breasts[26]). Although a phallus substitute seems to have been attested on the mummy of Padineith at Sakkara (a small golden amulet in the form of phallus placed between the legs),[27] such an interpretation of a roll of bandage on a female mummy seems hardly convincing. It might well have played a role of a substitute of a *Book of the Dead* on papyrus or linen, but also of anything else placed between the legs (this spot forming an art of natural groove was especially suitable for any deposit): a package of embalmed viscera[28] or an *ushebty*-figure.[29] It is worth mentioning Daressy's observation made on the occasion of the examinations of the mummies of the Amun priests of the 21st Dynasty, that on the mummy n° 130 a stick, 35 cm long has been found between the legs instead of the usual papyrus-scroll.[30]

It seems that the same role of substitutes of amulets of indefinite nature could have been played by two other objects, similar to each other in appearance, found on the mummy Aset-iri-khet-es. These small pseudo-amulets of irregular shape were made of pieces of linen soaked and stuck together with a resinous substance; both objects were found sandwiched between bandages covering the breast and abdomen. As a number of various amulets have been found in similar spots on mummies, it is rather impossible to determine the exact purpose of the original amulets, envisaged by the performers of the bandaging ritual in this case.

Another linen object found upon the mummy is of a quite unusual character, and is so far unparalleled.

A ring of ca. 5 cm in diameter was originally placed between some compresses (made of small pieces of linen and short bandages) covering the stomach, evidently over the navel (Photo 4). On an analogous spot a small round golden plate (about 1 cm in diameter) was discovered in 1984 on a Ptolemaic mummy ÄS 73b in Munich,[31] and the plans of the disposition of amulets on some mummies of the same period found at Dendera show a similar circular shape in the navel area.[32]

Although various occurrences of the word _hp'_ meaning "navel" or "umbilical cord" have been discussed long since,[33] little can be found in the Egyptological literature on the religious connotations of the navel.[34] The word "umbilical cord" already appears in the Spell 317 of the _Coffin Texts_,[35] and then in the Chapter 17 of the _Book of the Dead_,[36] but for the matter studied here, two other texts are of importance. In the medico-magical papyrus in the Berlin Museum (P. 3027) an illness _nšw_ is being charmed with a long spell enumerating various parts of the body, including the navel: "Go out, _nšw_, fall on the earth! Do not fall on his navel [because] it is the «Morning Star»."[37] Chapter 172 of the _Book of the Dead_, thus far known only from one source, the papyrus of Nebseni, possesses a similar enumerative character. This interesting text is divided into "houses" (stanzas) and begins with the words: "I am purified with natron..." which evokes associations with a mummification process. In the first "stanza," a kind of invocation, the deceased is addressed among others as "lamented one," and beginning with the second part of this composition, different parts of the body are named, starting with the head, and ending with the toes, as if an operation on the mummy (perhaps consisting of anointments preceding the process of wrapping) would have been followed by ritual magical spells. In the fourth stanza, after having named, among others, breasts, arms, shoulders, and thighs, the text says: "your belly is the peaceful sky, your navel is the Morning Star which makes judgement and promises light in darkness, and whose offerings are the plant _anchimy_."[38] Erik Hornung suggests to translate the word _dw't_

[31] G. Ziegelmayer, op. cit.

[32] W. M. F. Petrie, _Amulets_, London 1914, pl. LII.

[33] Cf. among others A. Blackman, _Some remarks on an emblem upon the head of an ancient Egyptian Birth-goddess_, JEA 3 (1916), 203-206; B. Ebell, _Ein missverstandenes ägyptisches Wort_, ZÄS 65 (1930), 61-63; A. Gardiner, _Umbilical cord_, ibidem 66 (1931), 71.

[34] Some considerations are found in the article of A. Blackman, op. cit., 199-206.

[35] R. Faulkner, _The Ancient Egyptian Coffin Texts_, vol. I, London 1973, 241.

[36] R. Faulkner, _The Ancient Egyptian Book of the Dead_, London 1985, 45.

[37] A. Erman, _Zaubersprüche für Mutter und Kind aus Pap. Berlin 3027_, Berlin 1901, 21.

[38] R. Faulkner, _The Ancient Egyptian Book of the Dead_, 171.

[39] E. Hornung, *Totenbuch der alten Ägypter*, Zurich 1979, 354 ("Der Himmel ist dein Leib, wenn du zu Ruhe gehst, und die Unterwelt ist dein Nabel").

[40] W. M. F. Petrie, *Dendereh 1898*, London 1900, 33.

[41] On the navel of a girl's mummy of the Ptolemaic or Roman period in the collection of the Egyptian Museum, Berlin (Inv. no 837), originated from Thebes, a cover made of gilded wax has been found. Interesting is also the text appearing on the coffin belonging to this deceased: "The sky is closed over the earth, the earth is closed over the underworld, the underworld is closed over this strong coffin, this strong coffin is closed over the Osiris-Hathor NN;" the mummy is therefore, understood as lying in the centre of the universe. (A. Erman, *Ausfrührliches Verzeichnis der aegyptischen Altertümer; Kgl. Museen zu Berlin*, Berlin 1894, 343-344; for this information I am indebted to Prof. Renate Germer from Hamburg).

Figure 8.
Stars and solar discs representing an emanation of light and life from the God in the Netherworld (motif found on a coffin of the 21st Dynasty in the Egyptian Museum, Cairo, Inv. no CG 6259)

[42] *Nabel* in: *Die Religion in Geschichte und Gegenwart. Handwörterbuch für Teologie und Religionswissenschaft*, Tübingen 1960³, 1285-1286.

as "nether-world" rather than "Morning Star."[39] In this context it is interesting that an amulet in the form of a Star was found over the navel on a mummy in Dendera.[40]

The golden circle mentioned above, found on the navel of the mummy in Munich does not contradict this, because stars and (solar) discs are often painted side by side, when representing the emanation of light and the force of life from the God in the Netherworld (Figure 8); the activity of this beneficent god takes place in the night (the nightly sky, i. e. the invisible Osirian hemisphere of the Universe), which is alluded to by the star symbol, and during the day (the daily sky, i. e. the visible solar hemisphere of the world), symbolised by the disc. As man (= microcosm) was regarded as representing the whole universe (= macrocosm), the creation of the world was comparable to the personal birth and the human experience was echoed in many cosmogonic myths (the Creator is emerging from the darkness of the watery primordial ocean like a baby from the darkness of the liquids in the womb of its mother; the first light; the first cry, etc.). The navel is thus a symbolic join between the macro- and the microcosm, between the created world and the world before creation, where man returns after death, with the hope of a future rebirth.[41]

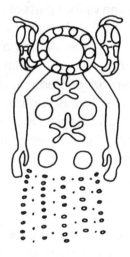

This crucial and central point of the body[42] needed a special protection, and the amulet found on the mummy of Aset-iri-khet-es evidently evokes this idea. It is probably not accidental that all the mummies upon which objects connected with the navel have so far been found, are Ptolemaic in date; the importance of the idea of "the navel of the earth (Omphalos) in Greek culture is well-known.

The form of the ring, no doubt of magical character, evokes associations with the knotted cords, sometimes also ending with a ring, which functioned as amulets on the necks of some mummies from Kafr Ammar."[43]

Another discovery on Aset-iri-khet-es' mummy, the pair of cords, is unparalleled; the object, measuring 31 and 36 cm, are made of twisted linen bandages (Photo 5) and placed upon the shins of the mummy among the bandages; the beginning of one cord was placed under the sole. These cords had certainly no technical meaning; they might have played a symbolic role of an unusual amulet, a substitute for something thin, long and anyhow related to legs and feet. The iconographic repertoire of some mummy-containers: the cartonnages and wooden coffins of the Third Intermediate Period and the Late Period offer indeed several figures with such thin oblong shapes, represented in pairs in the lower part of the coffins, corresponding to the legs: obelisks, the serpents and the so-called fetishes or sacred emblems of Nefertum. Among these various forms, obelisks, which are not at all flexible, are unlikely to have been substituted by cords. The choice between the remaining figures of serpents and Nefertum emblems was not easy, because these two pairs of symbolic representations offer appear together on coffins, as an example on the coffin in the Egyptological Institute of the University of Heidelberg, n° 1015 (Figure 9) shows. However, the fact that in this case the serpents have been painted on the bottom of the coffin (situated under the calves of the mummy) while the lotus-emblems of Nefertum appear on the interior of the coffin lid (painted over the shins) points to the latter symbol as the possible origin of the cord-amulets found on the shins of the mummy in Cracow. With this in mind a search for supporting proof in the form of a find during the recorded unwrappings of mummies was started again, with positive results.

[43] W. M. F. Petrie, *Heliopolis, Kafr Ammar and Shurafa*, London 1915, pl. XXXII; idem, *Amulets*, pl. XVII.

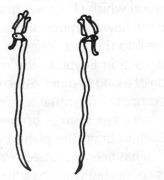

a   b

Figure 9.
Two pairs of the symbolic figures found on the coffin in the collection of the Egyptological Institute of the University of Heidelberg, Inv. no 1015

In 1837 Dr. Pettigrew found, again on a Ptolemaic mummy, on each knee "a thin piece of gold resembling the lotus-flower."[44] He also mentioned that the finger and toe-nails were gilt which is also the case in our mummy. Three years earlier the same scholar, on the occasion of the unwrapping of a mummy brought from Egypt in the XVIIth century by Henry Duke of Norfolk, made another interesting observation: "On cutting into the bandages of the sole of the left foot, they were found to enclose a bulbous root [...]. The right foot had also a bulbous root placed under the sole."[45] This discovery is not unique, it is not even the oldest recorded in the extant literature on mummies. As long ago as in 1764 a Dr. Hadley presented an article on the examination of a mummy in the *Transactions of the Royal Society in London*. "The mummy retained not the smallest vestige of the soft parts, except some of the tendons of the feet, to the sole of one of which a bulbous root, perhaps an onion, was discovered, firmly bound by fillets and pitch."[46]

In 1910 E. Naville published two stone slabs, probably of the Late Period, found at Horbeit and containing a ritual text.[47] The figure accompanying the beginning of this offers a perfect combination of all the elements mentioned above: the bulbous root (found under the soles of the feet), the lotus flower (found on the knees of another mummy) and the symbolic appearance of the sacred emblem of Nefertum (represented on the coffins and cartonnages near the feet and shins of the mummy inside) (Figure 10). The plant represented there was called *snnwt*, and is mentioned in the *Papyrus Ebers*;[48] it was tentatively identified with the binding weed *Convolvulus hystrix* and with scammony by J.-C. Goyon[49] and L. Manniche[50] respectively. However, this identification is hardly convincing, because the binding weed (scammony) is not a bulbous plant. In my opinion the *snnwt* was a kind of lily (probably *Lilium candidum* or *Lilium longiflorum*) which (1) grows from a bulb, (2) has strongly fragrant flowers much similar to the lotus, (3) corresponds well to the description in the *Papyrus Ebers*, and (4) was used in Egypt as the main component in the production of a kind of much esteemed ointment described by Dioskorides.[51] The ritual text from Horbeit known also from some other sources of funeral character, bears the title "Spell to bring the plant *anchimy* every day to the tomb;"[52] it has been discussed several times.[53] Although the text is connected with the offering ritual, it might have been used as well during the ritual

[44] W. Dawson, *Pettigrew's demonstrations*, 176.

[45] T. J. Pettigrew, *History of Egyptian Mummies*, London 1834, 102.

[46] A. B. Granville, *An Essay on Egyptian Mummies; with observations on the art of embalming among the ancient Egyptians*, in: *Transactions of the Royal Society*, London 1825, 282.

[47] E. Naville, *La plante de Horbéit*, ASAE 10 (1910), 191-192, pls. I-II; idem, *La plante magique de Noferatum*, Revue de l'Egypte Ancienne 1 (1927), 31-44.

[48] E. Naville, *La plante de Horbéit*. II, ASAE 16 (1916), 188, quotes the translation by V. Loret: "La plante dont le nom est *snnwt*, elle croit sur son bulbe comme le *k`rtw*, elle a une fleur comme le lotus."

[49] J.-C. Goyon, *Rituels funéraires de l'Ancienne Égypte*, Paris 1972, 347.

[50] L. Manniche, *An Ancient Egyptian Herbal*, London 1989, 93.

[51] Ibidem, 51.

[52] H. Altenmüller, *Zwei neue Exemplare des Opfertextes der 5. Dynastie*, Mitteilungen des Deutschen Archäologischen Instituts 23 (1968), 1-8.

[53] H. Kees, *Ein alter Götterhymnus als Begleittext zum Opfertafel*, ZÄS 57 (1922), 92-120; Naville, *La plante magique*, 31-44; Altenmüller, op. cit., 1-8.

of mummification. The fragrant plant identified with Nefertum (and in the iconography with his sacred emblem) is called at the beginning of the text: "this great-one who comes out as the lotus, who comes out from Nut, the great power born of Geb, who stops Seth in his fury."

Figure 10.
The *snnwt*-plant represented on a stone slab from Horbeit (after E. Naville, *La plante magique de Noferatum*, Revue de l'Egypte Ancienne 1, (1927), 33)

It is quite feasible that the spell found at Horbeit might have accompanied the act of putting linen imitation of the *snnwt*-plant on at least one shin of the mummy of Aset-iri-khet-es. Perhaps the second linen imitation found on another shin represented the lotus (or papyrus?) flower; hence the two plants might even have symbolized the Two Lands of Egypt. This seems to enrich our insight in the rituals performed during the mummification process in Egypt in the Ptolemaic period.

Photo 1.
Sarcophagus of Aset-iri-khet-es

Photo 2.
Falcon's head surmounted by solar disc

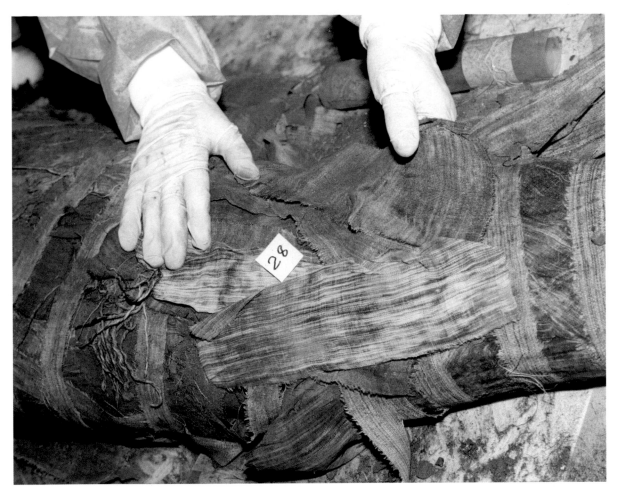

Photo 3.
Autopsy of the mummy of Aset-iri-khet-es

Photo 4.
Ring of linen placed on the navel of Aset-iri-khet-es'
mummy

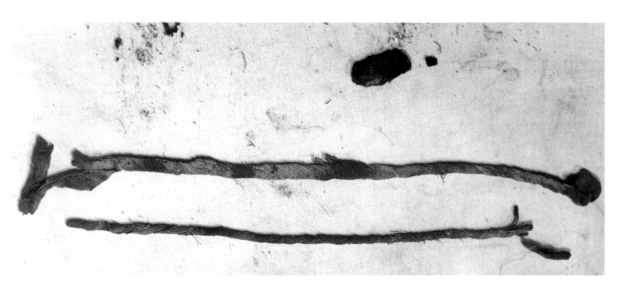

Photo 5.
Pseudo-amulets found during the autopsy of
Aset-iri-khet-es' mummy

Katarzyna Tempczyk

The mummy's wrappings

In January 1999, collecting materials for my M.A. thesis, I had opportunity to participate in the reconstruction proceeding of bandaging manner of Aset-iri-khet-es' mummy. The reconstruction was based on the observations made during the autopsy, relating to the disposition and course of each bandage, recorded in notes and photos, and it was controlled by the video records. Because of destruction of a considerable part of the wrappings caused by damage of the mummy's thorax, and by the strong impregnation of the bandages by resins, it was necessary to use additionally a few present-day sterile pieces of linen cloths.

The original wrappings of Aset's body consisted of:
1 – long narrow stripes of linen (approximately 2 cm in width) that once composed, among others, the first layer of bandages put on the body, and were then repeatedly used to fasten the broader bandages;
2 – long bandages (from 3 to 5 cm in width); these were used throughout the bandaging process to wrap the body in various ways: encircling the corps vertically or horizontally, or put across the body on its top and under the bottom;
3 – small rectangular numerous pieces of linen (average size 7 × 16 cm) laid on the top of the body, between the bandages, and used to shape the mummy;
4 – linen tampons used to fill the depression between limbs;
5 – long wide pieces of linen (10–16 cm in width) lying on the top of the mummy, or on both its sides; these cloths were divided at one end in two or three narrower stripes, girdling the feet;
6 – large rectangular shrouds completely enveloping the mummy.

The deceased was lying supine with arms positioned along the corps; the palms were placed on the pubic area of the womb. It has been observed that the lower part of both legs (from the knees to the feet) was wrapped separately, and then joined with the rest of the corps that had also been already bandaged. In the first stage of bandaging process[1] the arms, legs and also all the fingers were separately wrapped; the fingers were additionally supplemented with a gilded imitations of the nails (Photo 1).

The first layer of the wrappings was composed of numerous very narrow overlapping stripes of linen, dark brown in colour, girdling the members and the corps. Practically all these bandages were found joined with the deceased's skin, in result of strong soaking with a resinous liquid substance poured over the body. Next layers consisted of wider stripes encircling several times the mummy in various ways, and kept in position with another narrow bandages, which could be particularly well observed at feet. All the natural depressions of the body were at this stage packed in with numerous tampons; the mummy obtained therefore a relatively equal surface, which again was coated very abundantly with molten resin; this hardened and stuck together the layers of linen lying below (Photo 2).

The thorax, the abdomen, as well as the legs were then covered by numerous small rectangular pieces of linen of different sizes, used to reshape the natural convexities of the body. On a part of the torso, a shroud was laid, having about 70 cm in length, which was held in place by long narrow bandages crossing the chest area. Similar narrow stripes of linen ran around the legs, crossing over the metatarsus and girdling several times the calves, up to the knees. On the right side of the calves a wide piece of linen (approx. 16 cm in width) was found, bending under the heels, and then running upwards along the legs, on the left side. This bandage, too, was held in place by long narrow stripes (approx. 4 cm in width) of linen girdling obliquely several times the calves and the ankles.

At this stage the two parts of the mummy were joined, the fracture covered with a layer of small wraps, and the whole body was for the first time wrapped together with long narrow bandages (approx. 2 cm in width), which were running in certain distances around the whole body, girdling it ten-fold at least.

The upper layer of bandages consisted of long wide pieces of linen enveloping the mummy along both sides, from the shoulders to the feet. These were held in place, mainly at the ankles, by narrow stripes of linen. One bandage of this sort (approx. 10 cm in width and 176 cm in length) lying along the left side of the body was divided near its end in two parts 50 cm long that crossed under the feet; a similar bandage covered the right side of the corps. Another wide piece of linen was lying on the right side, bending under the heels, then running upwards the left side of the body, and finally disappearing under the mummy at the level of the pelvis. All these bandages were held in place by long narrow stripes of linen, which enveloped several times the mummy's legs at the level of ankles and feet, and crossed on the instep. Another narrow bandage was girdling not only the upper part of the limbs, but also the chest.

[1] Unfortunately, in consequence of activity of ancient robbers and the destruction of the original wrappings, it is impossible to reconstruct the bandaging manner of Aset's head, which has been found separated from the body, and deprived of bandages.

Afterwards, the top of the mummy was covered with a wide piece of linen (approx. 35 cm in width) divided into three pieces of different sizes: the central part – wider and shorter – ended on the instep, whereas the longer side-parts crossed themselves under the feet. Another similar three-fold bandage covered, with its two lateral parts, both sides of the body up to the shoulders, while its central part (ca. 20 cm in width) was laid under the heels. Then the mummy was wrapped with narrow stripes of linen, coated with molten resin, and again completely enveloped by a double shroud of fine quality linen. On the breast was found a "scarf" made of fine linen (12 cm in width, and 54 cm in length) ending with selvage and warp fringes. Above this, the mummy's torso was again girdled several times with narrow bandages, and finally numerous narrow linen stripes crossing the chest were laid upon the mummy. The central part of the chest was smeared with molten resin, and then the cartonnage covering was sewn on the upper layer of the wrappings.

Regarding the texture of the bandages, most of these were made of thickly woven linen; here belong:

- all narrow stripes used at every stage of the bandaging process, wrapping mummy around and holding in place the cloths lying underneath;
- wide long pieces of linen found lying along the corps;
- resin-soaked tampons and a major part of the packing wraps.

However, the shrouds, the "scarf" and some "wraps" were made of fine linen.

Although no inscriptions or figural scenes have been found on the bandages, some of these are specifically decorated.[2]

Among the numerous "wraps" there are specimens with double or triple self-bands (Photos 3 and 4) running in parallel near to the end of the cloth.

Other pieces are decorated with warp fringes (the fringes made as a result of twisting long threads of warp); here belong both short endings of the "scarf" (Photo 5).

That type of fringe exists exclusively on the fine linen bandages because the threads of warp are more soft, and consequently more supple to twisting.

Examples of another type of fringe have also been found, consisting of the loose warp threads (ca. 3 cm in length) left after the relinquishment of the weft; the threads of weft directly above the fringes are, at the same time, woven loosely, and a double self-band is woven in the weft ca. 5 cm from the edge (Photo 6).

This type of fringe is characteristic for a kind of linen woven compactly with the use of thick fibers as can be observed on some narrow long stripes, and also on wide bandages found on the mummy.

Some pieces of cloth offer examples of carefully executed selvages (Photo 7).

Seams showing spots of repaired tears in the cloth are represented, too, in the materials from Aset's mummy, as seen on the Photo 8 (single seam) and Photo 9 (double seam).

[2] Some analogous examples of the decoration of Ancient Egyptian mummy wrappings are offered by the collection of textiles in the National Museum of Antiquities, Leiden (cf. E. H. C. van Rooij and G. M. Vogelsang-Eastwood, *The Pharaonic textiles*, in: *Pharaonic and Early Medieval Egyptian Textiles*, Leiden 1994, 13-27, pl. 1-3, 9, 11, 12) as well as by the collection in the Museum Gustavianum in Uppsala.

Photo 1.

Photo 2.

Photo 3.

Photo 4.

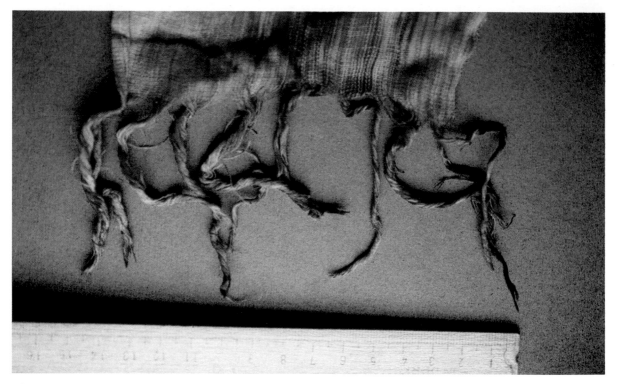

Photo 5.

Photo 6.

Photo 7.

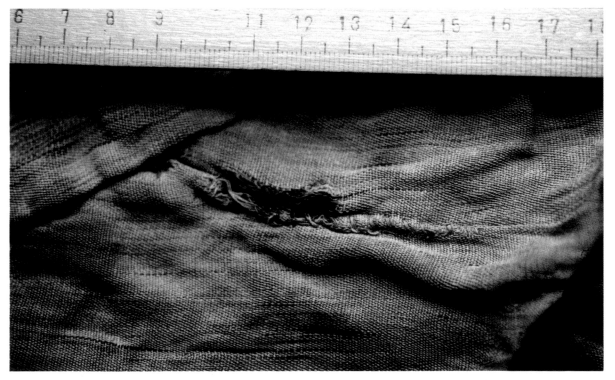

Photo 8.

Photo 9.

All photos by prof. A. Niwiński

Andrzej Urbanik

Comprehensive radiological examination

The object of the work is to publish the results of a comprehensive radiological examination (conventional radiology – X-ray and computed tomography – CT) of an Egyptian mummy. These results have also been compared with the physical results of the autopsy.

Material and method

A mummy from the collection of the Archaeological Museum in Cracow was submitted for the examination; the mummy was excavated at a site in el-Gamhud, conducted in 1907 by the first Polish Egyptologist, a Cracovian – Tadeusz Smoleński.

The mummy was removed from its polychromy-covered sarcophagus and from the cartonnage, on which hieroglyphic inscriptions name the deceased: Aset-iri-khet-es. Then the mummy was placed in three individually sealed (seam-welded) film bags and transported to the Department of Radiology of Collegium Medicum (Jagiellonian University), where radiological examinations took place. First a review X-ray films of particular portions of the mummy were made; these films facilitated a preliminary estimation. These standard X-ray films were converted into digital form with the use of a professional digitiser. Being stored in the memory of a computer they were later the subject of a very detailed analysis, which allowed enlargements to be made of selected parts; also, specific images, with parts of the mummy, were then assembled in order to obtain a complete image of the mummy.

Next, a CT examination took place (Somaton 2, Siemens). 182 scans were taken to a thickness of 8 mm, covering the whole body of the mummy and 40 2-millimetre scans of selected fragments of the mummy (Photo 1).

Photo 1.
Mummy in the gantry
of a CT apparatus –
view from the console

What was then analysed were elements of the skeleton, the soft tissue of the embalmed corpse, as well as other components of the mummy first of all the alignment of bandages. Taking advantage of the recent installation of a new of spiral CT device (Helicat Flash, Marconi) with the options of three-dimensional reconstruction (3D) and virtual endoscopy (VE), a subsequent examination was carried out, this time examining the head. The parameters of the scan: collimation 1.3 mm, pitch 1.5, increment 30%. The description and the CT images were compared with the actual state – the participation of a radiologist in the autopsy created a unique possibility to juxtapose the obtained radiological images against the actual state (Photo 2).

Photo 2.
Unwrapping of the
mummy and the
comparison of the
actual state with
radiological images

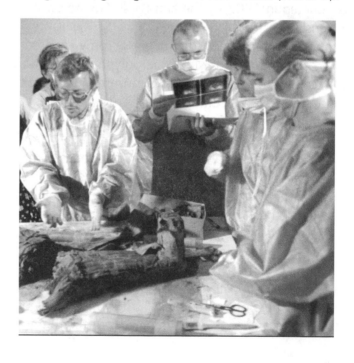

Analysed were images in the axial view, in 2-D reconstruction and also in 3-D reconstruction as well as images from virtual endoscopy (images of the cranium). In order to carry out this analysis a "window" was placed at a width of ca. 2000 H.U. (Hounsfield units) with the centre at the level from 500 to 800 H.U.

Results

On the basis of the X-ray review of films and CT images the findings were: damages to the bandages and also to the substance of: the cranium (maxilla and mandible), extensive damage to the chest, the upper extremities, the abdominal cavity and partly to the pelvis with dislocations. In these areas of the corpse a real "rubble" was found, consisting of elements with various degrees of X-ray obstruction. Those were identified as osseous elements, mud, fragments of bandages partly soaked with resin and also resin layers. Only lower extremities were preserved without any signs of damage. In spite of the fact that both the sarcophagus and the cartonnage looked very opulent, no presence of jewellery, amulets and beads, which were usually placed on a mummified corpse could be confirmed (Photos 3-5).

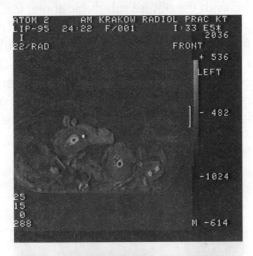

Photo 3.
CT examination – image in the transverse view at the chest level

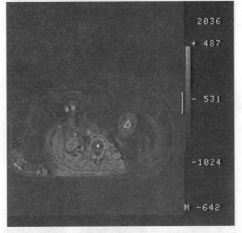

Photo 4.
CT examination – image in the transverse view at the abdomen level

Photo 5.
CT examination –
image in the transverse
view at the pelvis level

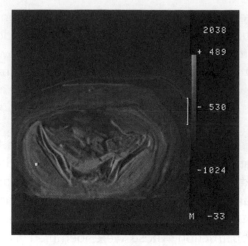

The radiological findings were confirmed during the autopsy; additionally, on the damaged phalanxes of fingers and toes remainders of gold were found. This proves that the mummy was robbed, in result of which considerable damage was done to the body.

During the analysis of the skeleton it was found out that the bone structure was friable. The pelvis with the obtuse sub-pubic angle; the pubic symphysis is low and its bottom edge being rounded archwise. These features are characteristic of a female pelvis. A transcondylar fracture of the right femoral bone was detected, without signs of synostosis (Photo 6). During the autopsy this finding was confirmed. Moreover, an atypical manner of embalming of the lower extremities was detected. With Aset's mummy it was found out that the lower extremities had been cut at the level of the knee joints; thighs and

Photo 6.
X-ray review film –
fracture of the right
femoral bone

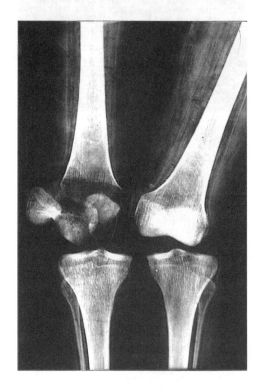

shanks were wrapped with bandage separately. Only the last layers of bandages formed the final shape of the bottom part of the mummy, creating the whole figure.

Considering the age of the woman (on the basis of anthropological examinations it was assumed to be between 25 and 30 years), the lack of pathological changes proving lesions (on the basis of all examinations carried out), and also the unusual manner of embalming of the lower extremities, one may reach a hypothesis about the reason for her death. In transcondylar fracture cases the popliteal artery may be damaged, which may result in exsanguination. Maybe this was the reason for the death of Aset-iri-khet-es.

For the aims of anthropological examination targeted X-ray films of the femoral and humeral bone were taken after these were unwrapped from the bandages.

In order to carry out a precise examination of the head an additional examination with the use of a high capacity state-of-the-art CT apparatus was made. From the image data thus obtained a 3-D reconstruction was possible, and VE images could also be taken. CT virtual endoscopy is a method recently introduced to medical diagnostics, whose basis is non-invasive image-taking of the interior of a body, as if observed through an endoscope. Analysing classical CT, 3D and VE images the lack of brain tissue was confirmed, and the interior of the cranium, from the occiput side, was partly filled with a mass at the contrast of 33-42 H.U., levelling into the horizontal. This substance, in the result of chemical and spectroscope analyses, was identified as resin (Photos 7-8). What was also found out were damages of osseous tissue of the nasal cavity and *sella turcica*, which indicates that the technique of brain removal through the nose of the deceased was used (Photo 9).

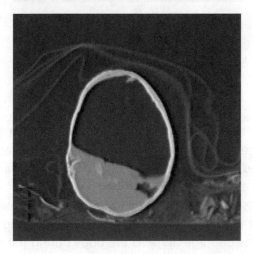

Photo 7.
CT examination – image in the transverse view at the cranium level – visible presence of resin after the brain had been removed

Photo 8.
CT images with
measurements of
density

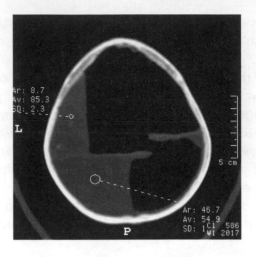

Photo 9.
Image in virtual CT
endoscopy – damage
of osseous structures
of the nose and *sella
turcica*

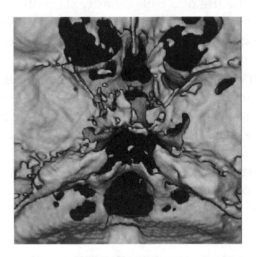

The state of the dentition was also examined, with the use of several techniques of image data processing. In particular the 2-D reconstruction along a curve was applied (this permitted to obtain images similar to those taken in pan-tomography technique), 3-D reconstruction, but the process was augmented by classic CT images taken in transverse cross-sections. It must be borne in mind that the dental defects were assumed during the autopsy to be consequences of the damage done to the body during the robbery. Analysing all the above-mentioned categories of images the following was found out: malocclusion ambimaxillary protrusion, considerable wear of the chewing surfaces of teeth, cavities and also signs of parodontal inflammation. All these changes were confirmed in the autopsy (Photos 10, 11).

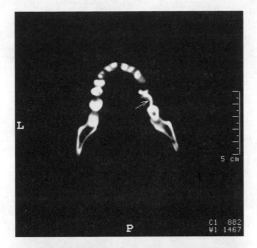

Photo 10.
CT examination – axial
view – cavities in the
teeth

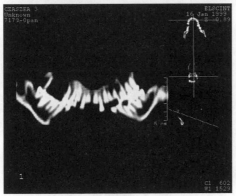

Photo 11.
CT examination –
reconstruction along
the dental curve

Using high-resolution technique and also the 3-D option, a spatial reconstruction of the cranium was obtained at very high precision (thickness of reconstructed layers – 1 mm). With the use of this method it was possible to show very precisely the elements of the configuration of the cranial area. The reliability of reconstruction, this technique being applied, can be confirmed via a comparison of reconstruction images and the photographs of the cranium with corresponding views. The images match absolutely. Therefore, attempts were made to obtain the lifetime appearance of Aset-iri-khet-es' face by means of a completely new method. Assumed as the basis for it was the 3-D reconstruction obtained during CT examinations of the wrapped mummy. To date, lifetime appearance of the face have been obtained on the basis of measurements of the cranium from completely unwrapped mummies, or, used as the basis were images of the cranium recorded in digital technology; in this case also after unwrapping them from bandages. The lifetime appearance of the face with the use of the new technique was carried out in the Institute of Forensic Medicine in Cracow. A modified Gierasimov's method was used. The cranium of Aset-iri-khet-es was defined as Mediterranean type with distinct Negroid features (Photos 12-14).

Photo 12.
3-D CT reconstruction –
the cranium in AP view

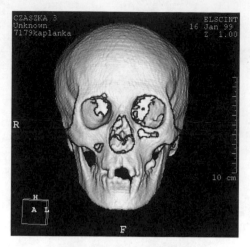

Photo 13.
Photograph of the
cranium – en face
(corresponds to Photo
12)

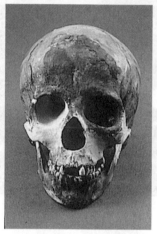

Photo 14.
Reconstruction of lifelike
appearance – en face

It should be re-emphasised that both the images of the interior of the cranium as well as the lifetime appearance image of the face were obtained on the basis of CT examinations, supplemented by modern computer methods of image transformation, without unwrapping the mummy.

In axial images, along the bones the presence of muscle tissue was shown, due to which one can analyse, with a high degree of precision, the course of particular muscle groups. This is especially clearly visible within the lower extremities. During the autopsy two fragments of structure defined as muscle were removed and subjected to histological examination – the image obtained resembling the interweaving of the striated muscle (Photo 15).

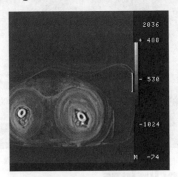

Photo 15.
CT examination – section on the thigh level – visible are muscle bands

CT examination permitted the reconstruction of, relatively precisely, the manner of bandaging, the thickness and alignment of bandage layers, the degree of their compression and their being soaked with resin. Within the trunk area the thickness of the bandage layers ranged from 5 to 10 cm. The extremities were wrapped tightly with bandage layers that adhered to one another closely. The upper extremities were wrapped separately. Also both lower extremities were wrapped separately with bands of a thickness of ca. 3-4 cm each, and then wrapped with an external layer at a maximum thickness of 2 cm. Bandages in the cranium area were badly damaged, thus not protecting this part of the body. What is of particular note is the very large degree of air content within the bandages, even in places where they were soaked with resin. The degree of X-ray absorption within the bandages amounts to, respectively: from -600 to -700 H.U. (relatively loose bands), through -500 to -20600 H.U. (tight bandaging, lack or poor soaking with resin) to -400 to -300 H.U. (tight bandaging, strong impregnation). Visible are also sections of bandages rolled up in a cylindrical shape, soaked with resin, inserted in many places among the layers of bandages in order to create an appropriate shape to the mummy. The high air content can also be found in the osseous structures of the mummy. This proves the efficiency of the activities aimed at a complete dehydration of the body (first of all covering with natritium). Loose spaces, such as those between the thighs, were filled with rolls soaked with resin. At the level of the central part of the thighs the presence of a cylindrical body was detected, at a diameter of ca. 3,5-4 cm, length of ca. 10 cm (Photo 16). A provisional hypothesis assumed the presence of a papyrus roll. During the autopsy it was found that it was a piece of tightly rolled canvas soaked with resin on the perimeter. Along the surfaces of bandages wrapping separately both the shanks, from the frontal side in mid-lines, linear structures were detected with a diameter of ca. 0,3 cm. In the course of the autopsy these turned out to be cords woven from canvas belts, aligned as it was found in CT examination. An interesting finding during the autopsy was a ring made of fabric located at the level of the navel. However, it was not revealed during CT examinations.

Photo 16.
CT examination
– a cylindrical structure
between the thighs
of the mummy

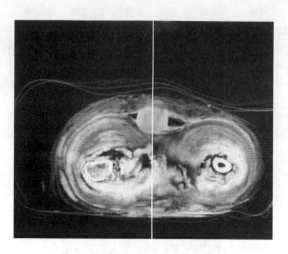

Discussion and conclusions

Mummies proved to be fruitful objects for radiological examinations, which later led to autopsies. The first examinations of a mummy with the use of X-rays were carried out in Frankfurt by König as early as March 1896 [König 1896; Notman, Tashjian, Aufderheide et al. 1986]. In Egypt, the first X-ray examination of the femoral bone of a mummy was made in 1898, and radiograms were added to reports from excavations in Dashasha [Brier 1996]. In 1924, for the first time with the use of X-rays, the mummy of a pharaoh was examined [ibidem]. That was Tutmosis IV. On the occasion of these examinations it turned out that it was the first pharaoh who went by taxi – it was this means of transport that took the mummy of the king to the X-ray laboratory of a Cairo hospital. Thenceforth X-ray photos of mummies were frequently taken, but they were treated more like a curiosity rather than an element of scientific examinations. Only due to a series of X-ray examinations of a mummy, carried out by doctor Ray Moodie in 1931 in Chicago [Moodie 1931], X-ray examination was acknowledged as a standard research procedure permitting to identify the sex, the age at the moment of death, pathologies and sometimes the reasons for death.

Carried out methodically all over the world, wherever mummy collections in museums could be found, radiological examinations yielded much information on mummification. A breakthrough in radiology, which was the introduction of computed tomography at the beginning of the seventies was not without influence on Egyptology [Harwood-Nash 1979; Vahey, Brown 1984; Marx, D'Auria 1986,1988; Levin 1988; Mankovich, Cheeseman, Stoker 1990]. The first CT examination of a mummy took place in 1976 for Royal Ontario Museum. It was the cranium with preserved brain, of a 14-year old, "Nakhut", who died ca. 3 thousand years before [Brier 1996]. In 1983, at St. Mary hospital in Rochester (USA) first MR examination of a mummy took place. However, clear images were not obtained, due the low water content of the embalmed body [Notman, Tashjian, Aufderheide et al. 1986].

Also in Poland such examinations have been carried out; among others in the seventies a team of Cracow radiologists and X-ray technicians, under the management of Prof. Olgierd Billewicz, made X-ray examinations of a mummy collection in Cracow Archaeological Museum. Also in Cracow, in 1993, the first CT Polish examination of a mummy [Gregorczyk, Hydzik, Moczulska et al. 1994] took place, but the examined corpse was not unwrapped. Current X-ray and CT examinations of mummies are a continuation of the work instigated by Prof. Billewicz, a man with broad interests, who was an advocate for the issue of radiologists' participation in interdisciplinary examinations, including paleo-pathology [Urbanik et al. 2001].

The unique value of the radiological examinations of the mummy of Aset-iri-khet-es was the opportunity to compare X-ray and CT images with the actual state verified during the autopsy [Kłys, Białka, Lech et al. 1998]. It should be remembered, however, that extensive damage and dislocations hindered complete imaging, as well as a comprehensive estimation of the reliability of X-ray and CT examinations. On the basis on the promising results, it should be said that the continuation of the project and the inclusion of other, well-preserved mummies is certainly justified [*Mumie und Computer* 1991; Seipel 1998]. In the described radiological examinations of the mummy completely new techniques were applied. In a classic radiological examination – digitisation of conventional X-ray images and their computer processing; in computer tomography – 3-D reconstruction, virtual endoscopy and reconstruction along a set curve. These give completely new possibilities of mummy imaging without unwrapping it. Apart from all this, it was the first time when an intravital reconstruction of a mummy's face, without unwrapping, was carried out [Marx, D'Auria 1988; Nedden, Knapp, Wicke et al. 1994; Kaczmarek, Lorkiewicz, Przybylski 1998].

References

B. Brier, *Egyptian Mummies. Unraveling the Secrets of an Ancient Art*, London 1996

A. Gregorczyk, A. Hydzik, K. Moczulska et al., *Obraz KT mumii egipskiej z okresu XXI dynastii*, Przegląd Lekarski 51,1 (1994), 57-61

D. C. Harwood-Nash, *Computed tomography of ancient Egyptian mummies*, Journal of Computer Axial Tomography 3, 6 (1979), 768-773

M. Kaczmarek, D. Lorkiewicz, Z. Przybylski, *Rekonstrukcja wyglądu twarzy na podstawie czaszki zmumifikowanych zwłok ludzkich ze stanowiska archeologicznego w El Gamhud datowanego na okres ptolemejski*, Archiwum Medycyny Sądowej i Kryminalistyki 48 (1998), 27-34

M. Kłys, J. Białka, T. Lech et al., *Badania fragmentów mumii – egipskiej kapłanki Iset Iri Hetes datowanej na okres ptolemejski*, Archiwum Medycyny Sądowej i Kryminalistyki 48 (1998), 13-25

W. König, *Photographien mit Röntgen-Strahlen, aufgenommen im Physikalischen Verein*, Frankfurt a.M.– Leipzig 1896

P. K. Levin, *First stereoscopic images from CT reconstruction of mummies*, American Journal of Radiology 151,6 (1988), 1249

N. J. Mankovich, A. M. Cheeseman, N.G. Stoker, *The display of three-dimentional anatomy with stereolithographic model,* Journal of Digital Imaging 3 (1990), 200-203

M. Marx, S. H. D'Auria, *CT examination of eleven Egyptian mummies*, RadioGraphics 6 (1986), 321-330

M. Marx, S. H. D'Auria, *Three-dimensional CT reconstruction of an ancient human Egyptian mummy*, American Journal of Radiology 150 (1988), 147-149

R. L. Moodie, *Roentgenologic studies of Egyptian and Peruvian mummies*, in: *Field Museum of Natural History Anthrolopological Memoires*, Chicago 1931

Mumie und Computer ein multidisziplinares Forschungsprojekt in Hannover, Hrsg. R. Drenkhahn, R. Germer, Hanover 1991

D. Nedden, R. Knapp, K. Wicke et al., *Skull of a 5300-year-old-mummy: reproduction and investigation with CT-guided stereolithography*, Radiology 193 (1994), 269-272

D. N. Notman, J. Tashjian, A.C., Aufderheide et al., *Modern imaging and endoscopic biopsy techniques in Egyptian mummies*, American Journal of Radiology 146 (1986), 93-96

W. Seipel, *Mumien aus dem Alten Ägypten. Zur Mumienforschung im Kunsthistorischen Museum*, Kunsthistorischen Museum, Wien 1998

T. Vahey, D. Brown, *Comely Wenuhotep: Computed tomography of an Egyptian mummy*, Computer Assisted Tomography 8, 5 (1984), 992-997

Maria Kaczmarek

Reconstruction of lifelike appearance

Introduction

The culture of Ancient Egypt is symbolised by the concept of life after death. As a result of this belief Egyptians devoted a great deal of efforts to improve the effectiveness of preservation the body of the deceased in artificial means and the attendant aids for the protection of the spirit. The purpose of mummification was to render the body of the deceased incorruptible and to maintain the physical appearance as nearly as possible to what had been in life. It was accomplished by using various techniques and procedures of mummification. In general, the body was coated with sufficient resin-soaked linen to model its natural contours in the material. The facial features of the deceased, the most important part of the body for realistic treatment, were modelled in cartonnage, a combination of either cloth and glue or papyrus and plaster, and by the time of the Roman Period as a flat, painted portrait, which covered the face. The brain was often removed and the skull was filled with resin or bitumen-like substances. Internal organs, such as the lungs, liver, intestines, stomach, were also removed and placed in the canopic chests or wrapped separately in several layers of bandages and placed back into the body cavity. As modelling of the natural contours of the body was the primary goal of the embalmers, they filled the body cavity with stuffing of linen cloth, or placed the materials under the skin through incisions made for that purpose. The arms and legs were rounded out either from inside the trunk or through minor opening made in the limbs. The wrapping pattern revealed that each finger and toe were wrapped separately, and the nails were often painted red with henna. This general pattern of mummification has been observed in Ancient Egypt for thousand years and, as it is emphasised, the notion of preserving human and animal dead came about naturally in the dry climate of Egypt [Goyon 1972; Mokhtar et al. 1973; Brier 1994].

The mummified body of Aset-iri-khet-es had been a cause of concern due to rather poor state of preservation and possibility of destroys it. The X-rays examination and tomography, taken prior to autopsy, provided the first glimpse of what lays beneath the layers of bandages. I also enabled to clear images of the densely packed interior of the body. The unwrapping and an external examination of the body followed above-mentioned non-destructive methods of examination. After a general autopsy, an internal inspection of all major parts was to be made, using modern techniques of various scientific disciplines. The techniques applied in the project included human biology, zoology, botany, chemistry, histology and textile studies.

My efforts, as a physical anthropologist, were focused on recovering as much data as possible in order to establish the individual's sex, age, facial features, the stature, and some other physical characteristics. I also hoped to search for signs of any diseases from which Aset-iri-khet-es might have suffered, and which might have contributed to her death. I carried out my investigation to follow a logical sequence and use of updated methodology in skeletal biology [Buikstra, Ubelaker 1994; Ortner, Putschar 1997]. I began my study with general inspection of the mummy. After the unwrapping I undertook an external examination of the body and bones. Finally, I reconstructed the most probable lifelike appearance of the face with the use of computerised techniques.

General autopsy

The body of the deceased was laid on back in fully extended position and wrapped in several layers of resin-soaked linen. The state of preservation was rather poor. The upper part of the body around the head (in the region of maxilla and zygomatic bones, and mandible), neck and chest was badly damaged by tomb-plunderers that had tried to find out valuable objects placed under layers of bandages. The pattern of wrapping was characteristic for the mummy and described in details in another issue of this book [Niwiński in present volume]. No amulets or relics were visible in the wrappings. If presented, they might be robbed by tomb-plunderers. Both, the outer and inner layers of the body wrapping were without any decoration. The spaces between the arms and body and between the legs were filled with linen wads, to model the natural contours of the body. The contour of the body was rather flat. The legs were bound separately with numerous layers of bandages. The toes and fingers were wrapped separately in a very accurate fashion. According to my previous experience, I suppose that the use of the resin in embalming Aset-iri-khet-es consisted in the procedure of pouring the hot liquid resin over the body at many stages. This caused some parts of the body were to be converted into a hard, solid mass, which could often be removed only with hammer [Kaczmarek 2000]. The chest and pelvis made such hard and solid parts of the body that there were impossible to analyse single bone, such as ribs or single bone of the pelvis. Superficial changes of the pubic symphysis were fairly well visible and thus it was possible to contribute this part of the skeleton to the assessment of the individual's age at death. The skin was degenerated in some regions, as were the muscles. In other regions of the body the skin was glued to the bandages and removed together with bandages while unwrapping. The skin and bones were tinged with black or dark brown colours by the resin or bitumen-like substance. Bones were preserved well and provide me with as much information as it was possible.

There was no way of knowing details on how the head was wrapped because the head was separated from the rest of the body. The hair, sculp and external ears were missing. The orbits were filled with eyes. The mouths were closed and teeth were intact. No ante-mortem fracture was found in the skull. The brain had been removed from the skull through the nostrils and replaced with resin or bitumen-like substance, which formed a pool in the skull before it solidified. In the radiograph the filling of the skull appeared as a "water level".

The right leg was broken in the knee articulation. As it was suggested, the loss of blood due to the fracture, could contribute to the cause of death.

Sex determination

Sex determination was essential to our analysis since the inscription had told us the female name of the deceased – Aset-iri-khet-es. In order to estimate her biological sex I undertook a comprehensive approach that combined the morphological information with analyses of cranial and postcranial measurements [Acsadi, Nemeskeri 1970; Ubelaker 1989; Buikstra, Ubelaker 1994]. Unfortunately, I could not use additional methods, although accurate for estimating sex and age in forensic cases, such as, for example, age-related morphological changes at the sternal extremity of the fourth rib, because that rib was not available for analysis [Loth, Iscan 1989]. My preliminary records of dimorphic features in skeleton showed that bones were smaller and more gracile in comparison with referenced standards of males. I have focused my interest on two excellent sites for sexing and it was important to make the most of both. It is well known that sexual dimorphism is better expressed in the pelvis. However, my observations of this site were incomplete due to the fashion of mummification procedure. The only thing I was able to notice was the shape of greater sciatic notch. It presented a typical female morphology – its broad shape was scored as "1". Femoral and humerus heads diameters of 41 mm and 30 mm respectively, indicate a female individual. When we consider other postcranial and cranial measurements they also reveal femaleness (see Table 1).

In recording cranial morphology I have chosen five aspects: robusticity of the nuchal crest, size of the mastoid process, sharpness of the supraorbital margin, prominence of glabella and projection of the mental eminence. I used a five-point scale to all cases being studied. The feminine features were scored at the lower end of the range.The external surface of the occipital was rather smooth with minimal bony projection. The robusticity of nuchal crest was scored as in between "1" and "2". The size of mastoid process was scored by comparing its volume with the external auditory meatus and the zygomatic process of the temporal bone. The mastoid process very small, its slight expression was scored between "1" and "2". The border of supraorbital margin was the example of minimal expression and scored "1". I could feel an extremely sharp edge of supraorbital margin. Comparing the profile of supraorbital region with the

Measurement Code	Diameter in mm	Cranial indices	
Maximum Cranial Length (g-op)	175	Cephalic Index (eu-eu/g-op) × 100 Mesokranius: medium-sized length of head	77.1
Maximum Cranial Breadth (eu-eu)	135		
Minimum Frontal Breadth (ft-ft)	89	(ba-b/eu-eu) × 100 Akrokranius: head is very height	99.2
Bizygomatic Diameter (zy-zy)	129		
Mastoid Length (ms-ms)	103	Frontoparietal Index (ft-ft/eu-eu) × 100 Stenometopus: forehead is very narrow	65.9
Basion-bregma height (ba-b)	134		
Bizygomaxillare Diameter (zm-zm)	87	Total Facial Index (n-gn/zy-zy) × 100 Mesoprosopus: medium-sized breadth of face	86.0
Bigonial Width (go-go)	80		
Total Facial Height (n-gn)	111	Orbital Index (orbital height/mf-ek) × 100 Shape of orbit is high	91.4
Upper Facial Height (n-pr)	69		
Nasal Height (n-sn)	52		
Orbital height	32		
Interorbital Breadth mf-ek	35		
Breadth of Maxilla M2	29		
Breadth of Apertura Piriformis	27		
Height of Apertura Piriformis	29		
Mandibular Length (go-gn)	76		
Bicondylar Breadth (cdl-cdl)	112		
Chin Height (id-gn)	26		
Maximum Ramus Breadth	30		
Femur: Bicondylar Length	429	Stature: 54.10 + 2.47 × 42.9 = 160.06 cm 160 cm	
Maximum Head Diameter	41		
Epicondylar Breadth	75		
Humerus: Maximum Length	304	Stature: 57.97 + 3.36 × 30.4 = 160.11 cm 160 cm	
Vertical Head Diameter	30		
Epicondylar Breadth	53	**Mean stature = 160 cm**	

Table 1.
Cranial and postcranial
measurements
of the skeleton
of Aset-iri-khet-es

diagram, a minimal prominence of glabella was observed, the contour of the frontal was smooth with little or no projection at the midline. It was scored at "1". In case of the mental eminence above the surrounding bone it was expressed minimally and scored as "1". From among characters indicative of secondary sex traits described above all were ranked into grade "1" or sometimes "2". Therefore, in the final result of sex determination it has to be said that all traits indicate the sex of individual as female with little doubt [Buikstra, Ubelaker 1994: 21].

Age determination

Individuals can be aged quite precisely up to about 25 years from teeth and between 13 and 25 for girls and 15 and 25 for boys from the "epiphyseal union," the fusion of cartilaginous areas at the ends of long bones. In case of Aset-iri-khet-es it was more difficult to age, since changes connected with processes of maturation have been completed. As for adults, I applied a complex, combined method of age determination. The age ranges established with the use of this method belong to morphological states, which result in determination of a physiological age closest to the chronological age.

I had to limit the age-related changes in the skeleton of Aset-iri-khet-es to those that occur in the pubic symphysis, humerus and femur, and the cranial sutures. It was caused by state of preservation and postmortem damages. With the use of a complex, combined method I was able to approximate actual chronological age of Aset-iri-khet-es fairly well.

In Photo 1 structural changes in the spongy substance of the proximal epiphysis of the humerus and femur are shown. It is well visible that in case of the humerus, the apex of the medullary cavity is situated well below surgical neck, and trabeculae exhibit radial systems. The latter means that ogival arrangement of trabelculae appears in smaller portions. Comparing this picture with other six characteristic phases distinguished in the proximal epiphysis of the humerus it is seen that the phase observed here indicates the commencement of adult age – phase I [Acsadi, Nemeskeri 1970: 125]. When describing phases of age-changes taking place in the spongiosa of the proximal epiphysis of the femur seen in Photo 1, I used reference standards that consisted of six phases [ibidem: 127]. As in the humerus, I found that apex of the medullary cavity was situated well below the lesser trochanter, truss texture of trabeculae was thick, individual features hardly distinguishable. I identified the above-described stage as phase I.

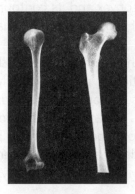

Photo 1.
The X-ray picture of proximal epiphyses of femur and humerus of Aset-iri-khet-es showing the structure of spongy substance

Turning out to the pubic symphysis it should be notice that morphological changes of the pubic symphyseal face are among the most reliable criteria for estimating age at death in adult human remains. Bearing this in mind, I made use of the Suchey-Brooks standards for estimating age at death based upon morphology of the pubic symphysis [Suchey, Katz 1986; Brooks, Suchey 1990]. The changes in the symphyseal face of pubic symphysis was closest to the description of the phase III according to which the symphyseal face showed lower extremity and ventral rampart in process of completion. It was marked by fusing ossified nodules, which formed upper extremity and extended along ventral border. Symphyseal face might either be smooth or retain distinct ridges. Dorsal plateau was complete. I did not observe any limping of symphyseal dorsal margin or outgrowth of bony ligamentous.

Taking into account the closure of cranial sutures I have to remember that although cranial sutures generally fuse with increasing age, there is considerable variability in closure rates. This fact reduces the value of suture closure patterns, as a single indicator, for age estimation. However, when used in conjunction with other attributes, as I have done in my study, they are quite useful. A detailed observation of stages of endo- and ectocranial suture closure showed that these stages ranged from open suture to minimal closure (scored as "0" and "1"). If we consider the final results of complex, combined method, it indicated the age at death of Aset-iri-khet-es as being young adult aged 25–30 years.

Morphometric description of the physical traits

The skull of Aset-iri-khet-es is presented in Photos 2–5, in the lateral, vertical, occipital and frontal views, respectively. One may see that the face was badly damaged in large parts of the maxilla, zygomatic bone and mandible. I suppose that the damage resulted partly from the activity of tomb-plunderers and partly from the state of skull preservation. During reconstruction procedure the damaged parts of the skull were replaced by the wax homologues. There was also evidence of the damage to the nasal bones, which resulted from removing brain from the skull cavity through the nostrils.

When viewing the skull vertically, its shape is rhomboid-like (Photo 3). Zygomatic arches are hidden (the skull is cryptozygous). Lateral view of the skull reveals alveolar prognathism and well marked projection of *protuberantia mentalis*. Occipital bone is convex and its contour is smooth. The forehead is perpendicular, its surface rather flat with slightly marked *protuberantia frontalis* (Photos 2 and 3).

Generally, the vault of the head is rhomboid-shaped with narrow and oval face. The forehead is positioned perpendicularly and frontal tubercles are pronounced. The region of supra-orbital ridge and glabella is slightly flattened. The setting of eye-sockets is horizontal with obliquely upwards their external corners. It seems that eyes could be set up deeply in eye-sockets. The region of zygomatic bones is marked clearly and zygomatic arches are narrow apart that is why they are hidden while viewing them vertically. The nose seems to be of a

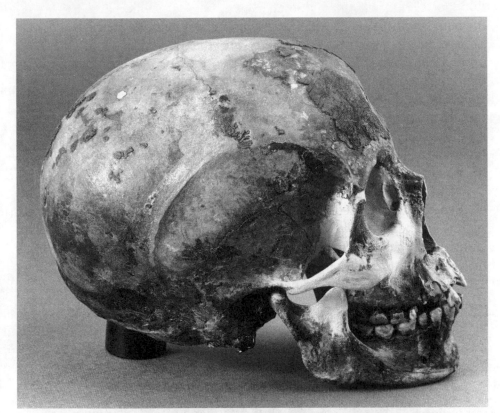

Photo 2.
The right side (*norma lateralis*) of the skull of Aset-iri-khet-es and wax replacement visible in the region of upper face and mandible. Closure of anterior saggital, right coronal, pterion, sphenofrontal, inferior sphenotemporal and right lambdoid sutures are visible

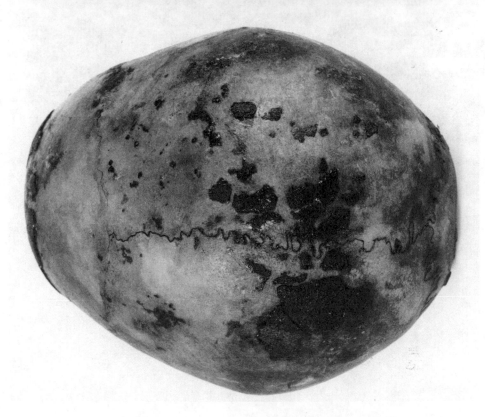

Photo 3.
Skull of Aset-iri-khet-es in *norma verticalis*. Closure of coronal, saggital and superior lambdoid sutures are visible

medium length, relatively wide, weekly prominent with the concave and well-profiled bridge of the nose. The lateral view of the skull reveals a marked alveolar prognathism. When jaws are firmly closed in their normal centric position an abnormal occlusion is revealed. Due to the prognathism and malocclusion it should be supposed that lips were of medium length, rather thick and the whole mouths prominent, with lower lip dominating over upper lip. Chins were probably moderate, high and narrow with strongly marked *protuberantia mentalis*. Mandible angles were rounded and apart in medium distance. Table 1 presents the descriptive characteristics in terms of quantitative data.

Quantitative data reveal the delicate structure of head of Aset-iri-khet-es. Her head was a medium length, high, with oval, medium breadth face, narrow forehead, and large eyes. The face was prognatic with malocclusion. Using Trotter and Gleser formula for the reconstruction of the lifelike body height, the stature of Aset-iri-khet-es was estimated as 160 cm [Trotter, Gleser 1958]. It means that Aset-iri-khet-es was a tall individual.

Photo 4.
Skull of Aset-iri-khet-es in *norma occipitalis*. Closure of saggital and lambdoid sutures are visible

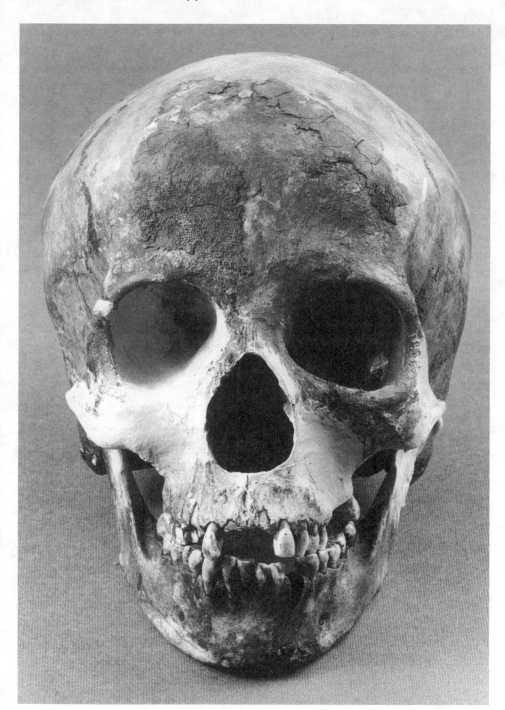

Photo 5.
Frontal view of the
skull of Aset-iri-khet-es
(*norma frontalis*). Wax
replacements are
visible in the region of
maxilla and
mandibular condyles

Dentition and dental health, evidence for palaeopathological changes

Dentition of Aset-iri-khet-es is illustrated in Photos 2, 3, 4, and 5. Methodology of dental morphology was taken after Kaczmarek [1979, 1980]. It is seen that major part of the maxilla, alveolar bone and the mandibular condyli are reconstructed post-mortem. All teeth in the right side of the maxillary dental arch are present, some of them are damaged and make measurements impossible (first incisor, canine, first and second premolars). In the left side of upper dental arch first and second molars are absent. I know that it is post-mortem absence caused by damage of maxilla. In mandible all teeth were present except for post-mortem loss of right canine. Lateral upper incisors exhibit traces of shovel-shaped lingual surfaces. This trait is not common among Ancient Egyptians. Hypocone reduction in upper molars is rather strong. M1 is a 4-cusped tooth and both, M2 and M3, are 3-cusped teeth. The descriptive impression is supported by mesio-distal and bucco-lingual measurements (see Table 2). There is evidence for slight crowding of lower incisors. It is difficult to recognize the number of cusps in lower molars because of the attrition, which flats dental cusps. It seems that M1 could be 5-cusped tooth and the other molars 4-cusped. Dental wear makes also impossible to observe groove pattern on occlusal surface of molars.

Table 2.
Mesio-distal and bucco-lingual measurements of teeth (in mm)

Diameter				Tooth				
	I1	I2	C	P1	P2	M1	M2	M3
M-D Maxilla		6.6		7.3	7.0	10.6	9.8	9.0
B-L Maxilla		6.8		9.7	9.8	11.3	11.2	10.4
M-D Mandible	5.6	6.4	7.0	8.0	7.9	11.3	10.8	11.2
B-L Mandible	6.8	7.2	8.3	8.4	8.4	10.6	10.2	10.2

Teeth are medium in size with reduction in their medio-distal and bucco-lingual diameters within tooth class and in distal direction of the dental arch.

There is alveolar prognathism and strongly marked *protuberantia mentalis*. The occlusion is not normal. The malocclusion may be classified after Angle as Class II [Angle 1907 cited after Mills 1963]. This malocclusion is recognised when lower posterior teeth (and usually also the lower jaw) are in a post-normal relations to their antagonists – in such case like that the upper incisors are frequently prominent (occlude in front of the lowers).

A general survey of dental morphology would be incomplete without some consideration of pathology. The greatest single problem in the dentition of Aset-iri-khet-es, shared with Ancient Egyptians, was attrition. Teeth were worn down throughout life by the consumption of a coarse diet. Attrition becomes so extensive that the enamel and dentine was eroded away until the pulp was exposed. The living tissue inside the tooth died, and the empty root canals become a source of chronic infection and abscess. In order to estimate the degree of occlusal surface wear I used a system developed by Murphy [1959], modified by Smith [1984] and useful in dietary reconstruction. In upper incisors moderate dentin exposure was observed with no longer resembling a line (see Photo 6). In first upper molar quadrant is flat due to attrition, and dentine exposure is one-fourth of quadrant or less. The second and third upper molars show flat quadrants without dentine exposure. In the third molar the cusps are becoming obliterated but yet not worn flat. In mandible teeth are less worn. In incisors moderate dentin exposure without resembling a line is observed (see Photo 7). Mandibular molars are less worn than their opposite teeth. The degree of the attrition may be characterised by the quadrant area, which is worn flat (horizontally) without dentin exposure. A large interproximal decay between canine and first premolar on the right side of mandible is seen. Dental cavity is also seen on the occlusal surface of the first, right lower molar (Photo 7). There are two major environmental causes one may speculate, that may have resulted in the lack of extensive dental decay: the absence from the diet of refined carbohydrates such as sugar and the extreme attrition which provides a more difficult environment for decay to begin.

The second problem found in Aset-iri-khet-es was periodontitis, visible in right canine in maxilla and central and lateral incisors in mandible. This disease results in loss of the bony support of the teeth and is often associated with plaque resulting in calculus or tartar deposits on the teeth. The ultimate result of periodontitis is extensive periodontal disease that results in the loss of teeth. There is evidence that extractions and the treatment of dental abcesses were undertaken in the eastern Mediterranean area as early as 3000 B.C. [Weinberger 1940; Sigerist 1951], and that the removal of calculus and prosthetic treatment was well established by about the middle of the first millenium B.C. However, such primitive dentistry is unlikely to have affected more than a very small segment of the population. It is therefore assume that the pathological lesions present in Ancient Egyptians represent the unrestricted results of natural process. It may reflect variations in the genetic, dietary, bacteriological and physiological aspects of man.

Reconstruction of lifelike appearance of the face

The face of Aset-iri-khet-es, that has already been described, was reconstructed in two major steps: the most likelihood facial appearance was found within an updated computerised system, and the reliability of reconstruction was assessed using the superimposition technique. A detailed description of this procedure is given in *Facial forensic reconstruction of a mummified body from an archaeological site at El Gamhud, dated on the Ptolemaic Period* [Kaczmarek, Lorkiewicz, Przybylski 1998].

The system we have used in reconstructing Aset-iri-khet-es' lifelike appearance, Pol-Sit Reconstruction, is a universal system for identifying individual's face. This system is based on the picture put to the computer's memory and consists of two parts. The first one is used for elaborating the picture of skull, the second one for composing elements of the face from the data base previously stored in the computer and put on the elements of the skull. Data base involves the results of detailed investigations of variation in

Photo 6.
Maxilla and teeth

Photo 7.
Mandible and teeth

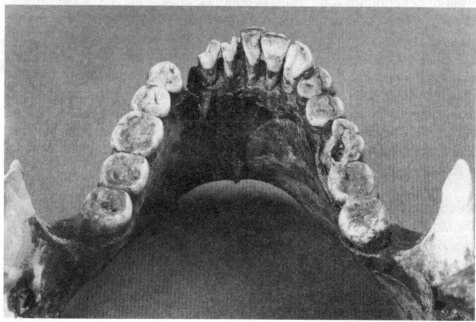

morphological structures of bones and soft tissues. Data base consists of many thousands of elements in photo or photographic forms the so-called masks which comprises various elements of the face, such as eyes, eyebrows, ears, lips hairs. The basic data base is supplemented by such elements, as for example: moustaches, beard and whiskers. All these elements are classified into groups and subgroups, according to their meaning for reconstructing procedure.

The starting point to our analysis was to put the frontal view of Aset-iri-khet-es' skull to the computer memory with the use of the camera VHS-C (for the picture of the skull see Photo 5). In the next step of this procedure the picture of the skull was normalised within X, Y co-ordinates. Having the picture of the skull in normalised position, the skull was covered with points and markers for the appropriate structural elements of the face taken from database in the next step of this procedure. Finally, the contour of the face was drawn. The landmarks on the skull for further procedure of reconstructing the facial elements are presented in Figure 1. The morphological characteristics responsible for individual physiognomy were matched to markers pointed out on the skull. They were selected from database. The following steps of this procedure is illustrated in Figure 2 (with landmarks in the background) and in Figure 3 (where landmarks are erased). In Figure 4 reconstructing lifelike appearance of Aset-iri-khet-es' face is shown. The result of superimposition of skull and appearance of face is shown in Figure 5. It is well seen that the reliability of reconstruction is very high.

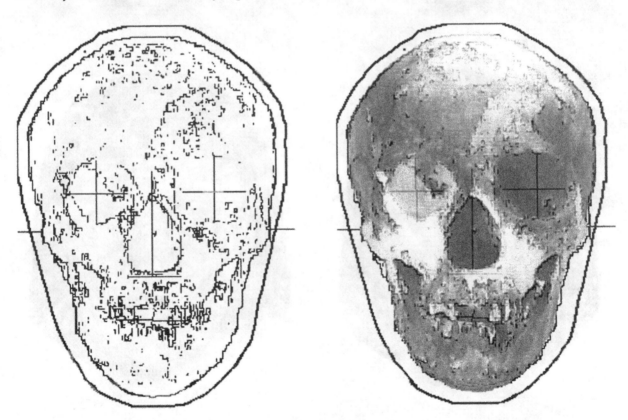

Figure 1.
Landmarks on the skull

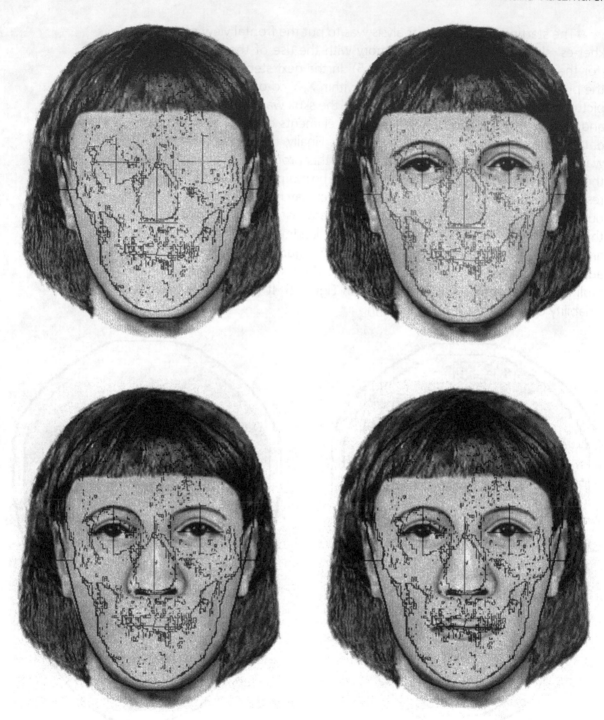

Figure 2.
Illustration of the
following steps in
facial reconstruction:
eyes, nose, lips.
Landmarks are visible
on the skull

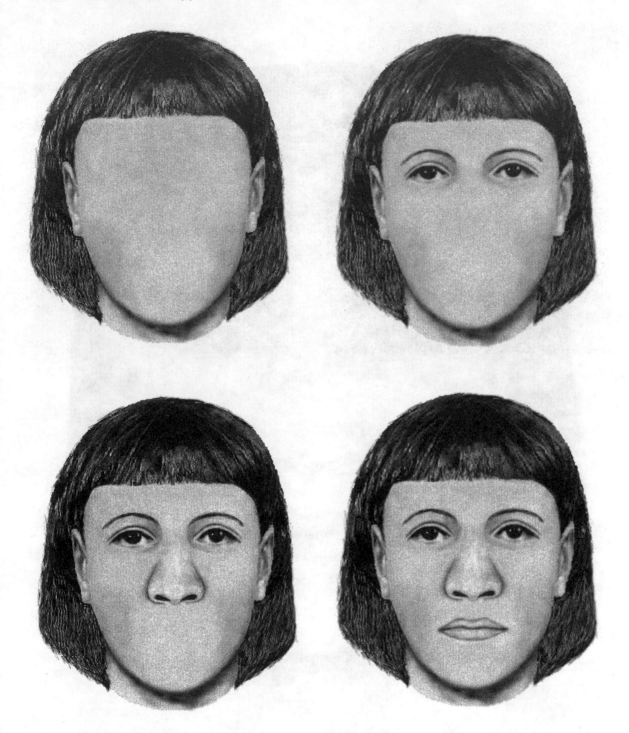

Figure 3.
Illustration of the
following steps in
facial reconstruction:
eyes, nose, lips.
Landmarks are hidden

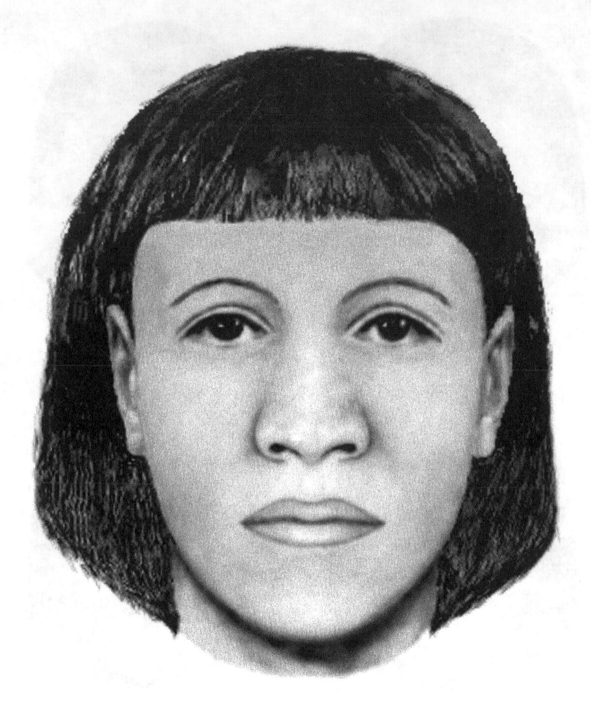

Figure 4.
Final result of the facial
reconstruction

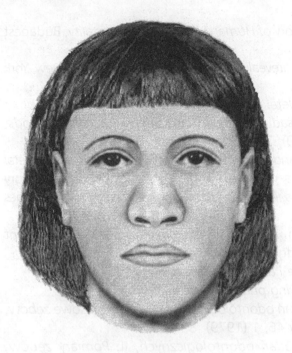
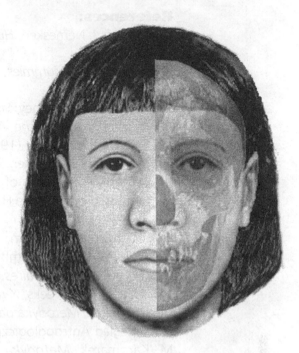
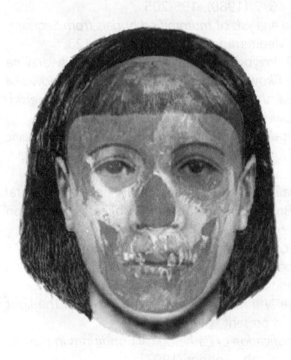

Figure 5.
The result of superimposition of the skull and appearance of the face

References:

G. Y. Acsadi, J. Nemeskeri, *History of Human Life Span and Mortality*, Budapest 1970

B. Brier, *Egyptian Mummies. Unrevealing Secrets of an Ancient Art*, New York 1994

S. T. Brooks, J. M. Suchey, *Skeletal age determination based on the os pubis: a comparison of the Acsadi-Nemeskeri and Suchey-Brooks methods*, Human Evolution 5 (1990), 227-238

E. Buikstra, D. H. Ubelaker, *Standards for data collection from human skeletal remains*, Proceedings of a seminar at the Field Museum of Natural History organised by Jonathan Haas, Arkansas Archaeological Survey Research, series n 44 (1994)

A. Cockburn, E. Cockburn, Th. A. Reyman, *Mummies, Disease and Ancient Cultures,* 2nd ed., Cambridge 1998

J. Goyon, *Rituels funéraires de l'ancienne Egypte*, Paris 1972

J. E. Harris, K. R. Weeks, *X-raying pharaohs*, New York 1973

M. Kaczmarek, *Metodyka badań odontologicznych*, I: *Cechy opisowe zębów*, Przegląd Antropologiczny 46, 1 (1979), 89-106

M. Kaczmarek, *Metodyka badań odontologicznych*, II: *Pomiary zębów*, Przegląd Antropologiczny 46, 2 (1980), 195-205

M. Kaczmarek, *Anthropological analysis of mummified burials from Saqqara*, Polish Archaeology in the Mediterranean 11 (2000), 118-123.

M. Kaczmarek, D. Lorkiewicz, Z. Przybylski, *Rekonstrukcja wyglądu twarzy na podstawie czaszki zmumifikowanych zwłok ludzkich ze stanowiska archeologicznego w el-Gamhud datowanego na okres ptolemejski*, Archiwum Medycyny Sądowej i Kryminalistyki 48 (1998), 27-34

S. Loth, M. Iscan, *Morphological assessment of age in adults: the thoracic region,* in: *Age Markers in Human Skeleton*, ed. by M. Y. Iskan, Springfield, Illinois 1989, 105-136

J. R. E. Mills, *Occlusion and mallocclusion of the teeth of Primate* in: *Dental Anthropology,* ed. D.R. Brothwell, Symposium Publications Division Pergamon Press 1963, 29-52

G. Mokhtar, H. Riad, S. Iskander, *Mummification in Ancient Egypt*, Cairo 1973

T. R. Murphy, *Gradient of dentine exposure in human tooth attrition*, American Journal of Physical Anthropology 17 (1959), 179-185

A. Niwiński, *Coffin, cartonnage and mummy of Aset-iri-khet-es in the light of Egyptological research* (in present volume)

D. J. Ortner, W. J. Putschar, *Identification of Pathological Conditions in Human Skeletal Remains*, Washington and London 1997

H. E. Sigerist, *A History of Medicine,* I: *Primitive and Archaic Medicine*, Oxford University Press, New York 1951.

B. H. Smith, *Patterns of molar wear in hunter-gatherers and agriculturists*, American Journal of Physical Anthropology 63 (1984), 39-56

J. Suchey, D. Katz, *Skeletal age standards derived from an extensive multiracial sample of modern Americans*, Abstract, American Journal of Physical Anthropology 18 (1986), 329-330

M. Trotter, G. C. Gleser, *A re-evaluation of estimation of stature based on measurements of stature taken during life and of long bones after death*, American Journal of Physical Anthropology 16 (1958), 79-123

D. H. Ubelaker, *Human Skeletal Remains*, 2nd ed., Washington D.C. 1989

B. W. Weinberg, *Did dentistry evolve from the barbers, blacksmith or from medicine*, Bulletin History of Medicine 8 (1940), 965-968.

Małgorzata Kłys
Teresa Lech
Janina Zięba-Palus
Józefa Białka

A chemical and physicochemical investigations

Introduction

The Egyptians believed that only a body that was preserved could fulfil the prerequisite of living forever. This belief came from religious observations that the dry sand of the desert acted to preserve buried bodies. Such beliefs were extant as early as the Neolithic and Predynastic periods of 5,000-4,000 B.C.[1] An example of the importance of the preservation of the body is seen in the invocation from The Ancient Egyptian Book of the Dead: "My body is everlasting, it will not perish and it will not decay for ages."[2]

Interestingly, the first people who mummified bodies were not the Egyptians. In prehistory, members of the cultural group Chinchorro, who came from northern Chile, practised a selective, elaborate form of artificial mummification which took place more than 4,000 years ago, i.e., more than 1,000 years before the Egyptian mummification began.[3]

The mummification process as described in detail in many fundamental works indicates that it was very complicated.[4] It was not only a highly technical procedure, but it was accompanied by a ritual ceremony, imitating in great detail the process by which the god Osiris was prepared for resurrection.[5]

While initially the study of mummies was confined to observing a small number of accidentally discovered specimens, later research has come from a wider variety of mummies. These newer studies have involved the co-

[1] E. Strouhal, L. Vyhnanek, *Egyptian Mummies in Czechoslovak Collections*, Narodni Muzeum v Praze, Prague 1980, 7-11; A. Niwiński, *Mity i symbole starożytnego Egiptu*, Warszawa 1995.

[2] R. Clark, *Myth and Symbol in Ancient Egypt*, London 1959; R. O. Faulkner, *The Ancient Egyptian Book of the Dead*, London 1985.

[3] A. C. Aufderheide, I. Munoz, B. Arriaza, *Seven Chinchorro mummies and the prehistory of Northern Chile*, American Journal of Physical Anthropology 91/2 (1993), 189-201.

[4] Clark, op. cit.; Faulkner, op. cit.; Strouhal, Vyhnanek, op. cit., 16-24, 155-164; A. Lucas, J. R. Harris, *Ancient Egyptian Materials and Industries*, 4th ed., London 1962, 270–326; A. T. S. Sandison, s.v. *Balsamierung*, Lexicon der Ägyptologie I (1975), 610-616; H. Riad, Z. Iskander, *Mummification in Ancient Egypt*, Cairo 1973.

[5] Strouhal, Vyhnanek, op. cit., 12-15; A. Piankoff, *The theology of the New Kingdom in Ancient Egypt*, Antiquity and Survival 1/6 (1956), 488-500.

operation of archaeologists, anthropologists, chemists, and physicians. Progress in research methodology has produced new examination procedures resulting in greater detail of the description of external body features, and in dissections using highly technical methodology, i.e. histological, pathohistological, and chemical analysis, and sophisticated radiographic techniques. Such investigations have concentrated on a detailed study of mummification techniques and on finding pathological changes in the specimens.[6] This research has been aimed at determining the characteristic features of each mummy.

The present study is an examination of a single mummy – an Egyptian priestess – and was undertaken with these factors in mind.

The mummy belongs to the collection of the Archaeological Museum in Kraków, Poland.[7] It was discovered by the Polish Egyptologist Tadeusz Smoleński in 1907 in the Ptolemaic necropolis in El-Gahmud, and is dated between the third and the first century B.C.

Before the mummy's restoration was begun, a multidisciplinary program was undertaken including anthropological,[8] histological and serological,[9] physicochemical, hemogenetic, paleobotanical examinations, the examination of pollen, computer tomography of the skeleton, and other studies analysing fibers and material taken from the sarcophagus.[10]

Some of these studies – the chemical and physicochemical – are discussed in the present paper. The purpose of the chemical and physicochemical evaluations was to identify the materials used for preservation, such as resin or/and bitumen, and to determine the chemical composition of the samples.

Materials and methods

The fragments of an Egyptian mummy were examined. The following samples taken from the sarcophagus were analysed:

- {1} powder scrapings from cervical (neck) vertebrae;
- {2} fragments of the bandages taken from different parts of the mummy;
- {3} a fragment of unknown substance lying under the mummy's back;
- {4} a fragment of unknown substance lying on the abdomen;
- {5} fragments of unknown substance lying on the chest;
- {6} a fragment of mass from the cranial vault;

[6] Strouhal, Vyhnanek, op. cit., 7-11.

[7] B. Aleksiejew-Wantuch, M. Paciorek, *Program of conservation works of the object "Cartonnage from the Egyptian Sarcophagus of Priestess Aset-iri-khet-es"*, Documents of the Archaeological Museum in Kraków, 1995; K. Babraj, H. Szymańska, *Badania mumii egipskiej w Muzeum Archeologicznym w Krakowie*, Filomata 433-434 (1996), 3-10; iidem, *Eine Mumie unter dem Mikroskop. Die Untersuchungen an der ägyptischen Mumie in Archäologischen Museum zu Kraków*, Antike Welt 5 (1997), 369-374.

[8] M. Kaczmarek, *Anthropological investigations on mummified burial from Ptolemaic Period in Egypt*, Journal of Paleopathology (in press).

[9] *Protokół wizytacji otwarcia grobu króla Kazimierza Jagiellończyka w kaplicy Świętokrzyskiej w katedrze na Wawelu w dniu 19 maja 1973*, Studia do Dziejów Wawelu 4 (1978), 477-506.

[10] Aleksiejew-Wantuch, Paciorek, op. cit.; Babraj, Szymańska, *Badania mumii egipskiej...*, 3-10; iidem *Eine Mumie...*, 369-374.

{7} a fragment of mass from the cartonnage wrapping the mummy;

{8} two molar teeth and one unidentified tooth;

{9} fragments of fingernails;

{10} fragments of humeri (arm bones).

The analysis of the resin and bitumen samples was performed by means of physico-chemical tests, infrared spectroscopy and spectrographic method. The following chemical features of samples were taken into consideration according to Lucas:[11] NaOH saponifiability, solubility in C_2H_5OH, UV fluorescence, reaction with $CH_3COO \cdot CO$ and H_2SO_4, microscope appearance, characteristic of resins upon heating.

Infrared spectra were obtained with a Digilab FTS 40A Fourier transform spectrometer using both KBr technique and a UMA 500 microscope attachment. Each spectrum represented a collection of 512 scan at a resolution of 4 cm^{-1}. The spectra were searched automatically by the computer for the maximal and peak positions.

The screening to evaluate the presence of trace elements such as V, Mo and Ni was performed using quartz spectrograph Model ISP 22, SU. The samples were grinding, mixed with carbon and excited in carbon electrode by interrupted AC arc.

The physicochemical analysis consisted of:

1 – qualitative analysis using a JSM 5800 JEOL scanning electron microscope equipped with X-ray microspectrometer Link-ISIS OXFORD Instrument (SEM/EDX) and a spectrograph Model ISP 22;

2 – quantitative analysis: a) by atomic absorption spectrometry (AAS) using a spectrophotometer SP 9-800 Pye UNICAM (the flame AAS technique for Ca, Mg, Na, K, Fe, Zn, Cu, Mn, Pb, Tl); b) the flame atomic emission spectrophotometry technique for Na according to Haswell[12], a Sanger-Black test for arsenic and the spectrophotometric with molybdovanadophosphoric acid method for phosphorus according to Boltz[13].

The samples of teeth (1.02 g), nails (0.95 g), bones (1.05 g), and fragments of resins {3 & 6} (2.6 g) were crushed in a grinding machine (Retsch KG, Germany), then ashed in a muffle-oven (Griffin, UK) at 450°C for 16 hours (the sample of teeth was treated additionally with 2 ml concentrated HNO_3, Suprapur, and then reashed until a white residue at 500°C for 5 hours). After ashing the percentage of mineral and non-mineral compounds was calculated on the basis of the loss

[11] Lucas, Harris, op. cit., 270-326; *Protokół wizytacji otwarcia grobu...*, 477-506.

[12] S. J. Haswell, *Atomic Absorption Spectrometry. Theory, Design and Applications*, Elsevier, Amsterdam 1991.

[13] D. F. Boltz, *Colorimetric Determination of Non-metals*, New York 1958.

of mass during the procedure. The ashing samples of teeth, nails, bones and resins were mineralised and treated with HNO_3 and HCl and diluting with deionised H_2O. The samples were analysed by AAS as above or AES method as above and the main (Ca, Mg, Na, K) and trace (Fe, Zn, Cu, Pb, Mn, Tl) chemical elements were determined. The solutions were aspirated into an air/acetylene flame prior to the analysis. A lanthanum diluent (0.1% w/v La in 1% v/v HCl) was necessary prior to aspiration for measurement of calcium. Blanks and matched standards were simultaneously quantified. The methods of standard additions was used to validate calibration.

The analysis for arsenic was performed by Sanger-Black method (detection limit 1 μg As/sample) using 2 ml of basic solutions (residue dissolved after ashing).

The determination of orthophosphate ions was carried out by spectrophotometric method as above using mineralised samples of biological material (diluted samples of teeth and nails or resin). All standard solutions (1000 mg/l) were obtained from Merck (Germany). Working standards were prepared by diluting with water to an appropriate level immediately before analysis.

Results and discussion

All the fragments of the mummy were dark-brown, while the deeper layers of the bandages were light-brown. There was a characteristic chemical reaction of the resins in fragments {1, 2, 4, 5, & 6}. This consisted of the saponifiability of NaOH, weak solubility in C_2H_5OH, yellow uv fluorescence, a wine-red colour in reaction with CH3COO•COCH3 and H_2SO_4, the appearance of yellow-brown particles under the light microscope, and fragment {6} melting upon slight heating. Chemical identification of the presence of resin was confirmed by infrared spectrophotometric analysis.

Resins are identified by their infrared spectra (IR). Two different kinds of spectra were found in the present study (Figure 1 A & B): one from the scrapings from the cervical vertebrae {1} and another from the fragments in groups {2, 4, 5, & 6,}. Fragments {3} and {7} did not display the properties of resin. While bone scrapings were present only in group {1}, resin was found in all groups {1, 2, 4, 5, & 6}. Spectra obtained for examined samples were very similar to IR spectra of some natural resins being mixtures of resin acids. The differences between particular natural resins concerns some weak absorption bands in the region 7.5–11 microns. Although the discriminating power of IR spectroscopy in

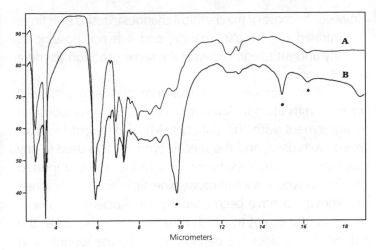

Figure 1.
Infrared spectra of:
(A) examined samples,
(B) examined samples with probable talc

examination of natural resins is rather poor, it is possible to suggest that the examined resin samples belong to the "Copal" family. This family contains about 23 different resins as shown in the Hummel/Scholl *Atlas*,[14] but a pine resin such as "east African copal" seems to be the most likely much (Figure 2).

[14] D. O. Hummel, F. Scholl, *Atlas der Kunstoff – Analyse*, Weinfeim/Bergstr. 1968.

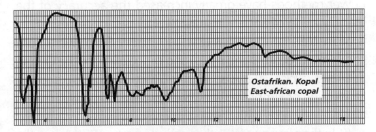

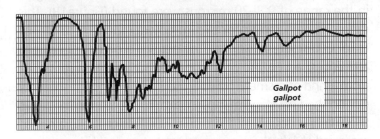

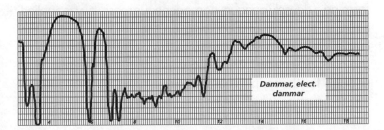

Figure 2.
Infrared spectra of some natural resins according to the Hummel/Scholl *Atlas*

[15] Strouhal, Vyhnanek, op. cit., 12-15.

[16] Lucas, Harris, op. cit., 270-326.

[17] A. D. Cross, *An Introduction to Practical Infrared Spectroscopy*, London 1960; F. M. Helmi, *Infrared analysis of some ancient resin residues on pottery sherds from Tell el-Amarna*, Seventh International Congress of Egyptologists, Cambridge 1995, 82.

[18] M. Serpico, *Chemical analysis of coniferous resins from Ancient Egypt using Gas Chromatography/Mass Spectrometry (GC/MS)*, Seventh International Congress of Egyptologists, Cambridge 1995, 163-164.

However, because of the chemical changes in resins over time, the infrared spectra also change, and it is not possible to identify ancient specimens with the same precision as more recent specimens.

It is well-known in the literature that resin was used for mummification in Ancient Egypt.[15] Our conclusions are in agreement with this concept. Many different kinds of resins were used, and the specific type of resin used in any given instance provides the basis for further study. Imported coniferous woods such as cedar, pine, fir, juniper, and cypress are known to have been used by the Ancient Egyptians, although the extent to which they were used has been the subject of considerable debate. Similarly, the identity and availability of coniferous resins has also remained unclear. Lucas[16] and his contemporaries performed chemical analyses of ancient resins, often proposing quite specific identification of the resin. It is now apparent, however, that much of their earlier work needs revision in light of the recent advances in resin chemistry and improvements in the techniques used for chemical analysis. Different ancient resin specimens have more recently been analysed by infrared spectrometry[17] and gas chromatography/mass spectrometry (GC/MS). These newer methods have greatly increased the accuracy of the identification of ancient natural products such as resins.[18] It is probable that the resins used in Ancient Egypt were from coniferous trees (firs and pines) and probably from the Cilician fir (*Abies cilicica*), the Aleppo pine (*Pinus halepenis*), and the Stone pine or Umbrella pine (*Pinus pinea*). Our examinations are in agreement with these suppositions.

In the scrapings from the cervical vertebrae, wavelengths in the range of 9,8–20 microns were found (Figure1B). This range is characteristic for talcum powder (mineral talcite, or magnesium silicate hydrate). This mineral probably came from a chemical admixture of natron used for mummification, or from a kind of cosmetic powder used for painting the mummy during the final stage of mummification. Also examined was the material found in the cranial vault after the brain was removed. Melted resin was most often used as a filling, forming a densely opaque, homogeneous mass. It was applied either in the form of a covering on the inner surface of the cranial vault, or it was poured into this cavity with the nape of the neck downward. The head was left in this position long enough for the resin to harden with a typical craniocaudally-aligned surface which delimited the front edge of the cast. Sometimes small slips of resin ran out of the edges of the filling. In a few cases the filling consisted of linen soaked with resin.

Filling the skull with resin was not so widespread.[19] Since it was an expensive procedure, it was used only on those of a relatively high socioeconomic position. According to Herodotus the brain was removed only in the most expensive cases of embalming. In different periods in history, the practice was used to a greater or lesser extent. For example, the frequency of fillings seems to have been less in Greek and Roman periods than in the earlier periods. In the case of Aset-iri-khet-es, the social position of the priestess was undoubtedly high, so it could be expected to find resin filling the entire cranial vault.

A resinous substance found in the bandages and taken from different parts of the cartonnage was of the same origin as that in the skull and in other of the mummy's fragments. Other fragments contained substances additional to resin. The sample which consisted of a fragment of unknown substance from under the mummy's back, a fragment of mass from the cartonnage wrapping the mummy and the samples of bandages, especially taken from the parts covering the abdomen, displayed characteristic findings. These were reactions which consisted of good solubility in C_2H_5OH and $C_6H_5CH_3$, unsaponifiability in NaOH, and a melting point under combustion between 120°C and 130°C. Additionally, the samples presented a polished surface of dark brown particles under the light microscope. These findings are characteristic for bitumen, or pitch.

Undoubtedly natural bitumen coming from the Dead Sea was employed extensively in Egypt during this period, and always contained V, Ni and Mo. The resinous substances, by contrast, were free or almost free of these elements.[20] Our spectrographic analysis did not reveal the presence of these elements. Since it is generally accepted that spectrographic analysis is more specific than chemical analysis, positive chemical tests alone would not be convincing evidence that bitumen was used in the embalming procedures of Aset. Spielman[21] stated that bitumen was often used for human mummification, but primarily in periods earlier than the Ptolemaic. If bitumen had been used for mummification in the Ptolemaic period, it seems likely that it would have been used more for non-human mummies, such as birds, than for humans. The reasons for this are that the procedure for mummification changed during the Ptolemaic, and bitumen was probably a cheaper material than

[19] F. LLagostera, *Radiological Aspects of the Egyptian Mummies*, V Congress of the ISRRT, Madrid 1973 (personal communication); Strouhal, Vyhnanek, op. cit., 16-24; L. Leek, F. Fielce, *The problem of brain removal during embalming by the ancient Egyptians*, Journal of Egyptian Archaeology (JEA) 55 (1969), 112-116.

[20] Lucas, Harris, op. cit., 270-326.

[21] P. E. Spielman, *To what extent did the Ancient Egyptians employ bitumen for embalming*, JEA 18 (1932), 177-180.

resin. The use of bitumen, then, became relegated to non-humans as history progressed.

Spielman further suggested that the appearance of the specimens, when exposed to ultraviolet rays, demonstrated that black substances obtained from mummies "occupied positions between the undoubted bitumen and undoubted resins." This means that there are elements of both bitumen and resin in the samples. The difficulty in making a more definitive analysis arises from the changing chemical composition of mummification materials with the passage of time, especially with those samples from later mummies which are black and behave like bitumen. This would tend to increase the probability of obtaining false positive results for bitumen. The most reliable determination in this situation is spectrographic analysis. Because our spectrographic analysis was negative for V, Ni and Mo, it can not be verified that bitumen was used in the mummification. The admixture contaminating the resin such as waxes, oils, and ointments could result in the display of the chemical properties of bitumen.

The analysis of the fragments of teeth, nails, extremity bones, and the other fragments identified as resin, showed a fresh weight of substances (% of the total) and ash weight of mineral compounds (% of the total) as shown in Table 1. The data on the bones, teeth and nails are comparable to those occurring in similar specimens of contemporary cadavers.[22]

[22] G. W. Iyengar, W. E. Kollmer, H. J. M. Bowen, *The Elemental Composition of Human Tissues and Body Fluids*, New York 1978; W. Plenert, W. Heine, *Normalwerte*, Berlin 1978, 142.

Material	Fresh weight (%)	Ash weight (%)	Ash weight (%)
Teeth	33,0	67,0	73,9
Nails	80,1	19,9	–
Bones	47,6	52,4	54,0
Resin (from skull)	97,3	2,7	–

Table 1.
Percentage of fresh and ash weights in mummy's fragments

In Table 2 the results of qualitative analysis are presented. This is the preliminary physicochemical analysis. The first part of the analysis is a point-microanalysis of whole fragments, which examined their chemical composition. The data suggest that the composition of fragments {3} and {7} is different than that of the other fragments. This means that fragments {3} and {7} came not from the mummy, but from the material from the space outside the mummy and filling the sarcophagus. This agrees with our chemical and infrared analysis indicating that fragments {3} and {7} are not resin. Additionally, powder scrapings from the cervical vertebrae {1} contained Si and Mg, which are the components of talcum powder. The second part of the microanalysis concerned powdered fragments of resin {6}, teeth {8}, nails {9}, and bones {10}. It suggests a similar chemical composition of the teeth, nails, and bones, all of which are different from resin.

Material	Chemical elements
Teeth	C, O, P, Ca > Na, Mg, Al, Si, S, Cl, Cu
Nails	C, O, P, Ca > Na, Mg, Al, Si, Cl, K
Bones	C, O, P, Ca > Na, Mg, Al, Si, S, Cl, K
Resin (from skull)	C, O, Na, Si, S, Ca > Mg, Al, P, K, Fe
Powder from cervical vertebrae	C > O, Si, S > Na, Al, P, Cl, K, Fe, Mg
Fragment of mummy's abdommen	C > O, Na, S, Ca > Mg, Al, Si, P, Cl, K
Mass from cartonnage	C > O, Cl, Ca > Mg, P, S, K
Mass from mummy's back	C > O, Na, S, Ca > Si, P, K

Table 2.
Chemical qualitative composition of mummy's fragments by point – X-ray microanalysis

Table 3 presents the results of quantitative physicochemical investigations of these fragments, which indicate the amount of basic and trace elements. In Table 3 is the content of trace elements in bones, teeth, and nails taken from an exhumed contemporary body,[23] and in Table 4 normal values occurring in living people, according to Iyengar, Kollmer, Bowen.[24] A comparison of the data in Tables 3 and 4 leads to the several observations. In the fragments of bones, main elements such as Ca, Mg, Na, K, and P, and trace elements such as Fe, Zn, Mn, Cu, and Pb, are comparable quantitatively with those of contemporary living people.[25] In teeth, most of the main and trace elements were in the range typical for contemporary living people, however, the concentration of some elements was significantly lower in the mummy. For example, K and P were about 50% lower, Zn was 10 times lower, and Pb was not detected. In the nails, the analysis revealed Ca, Mg and P at concentrations 10-30 times higher than the levels in contemporary living people, while Mn was 50 times higher, Fe was 8 times higher, and Na was twice as high. On the other hand, the concentrations of Pb and Cu were significantly lower.

[23] Archivum of Institute of Forensic Research, Kraków, Expertise from exhumate nr Dz.E. 12/97/T.

[24] Iyengar, Kollmer, Bowen, op. cit.

[25] Ibidem; W. Plenert, W. Heine, op. cit., 142.

Material	Main chemical elements (mg/g)				
	Ca	Mg	Na	K	P
Teeth	301	7,68	5,46	0,257	67,8
Nails	73,1	1,67	7,17	0,412	28,7
Bones	200	0,778	14,3	2,11	73,3
Resin	2,2	0,309	2,37	0,868	0,55
Exhumate bones	–	–	–	–	–
Exhumate nails	–	–	–	–	–

Material	Trace chemical elements (µg/g)				
	Fe	Zn	Cu	Pb	Mn
Teeth	68,0	14,0	12,8	0	9,60
Nails	311	63,0	8,1	10,2	99,5
Bones	269	118	23,8	21,5	15,5
Resin	174	24,7	37,9	39,5	7,06
Exhumate bones	70-298	50-71	1,3-2,0	20,4-112	0,81-1,53
Exhumate nails	29	130	3,61	13,6	1,29

Table 3.
Contents of main and trace chemical elements in
mummy's fragments and in the exhumate*
*Exhumate – Archivum of Institute of Forensic
Research (Nr 120/97/T)

[26] Lucas, Harris, op. cit., 270-326.

[27] Strouhal, Vyhnanek, op. cit., 12-15.

The presence of nail-painting material or other materials used for mummification can provide an explanation for the differences between the chemical content of Aset's nails and those of people living today. It is well-known in the literature[26] that during the mummification procedure, the natron bath usually resulted in depilation (if it had not been done before embalming) and nail removal. So it might be assumed that in mummification a special substance, containing, among other elements, K, P, Fe, Mn, and Zn, was used either as a painting cosmetic, or simply as a substance used to counter the damage to the nails during the dehydration process. As an alternative to this practice it is possible that in certain cases the nails on the hands and even on the feet were sometimes sewn on with a linen thread[27].

Material	Main chemical elements (mg/g)				
	Ca	Mg	Na	K	P
Teeth Enamel	360 (34-390)	4,20 (2,5-5,60)	7,70 (6,80-11,6)	0,50	175 (170-180)
Dentine	250-282 270 (250-290)	6,18-8,60 8,40 (7,3-9,6)	5,30-7,50 7,50	– 0,70	121-135 130 (120-140)
Nails	0,368-0,863-3,40	0,066-0,120	0,440-3,10	0,357-2,40	0,180-0,205-0,99
Bones	166-309	0,700-0,980	5,60-14,1	1,47	50-171

Material	Trace chemical elements (µg/g)				
	Fe	Zn	Cu	Pb	Mn
Teeth Enamel	4,4-338 200,0	199-366 276,0	0,26-33 0,26	3,6-36 16,0	0,28-30 0,54
Dentine	31,7-110 70,0	173-198 199,0	0,20-28 0,21	7,2-28 45,0	4,52-10,5 0,19
Nails	27-41 79 (MS) 347 (SAS)	73-200	17,8-53	13,8-39	0,04-2,1
Bones	3-115-707	50-187	1-25,7	10,0-69	0,19-116

Table 4.
Contents of some main and trace chemical elements in teeth, nails and bones according to Serpico, op. cit., 163-164; Iyengar, Kollmer, Bowen, op.cit.

Our physicochemical analysis permitted the differentiation between resinous and non-resinous substances, and confirms the results obtained by means of other methods, such as chemical analysis and infrared spectrophotometry. The quantitative chemical composition of the fragments of teeth and bones, which is similar to that of contemporary living people, indicates that the main and trace elements were not influenced by the passage of time. The chemical composition of the nails was probably influenced by the application of cosmetics and by the mummification process. The chemical composition of other fragments of the mummy has not been found in previous literature.

Małgorzata Kłys
Barbara Opolska-Bogusz
Barbara Próchnicka

A serological and histological study

Introduction

The study was performed on the fragments of an Egyptian mummy Aset-iri-khet-es which belongs to the collection of the Archaeological Museum in Kraków, Poland.[1] In our previous study,[2] chemical and physicochemical investigations of mummy's fragments were undertaken. Beginning with the end of 18th century, Egyptian mummies were the subjects of different kinds of examinations all over the world. Among these examinations, serological and histological studies have played a very important role.[3] On the basis of those results, scientists have attempted to evaluate both the efficiency of the mummification process, and any changes in mummy's tissue structure under the influence of time. Additionally, the determination of blood group could be used in identifying the genetic background of the mummy.[4] Histological and pathohistological studies were undertaken in order to find any cellular changes due to the preservation process, with pathological changes being evidence of possible disease.[5]

Materials and methods

The subjects were two fragments of calf muscle {11 & 12}. These fragments were located by means of computer tomography performed in the previous phase of the examination.[6] In the serological examination, particles of the fragments were harvested and then powdered in order to prepare a suspension in a physiological solution of

[1] K. Babraj, H. Szymańska, *Eine Mumie unter dem Mikroskop. Die Untersuchungeg an der ägyptischen Mumie in Archäologischen Museum zu Kraków*, Antike Welt 5 (1997), 369-374.

[2] M. Kłys, T. Lech, J. Zięba-Palus, J. Białka, *A chemical and physicochemical investigations* (in present volume).

[3] E. Strouhal, L. Vyhnanek, *Egyptian Mummies in Czechoslovak Collections*, Narodni Muzeum v Praze, Prague 1980, 7-11.

[4] R. G. Harrison, R. C. Conolly, A. Abdalla, *Kinship of Smenkhkare and Tutankhamen affirmed by serological micromethod*, Nature 224 (1969), 325-326.

[5] Strouhal, Vyhnanek, op. cit., 7-11; T. A. Reyman, M. R. Zimmerman, P. K. Lewin, *Autopsy of an Egyptian mummy*, 5, *Histopathologic investigation*, Canadian Medical Association Journal 117/5 (1977), 470-472; J. Mignot, P. F. Ceccaldi, M. Durigon, M. Bucaille, *Pathohistological study of the skin of a mummy*, Archives d'Anatomie et de Cytologie Pathologiques 24/4 (1976), 291-294; M. A. Ruffer, *Remarks on histology and pathological anatomy of Egyptian mummies*, Cairo Scientific Journal 4/40 (1910).

[6] Kłys, Lech, Zięba-Palus, Białka, op. cit.

[7] Z. Marek, K. Jaegermann, B. Turowska, *Oznaczenie gatunkowej przynależności białek przy pomocy precypitacji w polu elektrycznym w żelu agarowym*, Folia Medica Cracoviensia 6/1 (1964), 83-91.

[8] B. Turowska, *Badanie śladów biologicznych*, in: *Medycyna sądowa*, ed. B. Popielski, J. Kobiela, Warszawa 1971, 736-745.

salt (0.85% NaCl). The mixture was kept for 24 hours at 4°C and then centrifuged. An extract was examined by the immunoprecipitation method on agar gel, using serum precipitated from human protein[7] manufactured by Behringwerke (Germany). Blood group testing in the ABO system was performed by the absorption method with the use of standard anti-A, anti-B (1:128) and phytoaglutinin anti-H (1:30),[8] manufactured by Biotest (Germany).

The classical methods were used for the histological preparations:

a) Small particles from the fragments were placed in a physiological solution of salt (0.85% NaCl) for five days, then preserved in formalin. These fixed samples were next impregnated with paraffin, sliced, and stained with hematoxylin and eosin. The slides were viewed under light microscope at 125×, 200×, and 500×.

b) Small particles from the fragments were placed in a 3% solution of glutaric aldehyde in cacodyle buffer (0.2 M., pH 7.4), then preserved in osm tetraoxide (1% OsO_4 in cacodyle buffer). After dehydratation in ethanol and propylene oxide prepared tissue were impregnated with epoxide resin "Spur". Then fixed samples were cut with glass and diamond knife into very thin slides. The slides were viewed under electronic microscope.

Results and discussion

The presence of human protein in the calf muscles in our study is evidence that the fragments were of human origin. Additionally, it may be argued that the successful analysis of protein from a 2,400 year-old mummy is evidence of good preservation of the mummified tissue. Another study of mummy's protein leading to the identification and analysis of particular components of human protein has also been performed.[9] In addition to muscle, other tissue has been used for protein determination. Isolation of an enzyme in bones taken from a 2,300-year old Ptolemaic mummy was carried out by Weser and Kaup.[10] These factors lead us to conclude that after about 2,400 years, muscle protein can remain identifiable, the calf and bones are adequate sites for sample harvesting, and the mummification process was sufficient to permit protein preservation.

[9] R. A. Barraco, *Autopsy of an Egyptian mummy. Analysis of protein extract*, Canadian Medical Association Journal 117 (1977), 474.

[10] U. Weser, Y. Kaup, *Intact mummified bone alkaline phosphatase*, Biochimica et Biophysica Acta 1208/1 (1994), 186-188.

There has been extensive blood group testing of mummies.[11] The perfection of micromethods has facilitated the testing of mummified tissues for the ABO and MN blood groups.[12] An interesting study performed by Hart et al.,[13] on the 3,200 year-old mummy of a 14 year-old Egyptian boy named Nakht, identified his blood as type B. The blood cells recovered from Nakht are believed to be the oldest preserved human red and white blood cells known. Using ABO group testing it is possible to differentiate between human nationalities. In the case of the mummy of Aset-iri-khet-es, the ABO phenotype was revealed as type B. It is said that this phenotype occurs more often among people coming from eastern Europe and Asia than from other sides of the world.

ABO blood typing has been used to study mummies of other geographic origins. Allison et al.[14] found that in Peru all ABO blood groups were found in the period from 3,000 B.C. to 1,400 A.D. From 1,400 A.D. to 1,650 A.D., however, only types A and O were found. In Chile no type B or AB was noted either in pre-Columbian or Colonial mummies. These findings confirm the archaeological concept that the Chilean Indian was culturally as well as genetically different from the Peruvian Indian.

The histological examination of each of the two calf muscle fragments of mummy Aset-iri-khet-es revealed very similar histological pictures. Both preparations obtained with (a) method displayed a characteristic skeletal muscle structure. The cell organelles were only partly preserved, with the nuclei not visible. The muscle fibers appeared fragmented. The colour of the cells varied distinctly from normal, being very pale. Between the cells there was some amorphous brown substance, and in some places there was a granular mass similar to extravasated blood.

With the used of second method (b) the material crumbled into dust during cutting with the glass knife and the diamond knife as well. Under electronic microscope preserved fragments of tissue were not seen. Only residual fragments of riddle resin were observed.

The pictures obtained with only one histological method (a) represented just residual biological structure.

Both the osseous and the soft tissues permit the identification of pathological changes. Since the osseous tissue is considerably less deformable, however, pathomorphological changes are more easily and more definitively recognizable in osseous than in soft tissue. This disparity is increased during

[11] G. D. Hart, I. Kvas, M. L. Soots, *Blood group testing of ancient material with particular reference to the mummy Nakht*, Transfusion 18 (1978), 474-478; iidem, *Autopsy of an Egyptian mummy. Blood group testing*, Canadian Medical Association Journal 117 (1977), 476; Z. Lin, T. Kondo, T. Minamino, E. Sun, G. Liu, T. Oshima, *Genotyping of ABO blood group system by PCR and RFLP on mummies discovered at Taklamakan desert in 1912*, Japanese Journal of Legal Medicine 50 (1996), 336-342; M. J. Allison, A. A. Hossini, J. Munizaga, R. Fung, *ABO blood group in Chilean and Peruvian mummies, II, Results of agglutination-inhibition technique*, American Journal of Physical Anthropology 49 (1978), 139-142; W. C. Boyd, L. G. Boyd, *An attempt to determine the blood groups of mummies*, Proceedings of the Society of Experimental Medicine 31 (1934), 671; iidem, *Blood grouping tests on 300 mummies*, Journal of Immunology 32 (1937), 307-319; K. Berg, F. W. Rosing, F. Schwarzfischer, H. Wischerath, *Blood groupings of old Egyptian mummies*, Homo 26 (1975), 148-153.

[12] Berg, Rosing, Schwarzfischer, Wischerath, op. cit., 148-153.

[13] Hart, Kvas, Soots, *Autopsy of an Egyptian mummy*, 474-478.

[14] Allison, Hossini, Munizaga, Fung, op. cit., 139-142.

15 Strouhal, Vyhnanek, op. cit., 16-24.

16 Reyman, Zimmerman, Lewin, op. cit., 470-472; Mignot, Ceccaldi, Durigon, Bucaille, op. cit., 291-294; Ruffer, op. cit.; E. Fulcheri, *Immunochemistry: a new outlook in histopaleopathology*, Societa Italiana Biologia Sperimentale 71 (1995), 105-110; A. G. Nerlich, F. Parsche, T. Kirsch, I. Wiest, K. von der Mark, *Immunohistochemical detection of interstitial collagens in bone and cartolage tissue remnants in an infant Peruvian mummy*, American Journal of Physical Anthropology 91 (1993), 279-285; P. D. Horne, P. K. Lewin, *Autopsy of an Egyptian mummy*, VII, *Electron microscopy of mummified tissue*, Canadian Medical Association Journal 117/5 (1977), 472-3.

17 Ruffer, op. cit.

18 Fulcheri, op. cit., 105-110; Nerlich, Parsche, Kirsch, op. cit., 279-285.

the mummification process, in which postmortem surgery, washing and anointing, and wrapping all serve to mechanically deform the cadaver.[15] This deformation is considerably more marked in soft rather than in osseous tissue.

Histological changes have been the subject of research of various authors.[16] In comparing these studies, method standardisation has been a serious problem in the study of mummified tissues. A significant improvement in the histological and pathohistological study of mummies is connected with the name of the Cairo bacteriologist Ruffer.[17] He first succeeded in unfolding the methodology for returning elasticity to dried and friable tissues, and to modify the staining method which helped to obtain perfect thin sections. In this manner conditions were suitable for defining pathological changes in mummified tissues, and thus a new scientific branch was born which Ruffer defined as paleopathology. This has permitted histological study in recent times to reach a relatively high level of development.

Mummified tissues varying from subject to subject and even within the same subject, depend on the topographic region and the site. These changes result from to different mummification methods and subsequent environmental conditions in which the mummy was preserved.[18]

Conclusions

Identification of human protein or group substance could be an evidence of remain of human life in the mummified body and efficiency of mummification process. However, preservation of the body unchanged and undecayed for ever, into which believed Ancient Egyptian is not possible. Biological structures have to die finally what different more or less sophisticated histological studies confirm. The present study is an examination of a single mummy – an Egyptian priestess Aset-iri-khet-es – and just confirms factors known from different studies of mummies in the world.

Agnieszka Sutkowska

Molecular analysis of ancient DNA isolated from mummy's tissues

Introduction

First efforts concerned examining of ancient DNA were undertaken at the beginning of the eighties by Svante Pääbo who has worked at the Uppsala University (Sweden), he cloned DNA fragments isolated from Egyptian mummy, then he searched *alu* sequences.[1] At the same time Rassel Higuchi and Allan C. Wilson from Californian University – Berkeley have analysed mitochondrial DNA fragments obtained from quagga – an extinct representative (proxy, agent) of horse family from South Africa region.[2]

Since then ancient DNA was examined many times. The source of DNA were various e.g. insects captured in amber, fossil plants, bones, skin and parts of many tissues of extinct animals, museum specimen, Egyptian and Peruvian mummies and human remnants, which yielded natural mummification (Windover Cemetery – Florida), or were preserved in ice (Tyrol human from ice).[3]

The oldest examined human DNA originated from Windover site, and was 7,500 years old.[4]

The aim of the research conducted on DNA isolated from ancient human remnants was to solve the mechanisms responsible for evolutionary changes in human species. It is necessary to collect sufficient data from various human developmental stages. All aims could be worked out by examining conservative DNA fragments as well as polymorphic genetic system e.g. MHC system and its products which are

[1] S. Pääbo, *Molecular cloning of Ancient Egyptian mummy DNA,* Nature 314 (1985), 644-645.

[2] R. Higuchi, B. Bowman, M. Freiberger, O. A. Ryder and A. C. Wilson, *DNA sequences from the quagga, an extinct member of the horse family,* Nature 312 (1984), 282-284.

[3] T. Maniatis, E. F. Fritsch, J. Sambrook, *Molecular Cloning. A Laboratory Manual,* Cold Spring Harbor Laboratory, New York 1982.

[4] D. A. Lawior, C. D. Dickel, W. W. Hauswirth and P. Parham, *Ancient HLA genes from 7,500-year-old archaeological remains,* Nature 349 (1991), 785-787.

[5] Ibidem, 785-787; S. Pääbo, R. G. Higuchi and A. C. Wilson, *Ancient DNA and the Polymerase Chain Reaction*, Journal of Biological Chemistry 264 (1989), 9709-9712; S. Pääbo, *Ancient DNA: Extraction, characterisation, molecular cloning, and enzymatic amplification*, Proceedings of the National Academy of Sciences USA 86 (1989), 1939-1943.

[6] W. W. Hauswirth, C. D. Dickel, D. J. Rowold and A. Hauswirth, *Inter- and intrapopulation studies of ancient humans*, Experientia 50 (1994), 585-591.

[7] Pääbo, Higuchi and Wilson, op. cit., 9709-9712.

named in human body HLA system (Human Leucocyte Antigens), mitochondrial DNA analysis, mainly V region, "D-loop" fragments and *alu* sequences dispersed in the genome.[5]

Research presented in this paper was aimed to isolate ancient DNA which possess as high molecular weight as possible and as a result to obtain longer DNA fragments amplified by PCR technique.[6]

The first step of the survey was focused on duplication *alu* sequences. These sequences in ancient DNA were examined first time by Svante Pääbo at the beginning of the eighties.[7]

Materials and methods

Material for the experiment consisted of samples from two mummies. One of the mummies was embalmed body of Isis priestess Aset-iri khet-es originated from el-Gamhud (Middle Egypt) dated to the Ptolemaic period.

The second sample was from naturally post Meroitic mummified human remnants originated from Kassinger Bahri (IV cataract) in Sudan, dated to 5th-7th century.

Ancient DNA was obtained from forehead skin of Egyptian mummy and from eyehole of Sudanese mummy. Control sample was contemporaneous human DNA isolated from blood cells.

DNA isolation

Before DNA isolation the skin of the mummy Aset-iri-khet-es was treated in xylene. Then skin from both mummies were successively rinsed in ethanol solution (100%, 70%, 50%, 30%) and then in phosphate buffer. Samples prepared that way were digested by colagenase (1,25 mg/ml) in phosphate buffer. Each sample were divided in two parts. One of them were used to get DNA followed standard phenolic extraction method.[8] DNA from second part was isolated with application of DNAzol Reagent (GIBCO BRL) followed producer's protocol. Contemporaneous human DNA was isolated both by phenolic extraction method and with DNAzol Reagent. After isolation, DNA was purified by Low Melting Point agarose gel electrophoresis, then agarose blocks with cleaned DNA were cut out.

[8] A. Merriwether, F. Rothhammer and R. E. Ferrell, *Genetic variation in the New World: ancient teeth, bone, and tissue as sources of DNA*, Experientia 50 (1994), 592-601.

Amplification of DNA by PCR.
PCR conditions for *alu* sequences

For PCR amplification used primer: 5'-GTGGATCACCTGAG-GTCAGGAGTTC-3' designed to anneal to the 5' end of human *alu* interspersed-repeat sequences. PCR mix included for 50µl reaction: 1 unit Taq DNA Polymerase and supplier's buffer (GIBCO BRL), 200µM dNTP's, 400nM primer and genomic DNA. Amplification cycle: 95°C/4,5 min; 35× (50°C /50 s., 72°C/2 min, 94°C/30 s.); 72°C/5 min. Products were analysed on 1,2% agarose gel with 0,5 µg/ml ethidium bromide using lambda DNA HindIII/EcoRI digested as molecular weight standard.[9]

[9] J. Thacker, *Fingerprinting of mammalian cell lines with a single PCR Primer,* BioTechniques 16 (1994), 252-253.

PCR conditions for ABO genotyping

Two different reagent mixtures were prepared contained various primer density.

For PCR amplification used Perkin-Elmer reagents. 25µl reaction included 2,5 µl 10×PCR Bufforl,1,25µl 4mM dNTP mixture, 0,25 µl (1,25u) AmpliTaq DNA Polymerase, 15 mM $(NH_4)_2SO_2$, 4µg/25ml reaction of Bovine Serum Albumine (BSA) and 12,50pM or 18,75pM of each primer:

```
Mix I: 5'Op    5'-GGAAGGATGTCCTCGTGGTA*-3'   12,50pM
       3'Op    5'-GGTGGTGTTCTGGAGCCTG-3'     12,50pM
       5'Bp    5'-GTGGAGATCCTGACTCCGCTG-3'   18,75pM
       3'Bp    5'-GAAGAACG*CCCCCAT*GTAG-3'   18,75pM


Mix II: 5'A/Op  5'-GTGGAGATCCTGACTCCGCTG-3'  18,75pM
        3'A/Op  5'-GAAGAACC*CCCCCAG*GTAG-3'  18,75pM
        5'A/Bp  5'-GGAAGGATGTCCTCGTGGTG*-3'  12,50pM
        3'A/Bp  5'-AATGTCCACAGTCACTCGCC-3'   12,50pM
```

Amplification cycle: 94°C/30 s.; 32×(94°C/10 s., 60°C/10 s., 72°C/10 s.); 72°C/10 min.

Product of amplification were electrophoresed on 3% NuSieve Agarose gel with 0,5 µg/ml ethidium bromide using 100 bp molecular weight standard.[10]

[10] C. Crouse and V. Vincek, *Identification of ABO alleles of forensic-type specimens using rapid-ABO genotyping,* BioTechniques 18 (1995), 478-483.

Discussion

The main problem which scientist have faced during antique DNA examining was high degradation level of the material, presence of cell autolysis products as well as contamination caused by substances used in antiquity for body embalming. The impurity has made more complicated or impossible both to determine DNA concentration in the sample and PCR reaction.[11] Egyptian mummy tissue pretreated in xylene partially lost substances used for embalming which were soluble in xylene. Treatment in the file of alcohol caused partial purification of skin sample and increased water content. The remain contamination in the sample obtained from Aset-iri-khet-es tissues were observed after LMP agarose

[11] Maniatis, Fritsch, Sambrook, op. cit; Pääbo, *Molecular cloning...*

gel electrophoresis as a fluorescent spots and smudges amaranth and turquoise dyed, which migrated in the gel with distinct speed than DNA. Described above phenomenon helped to purify DNA. After electrophoresis, agarose blocks with cleaned DNA were cut out. DNA isolated from Sudanese mummy and contemporaneous DNA were treated in LMP agarose gel the same way as described above to maintain the same procedure for all samples. All the present studies reported that the most stable was the DNA originated from skin and bone cells. Scientists have explained this occurrence in many ways e.g. enzymes caused cell autolysis need relatively high water content, however extraneous tissues have dried up before postmortem degradation process is completed. Moreover it is supposed that DNA could create mineral complex with some mineral compounds present in bones and as a result DNA become more stable. It has been proved that DNA degradation level is similar in samples possessed various age. That phenomenon pointed out that degradation process appeared in a very short time after death, before the tissue could dry up. It is also widely known that DNA decay faster under stress factors e.g. oxygen radicals, natural radiation, or water which can wash out DNA from death cells. Nevertheless it was possible to undertake precious survey of antique DNA, especially thanks PCR technique.[12]

Accessible literature reported that most of scientists apply phenolic extraction method to isolate antique DNA. However that technique allow to get relatively short DNA fragments and amplification products which posses the length no more than 200 bp. In a short time a new method which allow to make longer PCR products was developed.

In the presented research phenolic extraction method was applied and brought comparative results. Isolation with DNAzol Reagent resulted with higher DNA molecular weight (Photo 1). The primer used in the research made possible to amplify all *alu* sequences in studied DNA. Since human DNA has got bout a 100 thousand *alu* copies, as a result was obtained a mixture of vast quantity of DNA fragments which had various length and gave characteristic smudge after electrophoresis (Photo 2).

If longer DNA fragments were used in the research, the longer amplification products were received.

Genomes of primitive organisms posses lower number of *alu* sequences and followed by described above procedure characteristic bends pattern for certain species could be gain.[13]

Presented results are very interesting because the length

[12] S. Pääbo, J. A. Gifford and A. C. Wilson, *Mitochondrial DNA sequences from a 7000-year-old brain*, Nucleic Acids Research 16 (1988), 9775-9787.

[13] Thacker, op. cit., 252-253.

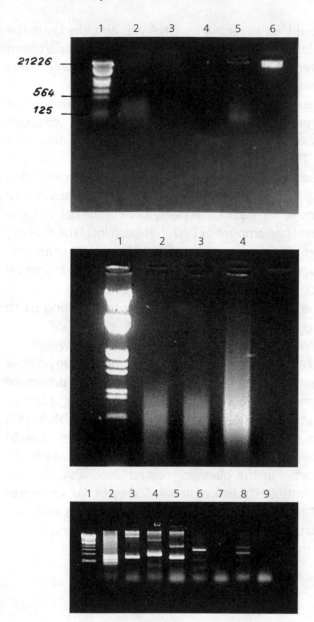

Photo 1.
Electrophoresis of isolated DNA.
1 – molecular weight standard, antique DNA isolated by phenolic extraction method (2,3) isolated with DNAzol Reagent (4,5):
2,4 – Egyptian mummy;
3,5 – Sudanese mummy; contemporaneous DNA

Photo 2.
Electrophoresis of PCR product with application of specific *alu* sequence primer. 1– marker;
2 – Egyptian mummy; 3 – Sudanese mummy;
4 – contemporaneous DNA

Photo 3.
Amplified ABO genotypes.
1 – molecular weight standard.
2, 3, 4, 5 – contemporaneous DNA;
6, 7, 8, 9 – Egyptian mummy

of amplification products are the same for DNA isolated from Egyptian mummy and Sudanese mummy, but much shorter then contemporaneous DNA. The results proved similar degradation level of DNA isolated from both mummies.

Results revealed in this paper confirmed other authors results, that DNA has been decayed in a very short time after death, and time after death to sampling time seems to be not critical.[14] It is important that received after amplification by PCR methods DNA fragments are much longer than described in the literature and posses 1300 bp.

After couple of months antique DNA was isolated again but from the sample originated from another part

[14] Pääbo, *Ancient DNA...*, 1939-1943.

of Aset-iri-khet-es remnants. DNA was amplified with the same *alu* specific primer. After electrophoresis apart from characteristic smudges, alien DNA contamination was observed.

The second part of the research was aimed to determine blood group of Aset-iri-khet-es with molecular technique application (Photo 3). The efforts didn't bring supposed results. The reason was that the set of primers applied in the research required very strictly determined genomic DNA concentration, what was impossible in the studied samples. There are some methods to purify DNA in the gel, but as a result the large amount of DNA has been lost. The quantity of ancient DNA was low, therefore DNA content in agarose blocks was low as well. The purification technique in agarose gel could caused total lost of antique DNA.

The results gained in this study might bring us to following conclusions.

DNAzol Reagent increased molecular weight of isolated ancient DNA. Inevitability to purify DNA in agarose gel as well as absence of sufficient method to determine DNA concentration in the sample could impede or restrict PCR method in molecular survey of antique DNA. PCR technique and specific primers for *alu* sequences allow to estimate the length of amplification products which can be expected in the planned research, and also allow to check purity of studied material. Survey of *alu* sequences by PCR technique confirmed principle which is said that degradation level of ancient DNA doesn't depend on the age of the sample.

Tomasz Grzybowski
Jakub Czarny
Marcin Woźniak
Danuta Miścicka-Śliwka

Sequencing of mtDNA region V from a 2.300 years old Egyptian mummy

Introduction

Over the last fifty years, among many achievements of biological sciences, the ability to identify an organism through an analysis of its nucleic acids seems to be among the most important. The ability to explore genetic polymorphism is applicable in many areas of biological sciences, such as evolutionary biology [Golubinoff, Pääbo, Wilson 1993], forensic medicine [Benecke 1997] and many others [Edwards, Caskey 1991; Powell et al. 1995]. The principal feature of living organisms which allows this type of analysis to be conducted is genetic diversity. Every organism and almost every living cell contains nucleic acids necessary to transfer its genetic information to the next generation. The genetic information itself consists of genes, their regulatory sequences and, usually, non-coding stretches of DNA [Lewin 1994]. It is quite obvious that non-coding DNA fragments are not direct targets for the environmental pressure and selection in the process of evolution and thus mutations occurring in such fragments may accumulate. In fact it has been observed that non-coding regions of nucleic acids exhibit higher mutation rates than coding regions and they harbor a major part of the genetic polymorphism found in living organisms, regardless of their taxonomical position [Kimura 1983].

Nucleic acids, DNA and RNA, are present in living cells and viruses in several forms, differing in their function, chemical composition and physical properties. For instance, nuclear DNA in Eucariota, together with many nuclear proteins, form a chromatin, which is organized in the form of chromosomes and clearly visible during cell divisions. Nuclear DNA contains an almost complete genetic information required for any organism to sustain its function [Lewin 1994]. Cellular organelles in Eucariota, mitochondria and chloroplasts, possess their own small genomes, consisting of circular DNA particles present in multiple copies. These genomes contain only a small number of genes, coding for proteins crucial to the organelle's function [Brown, Wallace 1994; Gray 1999]. RNA in living cells is utilized principally as an agent, transferring genetic information from the genomic/nuclear DNA to the protein synthesis path. RNA is also often referred to as a "molecular tool", as it is a component of many nucleoproteins involved in the cell's metabolic activity, such as ribosomes or signal recognition particles (SRPs) [Stryer 1995].

The mentioned differences in the physical and chemical properties of nucleic acids are crucial to the possibility of analyzing ancient genetic material. For instance, RNA particles are much less stable and chemically resistant than DNA, and so are of little practical use for this kind of analysis [Cheah, Osborne 1978]. Contrarily, organellar (mitochondrial or chloroplast) DNA particles are covalently closed and present in many thousands of copies in each cell so there is quite a high probability of finding some complete or only partially degraded particles even in very old biological samples [Hagelberg, Clegg 1991]. The chemical resistance of nuclear is similar to that of organellar DNA, but its particles are not closed and thus are more susceptible to the activity of nucleolytic enzymes. Moreover, nuclear DNA (chromosomes) is present in only a limited number of redundant copies in cells. For instance, an animal diploid cell contains only two copies of each chromosome while the same cell may contain a few thousands, or even a few hundred thousands, copies of mitochondrial DNA [Lawlor et al. 1991].

Numerous environmental factors influence our ability to analyze the genetic material of biological samples and they may be divided into two groups: biological and physical. The most prominent biological factor influencing the DNA stability are nucleolytic enzymes which are activated during an autolysis process after the death of an organism, or come from the bacterial flora present in a natural environment [Hummel, Hermann 1992]. Processes occurring naturally, such as mummification in dry or anaerobic conditions or freezing may inhibit the activity of these enzymes. Some papers describe successful genetic analyses of dried biological remains of different origin and age, coming principally from museum collections [Thomas et al. 1989]. Analyses are also reported of frozen ancient genetic material, the best known being the bacteria specimens obtained from a mummified body of the Tyrolean Iceman, found in 1991 in a glacier in the Alps [Cano et al. 2000]. Physical factors influencing the integrity of ancient DNA samples depend also on changing environmental conditions, principally the presence of oxidative agents [Pääbo 1989]. These factors are responsible for chemical modifications not only of the genetic material but also other chemical compounds found in living cells, such as proteins, fatty acids etc., that may even cause tissue fossilization [Niklas, Brown 1981]. Anaerobic and dehydrating conditions inside amber pieces were found to be favorable for the preservation of insect or tissue fragments. Microscopic examinations of some amber specimens, as old as 40 million years, revealed the presence of certain recognizable subcellular components such as mitochondria [Poinar, Hess 1982]. The analysis of DNA obtained from such specimens (a few bee species for instance) was also performed with good result [Cano et al. 1992]. Anaerobic environmental conditions similar to those in amber are also present in some wet bogs, allowing for a good preservation of organic remains much bigger than insects, ancient human bodies being the most often studied example [Pääbo et al. 1988]. Another specific form of remains' preservation is artificial mummification, popular in some circles of Ancient Egypt. Egyptian mummies, as an example of artificial tissue preservation, are very challenging as regards ancient DNA (aDNA) analysis. They are soaked with numerous chemicals of a different nature, such as asphalt, natron, alcohol, formaldehyde and many other substances of sometimes unknown origin, which may influence the results of analysis [Hummel, Hermann 1992].

The prolonged interaction between these diagenetic factors and the genetic material studied results in numerous changes in the DNA chemical compounds. These changes include inter-strand cross-links, oxidation of bases and deoxyribose particles, strand lesions and breaks, which eventually severely limit the number of intact, original DNA fragments [Pääbo et al. 1989]. This fact naturally favors the analysis of those DNA particles, which in living cells are present in a number of copies (i.e. mitochondrial or chloroplast DNA) and thus some intact DNA fragments may be preserved even after many years. One of the first experiments dealing with aDNA was the analysis of some 120 years old squagga skins kept in a museum. DNA from these skins was introduced into genetic vectors (plasmids) and then cloned (amplified) in a bacterial strand. The researchers were successful in obtaining the sequence of DNA nucleotides for some clones, although the cloning efficiency was very low due to heavy chemical modification of DNA. Nevertheless, the sequences obtained in this experiment allowed for repositioning the squagga species in the phylogenetic tree [Higuchi et al. 1984]. However, the large amount of samples necessary to obtain these results made it impossible to confirm the results in an independent set of experiments. The same was also the case for the DNA clones obtained from a 2.300-year-old Egyptian mummy [Pääbo 1985]. The additional drawback of cloning aDNA in bacteria lies in the activity of the DNA repair systems in bacterial cells, which was uncontrollable and might lead to changes in the original aDNA sequence due to an improper reconstruction of the primary DNA structure [Pääbo, Wilson 1988]. It then became obvious that the aDNA analysis calls for more sophisticated and, first of all, more efficient analytical tools. At the time when these experiments were performed the invention of Polymerase Chain Reaction (PCR) took place [Mullis, Faloona 1987]. PCR is an enzymatic reaction of DNA amplification, performed in vitro. The DNA template is placed in a reaction tube together with deoxyribonucleotides, enzyme (DNA polymerase), suitable reaction buffer and two short fragments of DNA (so called primers) delimiting the range of the amplified DNA region. The mixture is then heated and cooled down in subsequent cycles, each consisting of three stages: DNA denaturation, primer annealing and DNA synthesis. After 30 cycles the amount of the amplified DNA fragment in the reaction mixture is higher by a few orders of magnitude i.e. it is possible to synthesize ca.10^9 copies from one template DNA molecule.

The invention of the PCR method has had a tremendous impact on molecular biology. The ability to extract a selected sequence from the whole DNA of an organism and to amplify this sequence to virtually any desirable quantity has been used widely and with considerable successes [Mullis et al. 1994]. Among many applications of the technique there were some works dealing with aDNA from very old biological material, e.g. 17-million-year-old fossilized leaves of magnolia [Goldenberg et al. 1990] or human cadavers found in a peat bog [Pääbo et al. 1988]. PCR analysis of ancient remains of living organisms pose some very specific requirements as to the quality and integrity of the genetic material under investigation. Some of these problems are similar to those described for non-amplification methods, as for instance the problem of chemical modification of DNA. Additional questions regarding a possible contamination and inhibitory substances in the specimen studied must be asked before starting the analysis so that proper DNA extraction and quality control measures may be used. Each case of the wide variety of ancient specimens exhibiting different stages of decomposition and chemical changes requires individual treatment. Up till now, aDNA extraction and amplification methods were described for naturally mummified animal and human tissues such as brain or skin, but only few authors dealt with the problem of artificial mummification. Many of the chemicals used for the artificial mummification process exert an inhibitory effect on the activity of DNA polymerases, including Taq polymerase, utilized in the PCR amplification. In ancient material, even after obtaining an aDNA extract virtually free of foreign substances, one must face the problem of heavy DNA degradation and chemical modification (mainly oxidation). False results may be obtained as result of a bad quality of the PCR template, because DNA polymerase may erroneously introduce improper nucleotides in place of those chemically modified or it may "reconstruct" DNA fragment form shorter pieces present in the extract, not necessarily reflecting the structure of original sequence. This phenomenon calls for very stringent evaluation of experimental results and requires additional rules of interpretation so as to exclude the possibility of obtaining false results [Höss et al. 1994].

Since DNA extraction is always a crucial point to the successful aDNA analysis, this study aims to establish a reliable method for the extraction of DNA from an artificially mummified human corpse.

Materials and methods

Five samples of a ca. 2.300 years old Egyptian mummy, known as Aset-iri-khet-es from el-Gamhud were kindly provided by the Archaeological Museum in Cracow, Poland. These samples consisted of femur bones and muscles cut from a larger fragment of mummy's leg. As the mummy was preserved with a mixture of bitumen and cedar resin, all tissues were heavily modified chemically and macroscopically barely distinguishable from the inorganic parts of the mummy (i.e. bandages). Before extraction each sample was divided into four pieces which were extracted and analyzed separately, using two different extraction methods (organic – with or without decalcification – and silica). Two pieces of each sample were used for each extraction method. All work areas were cleaned with 7mM sodium hypochlorite solution and UV sterilized for 20 minutes before setting up any reactions. The labware was sterilized according to standard laboratory procedures. Details of the extraction methods utilized were as follows:

(a) Organic extraction (for soft tissue samples only). The samples were powdered in a mortar. About 2.0 g of sample powder was incubated at 56°C overnight with 100 μl of extraction buffer (10mM Tris, 100 mM NaCl, 39mM DTT, 10 mM EDTA, and 2% SDS) and 100 μl of 20mg/ml Proteinase K. After incubation, a single extraction was performed with phenol, followed by triple extraction with chloroform. The aqueous phase was next transferred onto the cellulose membrane of an Centricon 30 filtration device and concentrated to 100 μl.

(b) Organic extraction with decalcification (for bone samples only). The samples were powdered in a mortar. About 2.0 g of bone powder was incubated in 0.5 M EDTA solution, three times for 24 hours. Organic extraction was performed as described above.

(c) DNA extraction with silica and guanidinium thiocyanate was performed according to Höss and Pääbo [1993]. All buffers used for the silica-based extraction were incubated with silica overnight to remove any traces of a possible nucleic acids contamination. The samples were powdered in a mortar. About 0.5 g of sample powder was incubated for 12 hours in 1 ml of extraction buffer consisting of 10 M guanidinium thiocyanate (GuSCN), 0.1 M Tris-HCl, pH 6.4, 0.02 M. EDTA pH 8.0 and 1.3% Triton X-100. DNA was adsorbed on the silica and washed twice with a buffer consisting of 10 M guanidinium thiocyanate (GuSCN), 0.1 M Tris-HCl, pH 6.4, next twice with 70% ethanol and once with acetone. After drying the pellet at 56° C, DNA was eluted at 56° C in two aliquots of 65 μl H_2O.

The PCR reactions were performed to amplify 6 fragments of mt DNA: HV1 (positions 15997-16401 – 403 bp [Sullivan et al. 1992; Grzybowski 2000]), HV2 (positions 29-408 – 378 bp [ibidem]), 12S rRNA (positions 1091-1478 – 386 bp [Kocher et al. 1989]), Cyt b (positions 14841-15149 – 307 bp [ibidem]), region V (positions 8196-8316 – 121 p.z.) and region V (positions 8225 -8316 – 92 bp [Wrischnik et al. 1987]). PCR reactions were performed as described previously [Wrischnik et al. 1987; Kocher et al. 1989, Sullivan et al. 1992; Grzybowski 2000]. The physical map of mtDNA and localization of the amplified fragments is shown on Figure 1.

The quality and quantity of PCR products was checked in a 4% agarose gel.

Sequencing reactions of amplification products were performed using the BigDye Primer Sequencing Kit (Applied Biosystems) according to the manufacturer's instructions.

Both extraction and amplification controls were used in our study. Since the study employed PCR and dye-primer sequencing chemistry, 2 separate amplification reactions were required to generate templates for sequencing both strands of each segment analyzed. An extraction blank and a PCR negative control were run in all amplifications. Since small sets of samples were extracted at one time, extraction controls were multiplied. Mitochondrial DNA from contemporary humans was used as a positive amplification control.

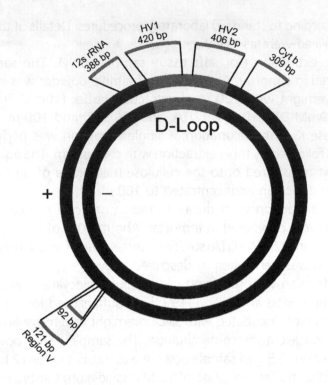

Figure 1.
A schematic map of the human mitochondrial DNA particle. Localization of all amplified fragments is indicated and the length of relevant amplification product is denoted

Results and discussion

During the organic extraction process a heavy contamination of the aqueous phase was observed, coming presumably from water-soluble preservative substances. This contamination was not removed when concentrating the samples on cellulose membranes. Amplification of the extracts obtained using an organic extraction method gave negative results. All 5 samples extracted by the silica method gave amplification products for the 92 bp fragment of region V. Additionally, 2 out of five samples extracted by the silica method gave a faint positive amplification signal for the 121 bp product of region V (Photo 1). None of the remaining mtDNA regions gave amplification products. Sequencing of five amplified 92 bp long DNA fragments revealed a sequence consistent between the samples, with a G->A transition at position 8270 (Figure 2), in comparison with the known sequence of positive control. The sequence obtained from the mummy was concordant with the Anderson's reference mtDNA sequence [Anderson et al. 1981]. The analyzed fragment of mtDNA region V comprised the region of a known mutation occurring in some individuals of East Asian origin and regarded as a valuable anthropological marker [Wrischnik et al. 1987]. This mutation was not present in the specimen studied.

As mentioned before, the choice of a proper DNA extraction method and stringent contamination precautions are the key steps in the analysis of aDNA [Höss et al. 1994]. In the present work a set of evaluation criteria have been adopted to ensure a proper interpretation of results. These criteria include: the use of reagent blanks and controls to track the presence of contamination in extraction reagents, no-template amplifications to control the

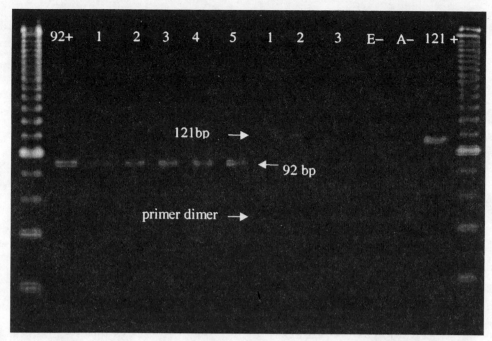

Photo 1.
Amplification results of two fragments obtained for the mitochondrial region V fragments. All samples were positive for the 92 bp amplification product while only samples 1 and 2 gave a detectable products for 121 bp fragment. Other samples (represented by sample 3 on the illustration) gave no product for the longer fragment similarly as negative controls of extraction and amplification

Symbol explanation:
1 – 5   – sample numbers
92+   – positive amplification control of the region V 92 bp product
121+   – positive amplification control of the region V 121 bp product
E-   – blank extraction control
A-   – blank amplification control

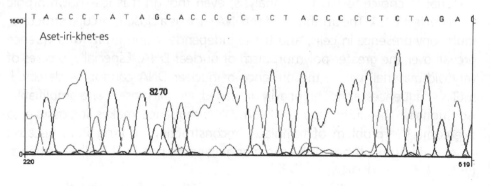

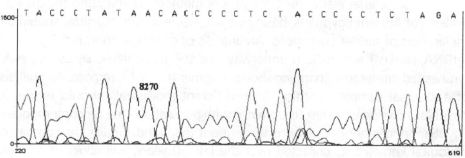

Figure 2.
Sequence of mtDNA region V of Egyptian mummy compared to the same sequence in positive control. A transition from G to A is clearly visible in position 8270 while the rest of the sequence is identical between these two samples

contamination in amplification reagents, multiple extracts from independent tissue samples, inverse relationship between amplification length and efficiency (due to aDNA degradation), unambiguous sequencing results and phylogenetic inference between ancient sequences and modern sequences of the same, or related, species. All the criteria mentioned were met in the course of generating the results presented in this work. Extraction blanks were processed together with the samples analyzed throughout the entire extraction, amplification and sequencing procedure and gave negative results in both amplification and sequencing reactions. Reagent blanks were also negative in all amplifications. Amplification of the 92 bp and 102 bp fragments of mtDNA region V revealed an inverse proportion between the length of the product amplified and the amplification efficiency. The sequencing results confirmed that the amplified mtDNA fragments are of human origin and that their sequence is different from the control human sequence in this region of mtDNA. All those facts strongly support the thesis, that the amplified material was in fact a DNA sample obtained from a mummy and not a modern contamination.

The principal goal of the present work was to establish a reliable method for the extraction of DNA from an artificially mummified human corpse. The silica method turned out to be a method of choice for such an analysis. The ability of silica to bind specifically even short fragments of DNA appears to play a crucial role in the procedure, allowing for a gentle, yet stringent purification of the genetic material from potential inhibitors of amplification. The next important factor in a successful genetic analysis of ancient tissues is the choice of the genetic material. Mitochondrial DNA has proved to be a material of choice for such an analysis, even though it is less polymorphic than nuclear DNA. The attributes of mtDNA such as a closed, circular structure, multicopy presence in cells, and tissue independent uniformity of sequence prevail over the greater polymorphism of nuclear DNA. Especially in cases of very old material, where the presence of nuclear DNA cannot be detected, mtDNA sequences, although heavily damaged, are still present and amplifiable. Additionally, the uniformity of the mtDNA sequence makes it possible to overcome the problem of template "reconstruction" during PCR, because amplified fragments are of the same origin and do not exhibit allelic variants, typical for nuclear DNA.

Next step, after elaborating the proper methods of analyzing the genetic material of Ancient Egyptians, basing on the tissues of one mummy, should be the analysis of further specimens. An analysis of other polymorphic regions of mtDNA, i.e. HV1 and HV2, is underway. This will be achieved by using newly synthesized primer sets, spanning shorter fragments of these regions. An analysis of additional samples, coming from different individuals, would render it possible to compare the results obtained with population data for contemporary Egyptians and other populations throughout the world. Finally, the combined biological knowledge, collected over the last 50 years, will allow us to look back into the life of our ancestors in a novel, fascinating way.

Afterword

The experience gained during the genetic analysis of the Egyptian mummy turned out to be very useful in the routine casework of the Institute, particularly in the project of genetic identification of victims from mass graves in the former Yugoslavia, run by the International Commission of Missing Persons (ICMP).

References

S. Anderson, A. T. Bankier, B. G. Barrell, H. L. de Bruijn, A. R. Coulson, J. Drouin, I. C. Eperon, D. P. Nierlich, B. A. Roe, F. Sanger, P. H. Schreier, A. J. H. Smith, R. Staden, I. G. Young, *Sequence and organization of the human mitochondrial genome*, Nature 290 (1981), 457-465

M. Benecke, *DNA typing in forensic medicine and in criminal investigations: a current survey*, Naturwissenschaften 84 (1997), 181-188

M. D. Brown, D. C. Wallace, *Molecular basis of mitochondrial DNA disease*, Journal of Bioenergetics and Biomembranes 26 (1994), 273-289

R. J. Cano, H. Poinar, G. O. Poinar Jr., *Isolation and partial characterization of DNA from the bee Proplebeia dominicana (Apidae: Hymenoptera) in 25–40 million year old amber*, Medical Science Research 20 (1992), 249-251

R. J. Cano, F. Tiefenbrunner, M. Ubaldi, C. Del Cueto, S. Luciani, T. Cox, P. Orkand, K. H. Kunzel, F. Rollo, *Sequence analysis of bacterial DNA in the colon and stomach of the Tyrolean Iceman*, American Journal of Physical Anthropology 112 (2000), 297-309

K. S. E. Cheah, D. J. Osborne, *DNA lesions occur with loss of viability in embryos of ageing rye seeds*, Nature 217 (1978), 593-599

A. Edwards, C. T. Caskey, *Genetic marker technology*, Current Opinions on Biotechnology 2 (1991), 818-822

E. M. Goldenberg, D. E. Giannasi, M. T. Clegg, C. J. Smiley, M. Durbin, D. Henderson, G. Zurawski, *Chloroplast DNA sequence from a Miocene Magnolia species*, Nature 344 (1990), 656-658

P. Golubinoff, S. Pääbo A. C. Wilson, *Evolution of maize inferred from sequence diversity of an Adh 2 gene segment from archaeological specimens*, Proceedings of the National Academy of Sciences USA 90 (1993), 1997-2001

M. W. Gray, *Evolution of organellar genomes*, Current Opinions on Genetic Development 9 (1999), 678-687

T. Grzybowski, *Extremely high levels of human mitochondrial DNA heteroplasmy in single hair roots*, Electrophoresis 21 (2000), 548-553

E. Hagelberg, J. B. Clegg, *Isolation and characterization of DNA from archaeological bone*, Proceedings of the Royal Society of London B 244 (1991), 45-50.

R. Higuchi, B. Bowman, M. Freiberger, O. A. Ryder, A. C. Wilson, *DNA sequences from the quagga, an extinct member of the horse family*, Nature 312 (1984), 282-284

M. Höss, O. Handt, S. Pääbo, *Recreating the past by PCR*, in: K. B. Mullis, F. Ferre, R. A. Gibbs (eds.), *The Polymerase Chain Reaction*, Boston 1994

M. Höss, S. Pääbo, *DNA extraction from Pleistocene bones by a silica-based purification method*, Nucleic Acids Research 21 (1993), 3913-3914

S. Hummel, B. Hermann, *General aspects of sample preparation*, in: B. Hermann, S. Hummel (eds.), *Ancient DNA*, New York 1992

M. Kimura, *The Neutral Theory of Molecular Evolution*, Cambridge 1983

T. D. Kocher, W. K. Thomas, A. Meyer, S. V. Edwards, S. Pääbo, F. X. Villablanca, A. C. Wilson, *Dynamics of mitochondrial DNA evolution in animals: amplification and sequencing with conserved primers*, Proceedings of National Academy of Sciences USA 86 (1989), 6196-6200

P. A. Lawlor, C. D. Dickel, W. W. Hauswirth, P. Parham, *Ancient HLA genes from 7500-year-old archaeological remains*, Nature 349 (1991), 785-788

B. Lewin, *Genes V*, New York 1994

K. B. Mullis, F. Faloona, *Specific synthesis of DNA in vitro via the polymerase – catalyzed chain reaction*, Methods in Enzymology 155 (1987), 335-350

K. B. Mullis, F. Ferre, R. A. Gibbs (eds.), *The Polymerase Chain Reaction*, Boston 1994

K. J. Niklas, R. M. Brown, *Ultrastructural and paleobiochemical correlations among fossil leaf tissues from the St. Maries River (Clarkia) area, Northern Idaho, USA*, American Journal of Botany 68 (1981), 332-341

S. Pääbo, *Ancient DNA: extraction, characterization, molecular cloning and enzymatic amplification*, Proceedings of National Academy of Sciences USA 86 (1989), 1939-1943

S. Pääbo, *Molecular cloning of ancient Egyptian mummy DNA*, Nature 314 (1985), 644-645

S. Pääbo, J. A. Gifford, A. C. Wilson, *Mitochondrial DNA sequence from a 7000-year-old brain*, Nucleic Acids Research 16 (1988), 9775-9787

S. Pääbo, R. G. Higuchi, A. C. Wilson, *Ancient DNA and the polymerase chain reaction. The emerging field of molecular archaeology*, Journal of Biological Chemistry 264 (1989), 9709-9712

S. Pääbo, A. C. Wilson, *Polymerase chain reaction reveals cloning artifacts*, Nature 334 (1988), 387-388

G. O. Poinar, R. Hess, *Ultrastructure of 40-million-year-old insect tissue*, Science 215 (1982), 1241-1242

W. Powell, C. Orozco-Castillo, K. J. Chalmers, J. Provan, R. Waugh, *Polymerase chain reaction-based assays for the characterisation of plant genetic resources*, Electrophoresis 16 (1995), 1726-1730

L. Stryer, *Biochemistry*, New York 1995

K. M. Sullivan, R. Hopgood, P. Gill, *Identification of human remains by amplification and automated sequencing of mitochondrial DNA*, International Journal of Legal Medicine 105 (1992), 83-86

R. H. Thomas, W. Schaffner, A. C. Wilson, S. Pääbo, *DNA phylogeny of the extinct marsupial wolf*, Nature 340 (1989), 465-467

L. A. Wrischnik, R. G. Higuchi, M. Stoneking, H. A. Erlich, N. Arnheim, A. C. Wilson, *Length mutations in human mitochondrial DNA: direct sequencing of enzymatically amplified DNA*, Nucleic Acids Research 2 (1987), 529-542

Maria Lityńska-Zając

Macroscopic plant remains from the sarcophagus

The research of plant remains in Egyptian sarcophagi was carried out in several sites of this kind. Because of the excellent preservation of the material, the most interesting results come from the tomb of Tutankhamun [Hepper 1990]. The study comprised the plants present both in the tomb and in the sarcophagus, that is, flowers and garlands placed in the tomb for the Pharaoh, supplies of food and drink, fabrics, as well as wooden equipment and objects, perfume, glue, resins, and others. A separate group consisted of species recognized on the basis of drawings, reliefs, and ornamental motifs used then, among others, in the production of jewelry. Several species of plants from the tomb were identified, for example lotuses *Nymphaea caerulea, N. lotus,* acacias *Acacia* sp., camomile *Anthemis pseudocotula,* tamarisk *Tamarix aphylla,* Lebanese cedar *Cedrus libani*, olive trees *Olea europaea,* poppy *Papaver rhoeas,* flax *Linum usitatissimum,* lentil *Lens culinaris,* coriander *Coriandrum sativum,* emmer wheat *Triticum dicoccon,* barley *Hordeum vulgare* and others [Hepper 1990]. The rich range of species found in the tomb of Tutankhamun, provides extremely precious and well dated information on the use of plants in Ancient Egypt.

A complex research, undertaken on the initiative of Krzysztof Babraj and Hanna Szymańska, of Egyptian sarcophagi from the Ptolemaic period, which are a part of the collection of the Archaeological Museum in Cracow [Szymańska and Babraj in this volume], comprised, among others, the analysis of plant remains. Unfortunately, in the sarcophagus of the most precisely examined mummy of Aset-iri-khet-es, few plant remains appeared. Some of them were found in the coffin. They were, first of all, tiny fragments of wood, which appeared as a result of the damage of the sarcophagus. Under the cartonnage, between the first layers of bandages, in the area of the hands of Aset-iri-khet-es, some fragments of ears, leaves, and grass culms were found.

In the deeper parts between the bandages, various size fragments of leaves and culms, as well as threads of plant origin appeared. Yet, the primary location of the plants is very difficult to trace. If they had deliberately been placed between the bandages, they should have traces of resin used for embalming. Because of the serious damage of the mummy – "in the area of the chest, the shoulders, and the head", and because of the bandages which cover it [Babraj, Szymańska 1998], it cannot be excluded that the plants penetrated between the bandages during a robbery "which was committed in the distant past" [ibidem].

The plant remains were preserved in a very dry condition; they had the yellow or yellow-brown colour, and were delicate and brittle. They were identified by a comparison with the contemporary material, on the basis of the characteristics of anatomical structure (wood, thread), as well as on the basis of morphology (spikelets, leaves and grass culms). In the process of their identification, the herbarium collections of the Institutes of Botany of the Jagiellonian University and Polish Academy of Sciences were used.

In the material under analysis, two fragments of empty (i.e. void of caryopsis) ears of common barley *Hordeum vulgare* were found. Both ear fragments consist of one rachis internode with three spikelets forming the so-called triplet. The internodes are ciliate on the edges. The spikelets are sessile, and are of approximately the same size. This kind of structure indicates the presence of the six-row form of common barley. The glumes preserved in the spikelets are narrowly lanceolate, usually with the broken top part. The lemmas show five nerves, the three of them being the main ones; the edges of lemma are strongly curved to the ventral side. The paleas have two nerves. The presence of husks attached to the internode indicates that this is the naked form of barley. Generally, barley can be divided into two types, the naked, and the hulled one. In the process of thrashing of the naked form, the grain falls out, while the glumes, lemmas an paleas remain attached to the internode, just like in our case.

The material under discussion also includes three fragments of the inflorescences (of panicle or raceme type) of a wild grass Gramineae indet. (Figure 1). The length of fragments is approximately 2,5, 3,3 and 5 cm. They consist of 4, 6 and 7 nodes, respectively, with two spikelets at each node. The spikelets are laterally compressed. The upper one is sessile, and the lower grows from a 6 mm long pedicel. The spikelets are empty. Separate spikelets have rather thick glumes with 3 distinct veins and a weakly marked nervation between them. The top parts of the spikelets are destroyed. Unfortunately, the lack of the reference material makes it impossible to identify this material in detail.

The preserved fragments of grass stems (culms) are circular in cross-section, divided into hollow internodes and closed joints. The leaf blades of grasses are linear, acute at the top. There is a characteristic parallel nervation on the surface of the leaves.

Also, shorter and longer fragments of threads of plant origin appeared between the bandages. The threads consisted of several up to about a dozen of fibres twisted in a spiral way. Separate fibres, observed in a light microscope,

Figure 1.
Gramineae indet. –
fragment of
inflorescence.
Magnification about 6×

have a cylindrical structure, are hollow inside, with transversal septa, their outer walls are smooth. They consist of separate, the so-called "fibrous cells", 20-40 mm long. The threads were made of flax *Linum usitatissimum* L.

As a supplement to this modest botanical data, there should be mentioned the identification, by Babraj and Szymańska [1997, 1998], of such kinds of flowers as lotus and camomile, which constitute the beads of the necklace. These motifs were common, among others, in the tomb of Tutankhamun [Hepper 1990].

The results achieved in the botanical research are modest. In the material from the coffin of Aset-iri-khet-es, only two species of cultivated barley and flax were found.

Barley has been cultivated in Egypt for at least 6000 years, which is proved by its numerous finds in settlements, in tombs, and inside mummies. It was used mainly as a grain for bread flour, and as cereal, as well as for the production of beer, and other alcoholic beverages [among others Hepper 1990; Nowiński 1970]. "Barley also had a ritual meaning, and as connected with the cult of Osiris", which is revealed in the research of the so-called corn mummies, among others, the ones from the collection of the Archaeological Museum in Cracow [Wasylikowa, Jankun 1997].

Flax was cultivated in Ancient Egypt as early as emmer wheat and barley, which is revealed in its earliest finds in Merimde and Fayum [Zohary, Hopf 1988]. It was used for textile goods as early as in the period of the Middle and the New Kingdom [ibidem]. The present find proves, once again, this use of flax.

In conclusion, I would like to indulge in a few words of "speculation". Empty spikelets of barley, found in the sarcophagus of Aset-iri-khet-es, cannot have been placed there as supplies of food for the afterlife. Presumably, a dry (?) bouquet of grass was placed for her in her coffin (put on the mummy). This is indicated by the lack of kernels. The spikelets of barley were ripe and thrashed. This may suggest the season of the year, in which the funeral of Aset-iri-khet-es took place. After the summer-autumn (July?) flow of the Nile, this grain was sown. Its short period of vegetation, lasting on average from 99 to 112 days [Nowiński 1970], suggests that this grain could have been harvested twice a year – in November and December, as well as in May and June. Maybe one of these months was the time of Aset-iri-khet-es burial. However, it cannot be excluded that she got a bouquet of full, ripe ears of corn. Repeated opening and moving of the sarcophagus could have caused the fact that the caryopsis fell out.

References

K. Babraj, *The ethics of research on mummified human remains*, in this volume

K. Babraj, H. Szymańska, *Eine Mumie unter dem Mikroskop. Die Untersuchungen an der ägyptischen Mumie in Archäologischen Museum zu Kraków*, Antike Welt 28/5 (1997), 369-374

K. Babraj, H. Szymańska, *Kapłanka Izydy z Krakowa*, Archeologia Żywa 3/8 (1998), 2-10

F. N. Hepper, *Pharaoh's Flowers. The Botanical Treasures of Tutankhamun*, Royal Botanic Gardens, London 1990

M. Nowiński, *Dzieje upraw i roślin uprawnych*, Warszawa 1970

H. Szymańska, *Tadeusz Smoleński. Excavations at el-Gamhud*, in this volume

K. Wasylikowa, A. Jankun, *Identification of barley from the Ancient Egyptian corn-mummies in the Archaeological Museum in Cracow*, Materiały Archeologiczne 30 (1997), 13-18

D. Zohary, M. Hopf, *Domestication of Plants in the Old World*, Oxford 1988

Birgit Gerisch

Archäoentomologische Untersuchungen an Mumien, Grabbeigaben und Gräbern des alten Ägypten unter besonderer Berücksichtigung der Mumie Aset-iri-khet-es

Abstract

The study of insect remains from Ancient Egyptian tombs, in particular from mummies and mortuary food, started already at the beginning of the 19th century. In the meantime, the importance of entomology in archaeology increased to a considerable extent and gave rise to the development of a new interdisciplinary field of research termed funeral archaeoentomology. In the present paper, results of records concerning the identification of insect remains from more than 40 sites are compiled. Special attention is drawn to the mummy Aset-iri-khet-es (Archaeological Museum in Cracow, Poland), which contained fragments of animals of the class insecta, belonging to the families of chrysopidae, cleridae, dermestidae, fanniidae, lathridiidae, and tenebrionidae, as well as a fragment of an animal from the class arachnida.

Einleitung

Insekten in Gerichtsmedizin und Archäologie

Nach dem Tod wird das Gewebe von Mensch und Tier zersetzt. An der Zersetzung sind, neben Bakterien und Pilzen, Insekten und deren Larven sowie andere Wirbellose beteiligt. Welche Arten in, auf und um den verwesenden Körper gefunden werden, ist von Umständen wie Klimaverhältnissen, Jahreszeit, Fundort, Alter und Zustand des Körpers abhängig. In der Forensischen Entomologie werden derartige Zusammenhänge benutzt, um zu gerichtlich verwertbaren Informationen über einen Leichnam zu gelangen. Anhand von Eiern, Larven, Puppen und Imagines können Hinweise auf das Zeitintervall seit dem Eintritt des Todes sowie auf Todesursachen und -umstände erhalten werden.

In der Archäologie gewann die Entomologie ab den sechziger Jahren zunehmend an Bedeutung [Kenward 1974]. Parasiten wie Flöhe und Läuse gaben Anhaltspunkte zum Hygienestandard und zur Krankheitsübertragung in damaliger Zeit [Harrison 1986]. Durch Funde von Insekten an Mumien und Grabbeigaben sowie an Vorräten in Speichern können Hinweise zur Verbreitung und zum Einfluß solcher Insekten als Schädlinge, insbesondere als Material-, Vorrats- und Hygieneschädlinge, auf das Leben im alten Ägypten erhalten werden. Insektenfunde an Mumien liefern dabei Informationen zum Umgang mit Insektenbefall sowie dessen Folgen für die Präparation und Aufbewahrung der Mumien. So wurde mit der Analyse von Insektenüberresten aus Gräbern und der Interpretation in einem archäologischen Kontext eine neue Richtung der Archäologie begründet, die heute als Grabstätten-Archäoentomologie ("funeral archaeoentomology") bezeichnet wird [Huchet 1996]. Mit solchen Ansätzen werden unter jeweils spezifischen Gesichtspunkten auch Vorstellungen von Celoria [1970] weiterentwickelt, wonach es darum geht, zwischen Entomologie und Archäologie eine interdisziplinäre Betrachtungsweise für die Wechselbeziehungen zwischen den Insekten und dem Menschen herauszustellen. Insekten und die von ihnen im alten Ägypten befallenen Mumien oder Grabbeigaben bilden dabei eines der ältesten, konkret belegbaren Beispiele für diese Wechselbeziehungen überhaupt.

Insekten im Alltag sowie in Kunst und Religion

Die Insekten beeinflußten sämtliche Lebensbereiche der Ägypter. In Überlieferungen zur Bedeutung der erwähnten Wechselbeziehungen überwiegt die Darstellung der Insekten als Lästlinge oder Schädlinge diejenige als Nützlinge bei weitem, und es wurden die durch Insekten bedingten Erschwernisse des Lebens in den Vordergrund gestellt.

Insekten beeinträchtigten das Leben der Menschen auf vielfältige Weise. Es wurde von Sandfliegen berichtet, vor denen man sich durch hochgelegene Schlafstätten, Wedel und engmaschige Netze schützte. Amulette sollten ebenfalls vor Angriffen von Fliegen schützen [Helck, Westendorf 1977]. Läusen, Flöhen und anderen Körperparasiten versuchte man durch Waschen, Kämmen bzw. Abrasieren der Haare und durch Einsalben sowie häufiges Wechseln der Kleidung entgegenzuwirken. Im Alten Testament wird über die Zehn Plagen berichtet, die die Ägypter heimsuchten. Drei der Plagen beruhten auf massenweiser Vermehrung von Schnaken, Fliegen bzw. Heuschrecken; drei weitere Plagen waren Folgen davon [Levinson, Levinson 1990]. Ernteverluste durch Insekten und ihre Larven mußten beträchtlich gewesen sein. In einem königlichen Dekret wirft ein Vorsteher der landwirtschaftlichen Verwaltung den Bauern vor, daß aufgrund ihrer Nachlässigkeit der "Wurm" einen großen Teil der Ernte vernichtet habe [Hoffmann 1963]. Eine besondere Rolle spielten Insekten, die in Haushalten, Vorratsräumen und -häusern vorkamen. Kornspeicher litten vermutlich unter besonders starkem Befall [Curry 1979]. Von Bedeutung war letztlich, daß viele der Insekten nicht nur zur Beeinträchtigung der Lebensqualität führten, sondern auch für die Krankheitsübertragung und die Ausbreitung von Seuchen verantwortlich waren.

Nicht nur im Alltagsleben, sondern auch in der Kunst spielten Insekten eine Rolle und beeinflußten das Schaffen der Menschen. Insekten wie Käfer, Heuschrecken und Schmetterlinge wurden zum Beispiel auf Wandbildern sowie in Form von Amuletten und als Schmuck dargestellt (Abbildung 1). Diese Darstellungen waren zum Teil so naturgetreu, daß Bestimmungen der Familie und in einigen Fällen sogar der Art möglich waren. Eine ausführliche Zusammenstellung hierzu wurde von Keimer [1938] gegeben.

a

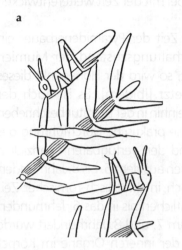

b

Abbildung 1.
Insektendarstellungen
[Keimer 1938]:
(a) Ausschnitt aus einer
Heuschreckendarstellung
aus der Mastaba des
Mereruka in Sakkara
(6. Dyn.);
(b) Kette aus Perlen in
Form von Käfern

In der Religion spielten Insekten ebenfalls eine wichtige Rolle. Der Gott Horus sollte vor giftigen, blutsaugenden und pflanzenfressenden Tieren und vor dem Schädlingsbefall im allgemeinen schützen [Levinson, Levinson 1990]. Es wurden Horus-Amulette gefunden, die auf der Rückseite die Inschrift trugen: "Wehre mir ab die Würmer, die mit dem Mund beißen" [Hoffmann 1963]. Andere Insekten wurden wiederum verehrt und als Amulette getragen oder dem Verstorbenen als Beigaben mitgegeben. Beachtung fanden Käfer von metallischer Farbe und solche mit ausgefallener Form. Auch aufgrund der Metamorphose zum erwachsenen Tier [Pettigrew 1834] und in Folge auffälliger Verhaltensweisen wurde bestimmten Insekten besondere Bedeutung beigemessen. So wurden Fliegen wegen ihrer Angriffslust als Sinnbilder der Tapferkeit betrachtet und deren Abbilder seit der 18. Dyn. als Auszeichnung an Soldaten verliehen. Der Käfer *Prionotheca coronata*, der wegen seiner sonnenähnlichen Körperform als Strahlender Sonnenkäfer bezeichnet wurde, war den Verstorbenen von der späten prädynastischen bis in die frühdynastische Zeit als Beigabe ins Grab mitgegeben worden [Levinson, Levinson 1996]. Im späten Alten Reich und in der 1. Zwischenzeit wurde der Heilige Pillendreher (*Scarabeus sacer*) verehrt. Auf seinem Verhalten basiert eine Mythologie, deren Kernpunkt die Wiedergeburt war. Es wurde angenommen, daß nur männliche Käfer existieren, die sich durch Selbstschöpfung fortpflanzen.

Insekten und Mumifizierung
In prädynastischen Zeiten wurden die Toten in eine Tierhaut, eine Matte oder in ein Kleidungsstück gewickelt und im Wüstensand begraben. Unter günstigen

Klimabedingungen wie Wärme und starker Luftzirkulation trockneten Haut und Muskelgewebe schnell, wodurch der Verwesungsprozeß im Inneren des Körpers zum Erliegen kam [Germer 1994]. Auf diese Weise entstanden natürliche Mumien. Durch die Bestattung der Verstorbenen in Gräbern verwesten die Körper demgegenüber rasch, und es wurde versucht, dies durch künstliche Mumifizierung zu verhindern. Prozeduren dieser Art wurden ab Ende der 3./ Anfang der 4. Dyn. bis in die byzantinische Periode durchgeführt [Fischhaber 1997]. Die Technik der Mumifizierung wurde dabei mit der Zeit weiterentwickelt und verändert [Sethe 1934].

Die künstliche Mumifizierung ist bis in die Zeit der Pyramidenerbauer ein königliches Vorrecht gewesen. Was die am Erhaltungszustand der Mumien gemessene Qualität der Mumifizierung anbetrifft, so wird der Höhepunkt dieses Kultes zwischen der 18. und 20. Dyn. angesetzt [ibidem]. Es ist auch der Mumifizierungsprozeß aus dieser Periode, der gemeinhin in der Literatur beschrieben wird, wobei allerdings zu bedenken bleibt, daß die praktische Durchführung des Prozesses auch vom Stand des Verstorbenen und den verfügbaren finanziellen Mitteln abhing. Durch Untersuchungen von Mumien aus dem 5. bis 8. Jahrhundert konnte die These gestützt werden, daß der noch in griechisch-römischer Zeit angewandte Prozeß der Mumifizierung im wesentlichen bis in das 6. Jahrhundert beibehalten worden war [Dawson, Smith 1924]. Im 7. und 8. Jahrhundert wurde der Mumifizierungsprozeß durch die Belassung der inneren Organe im Körper und die Ersetzung von Natron durch Kochsalz vereinfacht. Bei so behandelten Mumien wurden häufig ein schlechter Erhaltungszustand der Haut und Schäden durch Insektenbefall diagnostiziert [Anonymus 1997].

Während des Mumifizierungsprozesses wurden Gehirn und Eingeweide, abgesehen von Herz und Nieren, aus dem Körper entfernt. Durch eine etwa 30 bis 40 tägige Einbettung in kristallines Natron [Brier, Wade 1997] kam es zu einer Dehydrierung und teilweisen Entfettung des Leichnams. Danach wurde die Leibeshöhle mit Sägemehl, mit Natron gefüllten Beuteln, harzgetränktem Leinen und aromatischen Substanzen gefüllt. Die Körperoberfläche wurde mit Bienenwachs, Ölen, Milch, Natron, Gewürzen, Wein sowie mit Harz oder Bitumen eingerieben und der Körper in Leinen und Bandagen gewickelt, zwischen die Harz oder Bitumen gegeben wurde. Nicht nur Menschen, sondern auch Tiere wie Stiere, Katzen und Falken wurden mumifiziert [Hornung 1967]. Die Untersuchung der tierischen Überreste ist von großem Interesse, da bei Tieren der Prozeß der Mumifizierung weniger drastisch ablief, so daß möglicherweise vorhandene Parasiten wie Flöhe und Läuse, die bei menschlichen Mumien aus altägyptischer Zeit bisher nicht gefunden wurden, erhalten blieben [Harrison 1986] und auch zahlreiche andere Insekten identifiziert werden können. Ein "Mumienpaket" aus Theben enthielt zum Beispiel Ratten, Mäuse, kleine Vögel, Nattern, Kröten, Käfer und sogar Fliegen [Pettigrew 1834].

Durch eine sorgfältige Mumifizierung unterblieb eine weitere natürliche Zersetzung durch Bakterien, Pilze und Insekten, wobei aber auch Insektenüberreste erhalten blieben, die im Einbalsamierungsprozeß nicht entfernt wurden und die unter anderen Umständen verlorengegangen wären. Die Insekten können den

Körper zum Zeitpunkt des Todes, während der Mumifizierung, im Grab oder nach der Öffnung des Grabes befallen haben. Oftmals ist eine Bestimmung des Zeitpunktes, zu welchem der Insektenbefall stattfand, schwierig, wenn nicht unmöglich [Garner 1986]. Zur Klärung dieser Frage ist es unbedingt erforderlich, den Prozeß der Mumifizierung und die Lagerungsbedingungen der Mumie zu analysieren.

Ob Insektenbefall ein Hauptproblem bei der Mumifizierung war, ist nicht geklärt [Strong 1981]. Die Schäden, die durch Insekten verursacht wurden, waren zum Teil erheblich. Dies trifft für PUM[1] IV, die Mumie eines 8 bis 10 Jahre alten Kindes aus dem 1. Jh. n. Chr. zu [Riddle 1980]. Die Insekten waren so zahlreich, daß sie alle Körperteile dieser Mumie durchdrangen und große Löcher in Gewebe und Knochen hinterließen. PUM II, die Mumie eines 35 bis 40 Jahre alten Mannes aus der ptolemäischen Periode (ca. 170 v. Chr.), litt unter ähnlichem Befall. Die Einbalsamierer verhinderten jedoch größere Zerstörungen, indem sie die Mumie mit Harz behandelten und dadurch die Insekten abtöteten [Cockburn et al. 1980].

Viele Substanzen, die im Prozeß der Mumifizierung verwendet wurden wie Natron und Bitumen, wurden möglicherweise auch aufgrund ihrer Wirkung als Insektizid eingesetzt [Panagiotakopulu et al. 1995], ebenso verschiedene Pflanzensubstanzen. So wurden zum Beispiel bei der Untersuchung der Wirkung von ätherischen Ölen auf Schadinsekten überraschend starke Effekte festgestellt, und die meisten der Substanzen erwiesen sich als hochwirksam [Klingauf et al. 1983]. Unter Verwendung solcher Substanzen waren die Mumien für gewisse Zeit vor Insektenbefall geschützt [Levinson, Levinson 1994].

Jedoch selbst durch die Behandlung mit Natron konnten Insekten, zum Beispiel Dermestidae, die den Körper schon vor der Mumifizierung befallen hatten, nicht abgetötet werden. Solche Tiere überlebten aufgrund des durch das Natron entstandenen Mikroklimas unter experimentellen Bedingungen sogar länger als Vergleichstiere [Garner 1986]. Auch war es möglich, daß Insekten durch das Natron zu dem Körper vordrangen. Wahrscheinlich kann es sogar durch mehrmaliges Verwenden von mit Insekten kontaminiertem Natron zur Infektion von mehreren zu mumifizierenden Körpern gekommen sein [ibidem]. Erhebliche Beschädigungen durch Insekten an der Mumie Horemkenesi (21. Dyn., Theben) erfolgten wahrscheinlich während der Einlagerung in Natron [Strong 1981]. Stark beschädigte Körperpartien wie Arme, Beine und ein Teil des Hinterkopfes wurden vor dem Wickeln aus feinem Ton und Stroh nachgebildet. Möglicherweise waren in dieser Masse auch toxische Substanzen enthalten, die den Schädlingsbefall eindämmen sollten [ibidem].

Die Furcht vor der Zerstörung einer Mumie durch Insekten war groß, und es wurde versucht, den Verstorbenen auf magische Weise zu schützen. Hierzu steht im *Totenbuch* Kapitel 163 (Papyrus in Turin) geschrieben: "Um den Leichnam eines Mannes nicht in der Unterwelt zugrunde gehen zu lassen [...] und um sein Fleisch und seine Knochen vor Insekten zu schützen..." [Levinson, Levinson 1990]. In den Kapiteln 35 und 36 sind Vignetten gezeigt, in denen der Verstorbene ein Insekt mit einer Lanze durchbohrt bzw. mit einem Messer bedroht (Abbildung 2). Auch

[1] Pennsylvania Universtiy Museum.

sollten "gefährliche" Tiere von der Zerstörung der Mumie und der Vernichtung der Grabbeigaben abgehalten werden, indem sie in Gräbern ohne Kopf oder ohne Beine dargestellt wurden [Levinson, Levinson 1998]. Weiterer Schutz sollte durch Papyri erhalten werden. So wurde im Mund einer Mumie ein Papyrus mit folgender Inschrift gefunden: "Die Maden werden sich in dir nicht in Fliegen verwandeln" (Papyrus Giseh Nr. 18026:4:14 [Greenberg 1991]).

Abbildung 2.
Vignetten zur Abwehr von Insekten (Kapitel 36 des *Totenbuches* (19.-20. Dyn. in Keimer 1938). Der Verstorbene durchbohrt einen Mistkäfer (Familie Scarabaeidae) mit einer Lanze (a) und bedroht eine Schabe (Familie Blattidae) mit einem Messer (b)

Die symbolische Vernichtung oder Bedrohung von Insekten sollte zu deren Warnung und Abschreckung dienen [Levinson, Levinson 1994]. Es wurden auch praktische Maßnahmen zur Insektenabwehr eingesetzt. Im Ebers-Papyrus (ca. 1600 v. Chr.) sind hierzu verschiedene Rezepte aufgeführt, die auch im Alltagsleben Anwendung fanden. Diese beruhen auf der Verwendung von Substanzen, deren schädlingsabwehrende Wirkung durch empirische Beobachtungen ermittelt worden war [Levinson, Levinson 1990]. Eine Maßnahme gegen Insektenbefall war das Räuchern mit Harzen und anderen Substanzen. Räucherungen bildeten einen wichtigen Bestandteil des Götterkultes in Tempeln. Sie fanden auch bei verschiedenen Ritualhandlungen wie der Mundöffnungszeremonie, dem Darbringen von Opfergaben sowie beim Besuch der Grabstätte Anwendung [Levinson, Levinson 1994]. Das Räuchern hat auf verschiedene Insektenarten unterschiedlichen Einfluß. Es kann in Abhängigkeit von den eingesetzten Substanzen und deren Konzentrationen abwehrend, tötend oder sterilisierend wirken [Dibs, Klingauf 1983]. Auch Asche wurde aufgrund ihrer insektiziden Wirkung verwendet [Miller 1987].

Systematik und Übersicht über identifizierte Insekten

In der Grabstätten-Archäoentomologie ist vom systematischen Standpunkt her der Stamm Arthropoda (Gliederfüßler) von grundsätzlichem Interesse. Die an Mumien und Grabbeigaben gemachten Funde entfallen auf die Klasse der Insecta (Insekten)[2] und in geringem Maße auf die der Arachnida (Spinnentiere). Tabelle 1 enthält die wissenschaftlichen Namen für Kategorien des Stammes der Arthropoda, die im vorliegenden Beitrag erwähnt sind. Die Systematik zur hierarchischen Klassifizierung verwandtschaftlicher Beziehungen stützt sich dabei im wesentlichen auf die Taxa: Stamm, Klasse, Ordnung, Familie, Gattung und Art. Neben den wissenschaftlichen Namen in lateinischer Sprache existieren für die Repräsentanten einer Anzahl von Kategorien Trivialnamen in den lokalen Sprachen, von denen die deutschen ebenfalls in Tabelle 1 enthalten sind.

[2] Die Klasse der Insekten ist in ca. 1.000.000 Arten untergliedert. Schätzungen der Gesamtzahl von Insektenarten auf der Erde reichen von 5 Millionen bis zu 80 Millionen [Gullan, Cranston 1995].

Wissenschaftlicher Name	Deutscher Trivialname
Akis	Spitzkäfer
Akis reflexa	
Anobiidae	Bohrkäfer, Klopfkäfer, Nagekäfer, Pochkäfer
Anobium museorum	
Anobium punctatum	Klopfkäfer, Pochkäfer, Totenuhr
Anthrenus	Blütenkäfer
Anthrenus museorum	Kabinettkäfer, Museumskäfer
Anthrenus palaeoaegyptiacus	
Apocrypta	
Apocrypta longitarsus	
Arachnida	Spinnentiere
Arthropoda	Gliederfüßler
Atheta	
Attagenus	
Attagenus pellio	Dunkler Pelzkäfer
Blaps polychresta	
Blatta orientalis	Küchenschabe
Blattidae	Schaben
Blattodea	Schaben
Bostrychidae	Bohrkäfer
Bracon hebetor	
Braconidae	Brackwespen
Bruchidae	Samenkäfer
Bruchidius	
Buprestidae	Prachtkäfer
Calandra granaria	Kornkäfer
Calandra oryzae	Reiskäfer
Calliphoridae	Schmeißfliegen, Brummer
Calosoma	Puppenräuber
Cantharis	
Cantharidae	Weichkäfer
Carabidae	Laufkäfer
Chalcididae	
Chrysomya	
Chrysomya albiceps	
Chrysopidae	Florfliegen, Goldaugen
Cleridae	Buntkäfer
Coleoptera	Käfer
Copris scaraeus	
Copris midas	
Copris pithecius	
Corynetes rufipes	
Cucujidae	Plattkäfer, Schmalkäfer
Curculionidae	Rüsselkäfer
Dermestes	Pelzkäfer, Speckkäfer
Dermestes ater	Aas-Dornspeckkäfer
Dermestes cadaverinus	Aas-Dornspeckkäfer
Dermestes elongatus	
Dermestes frischii	Dornloser Speckkäfer
Dermestes leechi	

Tabelle 1.
Verzeichnis der wissenschaftlichen Namen der Klasse der Arthropoda und der verfügbaren deutschen Trivialnamen[3]

[3] Zur Klassifikation wurden Kiler [1963], Hinton [1963], Weber und Weidner [1974], Gozmany [1978], Hannemann et al. [1986, 1988] sowie Günther et al. [1994] hinzugezogen.

Wissenschaftlicher Name	Deutscher Trivialname
Dermestes maculatus	Dornspeckkäfer, Mumienkäfer
Dermestes pollinctus	
Dermestes roei	
Dermestes vulpinus	Dornspeckkäfer
Dermestidae	Pelzkäfer, Speckkäfer
Diptera	Zweiflügler
Ephestia	Speichermotten
Erodius costatus	
Fanniidae	Latrinenfliegen
Fannia canicularis	Kleine Stubenfliege
Gelechiidae	Palpenmotten
Gibbium	
Gibbium aequinoctiale	
Gibbium psylloides	Buckelkäfer, Kugelkäfer
Hymenoptera	Hautflügler
Insecta	Insekten
Lasioderma serricorne	Tabakkäfer
Lathridiidae	Moderkäfer
Lepidoptera	Schmetterlinge
Lepisma saccharina	Silberfischchen Zuckergast
Lymantriidae	Trägerspinner, Schadspinner, Wollspinner
Mesostenopa	
Mesostenopa picea	
Musca domestica	Große Stubenfliege
Muscidae	Echte Fliegen, Hausfliegen
Necrobia	
Necrobia mumarium	
Necrobia rufipes	Rotbeiniger Schinkenkäfer, Koprakäfer
Necrobia violacea	Blauer Kolbenkäfer, Brauner Schinkenkäfer
Ocnera philistina	
Oryzaephilus surinamensis	Gertreideplattkäfer
Pediculus humanus capitis	Kopflaus
Piophila casei	Käsefliege
Piophilidae	Käsefliegen
Pimelia spinulosa	
Plannipennia	Hafte, Echte Netzflügler
Plodia interpunctella	Dörrobstmotte
Prionotheca coronata	Strahlender Sonnenkäfer
Ptinidae	Diebkäfer
Rhizopertha dominica	Getreidekapuziner
Sarcophagidae	Aasfliegen, Fleischfliegen
Scarabaeidae	Blatthornkäfer
Scarabeus sacer	Heiliger Pillendreher
Scaurus puncticollis	
Silphidae	Aaskäfer
Sitodrepa panicea	Brotkäfer
Sitotroga cerealella	Getreidemotte, Weißer Kornwurm
Sitophilus	Kornkäfer, Reiskäfer, Maiskäfer
Sitophilus granarius	Kornkäfer
Staphylinidae	Kurzdeckenkäfer, Kurzflügelkäfer, Raubkäfer

Wissenschaftlicher Name	Deutscher Trivialname
Stegobium paniceum	Brotkäfer
Steraspis	
Steraspis squamosa	
Sycophaga	
Sycophaga sycomori	
Tenebrionidae	Dunkelkäfer, Schwarzkäfer
Thylodrias contractus	
Trachyderma philistina	
Trachyderma pilosum	
Tribolium	
Tribolium castaneum	Rotbrauner Reismehlkäfer
Tribolium confusum	Amerikanischer Reismehlkäfer
Trogoderma	
Trogoderma angustum	
Trogoderma granarium	Khaprakäfer
Zophosis	
Zygentoma	Fischchen

Obwohl an der Systematik der Zoologie seit weit über hundert Jahren intensiv gearbeitet wird, ist diese auch in der heutigen Zeit Änderungen unterworfen. So weisen selbst kürzlich veröffentlichte Vorschläge zur Systematik der Coleoptera beträchtliche Unterschiede auf. Auch die Schreibweise der wissenschaftlichen Namen war im Laufe der Zeit Modifizierungen ausgesetzt. Des weiteren wird die Übersichtlichkeit des Systems durch das Auftreten von Synonymen, die zum Beispiel durch unterschiedliche Benennung einer Art zustande kamen, beeinträchtigt. Besonders die Einordnung von Bezeichnungen aus Beiträgen der Anfangszeit der entomologischen Untersuchung von Mumien in die moderne Systematik ist dadurch teilweise schwierig.

Da die Namen in Tabelle 1 im wesentlichen aus Berichten über archäo-entomologische Untersuchungen von Mumien, Grabbeigaben und Gräbern aus altägyptischer Zeit stammen, kann durch die Zuordnung der Arten und Familien zu Ordnungen ein erster Eindruck über deren Verteilung gewonnen werden. 95% der Familien lassen sich den Ordnungen Coleoptera, Diptera, Lepidoptera und Hymenoptera zuordnen. Diese Ordnungen werden auch an Leichen der heutigen Zeit gefunden und spielen bei der Ermittlung der Liegezeiten eine wichtige Rolle [Benecke 1996].

Die Besiedlung eines toten Körpers mit Arthropoda erfolgt in verschiedenen Wellen [Shaumar et al. 1990; De Souza, Linhares 1997] und kann sich in Abhängigkeit von dem Zersetzungsprozeß und den damit verbundenen Veränderungen des Körpers über viele Jahre und auf unterschiedliche Arten erstrecken. Das Auftreten und die Abfolge der Arten sind, wie eingangs erwähnt, von einer Vielzahl von Faktoren abhängig. Trotz der Auswirkung solcher Faktoren ist ein Großteil der Taxa der Leichenfauna weltweit ähnlich [Gullan, Cranston, 1995] und auch die Funde an ägyptischen Mumien lassen sich diesen zuordnen.

Erstaunlich ist, daß sich in diesem Zusammenhang die bestehenden Parallelen zwischen Forensischer Entomologie und Grabstätten-Archäoentomologie nicht nur auf die höheren Taxa beziehen. Es spielen vielmehr konkrete Insektenarten sowohl im Zusammenhang mit ägyptischen Mumien als auch mit Leichen aus heutiger Zeit eine Rolle [Benecke 1996]. Man hat hier zu bedenken, daß ein Zeitunterschied von einigen tausend Jahren, gemessen an der auf über 350 Millionen Jahre geschätzten Zeit der Existenz von Insekten auf der Erde, vernachlässigbar klein ist, und daß offenbar auch unterschiedliche Umweltfaktoren keinen grundsätzlichen Einfluß ausgeübt haben. Des weiteren scheinen die an Verwesungs- und Zersetzungsprozessen beteiligten Arten vom kontinuierlichen Aussterben nicht unmittelbar betroffen gewesen zu sein. Auf Grund dieser Zusammenhänge muß erneut bemerkt werden, daß es nahezu unmöglich ist, in der Archäoentomologie das Alter von Insekten und Insektenteilen aus ihrer Art abzuleiten. Dies trifft insbesondere auf Insektenfunde zu, die von Mumien oder Grabbeigaben bereits losgelöst auftreten.

Im alten Ägypten wurden im übrigen Insekten nicht als eigenständige Gruppe von Lebewesen betrachtet. Die Einteilung des Tierreiches erfolgte nach dem Lebensraum [Hornung 1967]. So wurden alle Bewohner des Wassers als Fische und die Bewohner der Luft als Vögel bezeichnet. Zu den Vögeln zählten auch Insekten wie Fliegen, Bienen, Mücken und Schmetterlinge. Bewohner der Erde waren das Vieh bzw. Wild und das Gewürm.

Identifizierung von Insektenfunden

Die Insektenfunde werden anhand von Merkmalen des Exoskeletts, das aus Chitin besteht, identifiziert. Die Anwendung entsprechender Schlüssel zur Identifizierung von Insekten ist jedoch oftmals nicht möglich, wenn nur Fragmente erhalten sind. Hier ist vor allem der Vergleich mit rezenten Spezies erforderlich. Die Funde können meist nur Familien und Gattungen zugeordnet werden; eine Bestimmung der Art ist selten möglich.

Bei der Bearbeitung von Insektenfunden muß beachtet werden, daß durch Austrocknung Veränderungen der Oberflächenstruktur oder der Farbe eingetreten sein können. Farben wie Metallischblau, Grün oder Rot verändern sich bei Trockenheit in ein dunkles Blauschwarz [Coope 1970]. Bei verschiedenen Insektenfunden des alten Ägypten konnten entsprechende Farbveränderungen und fehlende oder reduzierte Behaarung festgestellt werden. Hope [1834] nahm an, daß der Käfer *Necrobia mumarium*, der lebend violett oder tiefpurpur gefärbt ist, durch aromatische Öle und Substanzen, die man bei der Einbalsamierung der Mumie einsetzte, teilweise entfärbt wurde. Eine ähnliche Annahme machte auch Alfieri [1931] insofern, daß Käfer, die an den Beigaben der Mumie Tut-anch-Amuns (18. Dyn.) gefunden wurden, aufgrund von Substanzen, mit denen sie in Kontakt kamen, entfärbt waren. Die hellere Farbe läßt die Käfer "unreif" erscheinen; abgesehen davon unterschieden sie sich jedoch nicht von *Necrobia rufipes* [Schenkling 1902]. Aufgrund solcher Veränderungen kann es zu Fehlern bei der Identifizierung [Huchet 1995] und auch zur Klassifizierung als neue Art kommen. So existieren für die Bezeichnung verschiedener Arten Synonyme. *Dermestes frischii* wurde *Dermestes pollinctus* und vermutlich auch *Dermestes roei* genannt [Hoffmann 1963]. *Dermestes maculatus*, *Dermestes vulpinus*, *Dermestes elongatus* und noch sieben weitere Namen bezeichnen ein und dieselbe Art [Hinton 1963]. *N. mumarium* und *N. rufipes* sind ebenfalls Synonyme.

Insektenfunde

Mumien

Anfang des 19. Jahrhunderts begann die Beschreibung von Insektenfunden aus altägyptischen Gräbern und an Mumien. Latireille [1819] berichtete von Necrobia-Funden an einer Mumie; die Tiere hatten sich in der Mumie entwickelt. Des weiteren beschreibt er eine Vase, in der Coleoptera-Fragmente enthalten waren, und erwähnt eine Mitteilung von Desmartes, die besagt, daß an einer Mumie Insektenfragmente, die möglicherweise zur Gattung Akis gehören, gefunden wurden. Atkinson [1825] berichtete von einer thebanischen Mumie, die tausende Larven von *D. vulpinus* und *Necrobia violacea* enthielt. Miller [1825] identifizierte an einer anderen Mumie ebenfalls *D. vulpinus* und *N. violacea*. Hope fand in der im Schädel verbliebenen Masse einer thebanischen Mumie der griechisch-römischen Periode, die ihm von Pettigrew zur Untersuchung übergeben worden war, verschiedene Insektenfragmente [Pettigrew 1834]. Es handelte sich um *N. mumarium*, eine Dermestes-Art, und eine beträchtliche Anzahl an Diptera-Puppen, die von ihrer Erscheinung her von zwei verschiedenen Arten stammten. Einige der Puppenhüllen waren leer, aber der Großteil enthielt fast vollständig entwickelte Fliegen. Im Kopf einer weiteren thebanischen Mumie fand Hope etwa 270 fast vollständig erhaltene Käfer und eine Vielzahl an Fragmenten, was auf etwa die doppelte Anzahl an lebenden Käfern hindeutete [Pettigrew 1834]. Die Käfer wurden von ihm als *D. pollinctus* bezeichnet und von Erichson [1846] als frisch geschlüpfte *D. frischii* identifiziert. Hope bestimmte des weiteren *D. roei* und *D. elongatus* an dieser Mumie [Pettigrew 1834]. An den thebanischen Mumien wurden des weiteren Fragmente, die wahrscheinlich von *Pimelia spinulosa* stammten, sowie eine große Anzahl von Puppen von mindestens drei verschiedenen Diptera-Arten gefunden. Eine Zuordnung der Funde zu einer der Mumien wurde nicht gegeben. Alluaud [1908] faßte zusammen, daß die an Mumien gefundenen Insekten im wesentlichen den Familien Cleridae und Dermestidae zuzuordnen sind.

Netolitzky [1911a, b] versuchte durch Magen- und Darmuntersuchungen von Mumien Hinweise auf Nahrungs- und Heilmittel der damaligen Zeit zu gewinnen. Unter seinen Funden waren auch Insekten. In der Bauchhöhle von zwei Mumien des prädynastischen Gräberfeldes bei Naga-ed-dêr fand er Fragmente, die vermutlich von *D. elongatus* stammten. Hoffmann [1963] vermutet, daß es sich eher um *Dermestes cadaverinus* gehandelt haben könnte. Keimer [1938] erwähnte eine Mumie aus Theben (Neues Reich), an der *Corynetes rufipes* gefunden wurde. Die Mumie Ramses II (Theben, 19.

Dyn.) enthielt Reste einzelner Exemplare von *D. frischii*, *Thylodrias contractus*, *Lasioderma serricorne* und *N. rufipes* [Steffan 1982, 1985; siehe auch Gerisch 1997]. Die Bestimmung dieser Fragmente war dadurch erschwert, daß sie entfärbt und abgerieben waren [Alluaud 1908]. Ausschlaggebend für die Insektenarmut dieser Mumie ist vermutlich, daß das Füllwerk nicht mehr vorhanden ist [Steffan 1985].

Mumien, die am Pennsylvania University Museum untersucht wurden, waren unterschiedlich stark durch Insekten zerstört. Die im folgenden aufgeführten Mumien sind, abgesehen von PUM II, mit wenig Sorgfalt präpariert worden. PUM II litt unter starkem Insektenbefall: vermutlich *Atheta* sp. und *Chrysomya* sp. sowie *D. frischii*, *Piophila casei* und *T. contractus* [Cockburn et al. 1975; Cockburn et al. 1980; Lynn, Benitez 1974]. PUM III und PUM IV waren ebenfalls von Insekten beschädigt. PUM III, die Mumie einer etwa 35 Jahre alten Frau (ca. 835 v. Chr.), enthielt *Chrysomya albiceps*, vermutlich *N. rufipes* und *T. contractus* [Riddle 1980]. Die Mumie PUM IV litt, wie PUM II, unter ähnlichem Befall [Cockburn et al. 1980]. Es wurden auch *Stegobium paniceum* Käfer erwähnt, die sich im Körper der Mumie PUM IV befanden [Riddle 1980].

Zahlreiche Insekten wurden in den Mumien und Kanopengefäßen der Manchester-Museum-Collection gefunden [Curry 1979]. Es handelte sich bei diesen hauptsächlich um Coleoptera und Diptera [David, Tapp 1992]. Einige der Sarkophage waren durch *Anobium punctatum* beschädigt worden [David 1978]. An der Mumie einer Frau namens Asru (möglicherweise Luxor, 25. Dyn.) wurde vermutlich *C. albiceps* identifiziert [David 1978]. Die Mumie "1770", bei der es sich wahrscheinlich um eine Frau handelt, die möglicherweise aus Hawara (römische Periode) stammte, enthielt *Anobium museorum*, *A. punctatum*, Carabidae, *C. albiceps*, *Gibbium psylloides*, *Musca domestica*, *N. rufipes*, vermutlich *P. casei* und *Dracunculus medinensis*[4] [David 1978; Harrison 1986]. Hinweise zur Lagerung der Mumie "1770" wurden durch *P. casei*-Puppen erhalten. Die Lage der Puppen im Inneren der Mumie sowie in den inneren Bandagen stützen die Vermutung, daß es möglicherweise durch Überflutung des Grabes zu einer Rehydrierung der Mumie kam, die daraufhin neu gewickelt wurde [David, Tapp 1992]. Durch eine C^{14}-Datierung wurde gezeigt, daß die Bandagen jünger als der Mumienkörper waren [Curry 1979]. Wäre die Mumie ohne Rehydrierung neu gewickelt worden, hätte man keine *P. casei* gefunden, da die Larven keinen trockenen Leichnam befallen [David 1978]. Die Mumie "1767", bei der es sich um einen Mann handelt (Fayum, römische Periode), enthielt *Blatta orientalis*, die Mumien der Brüder Nekht-Ankh und Khnum-Nakht (Rifeh, 12. Dyn.) vermutlich *C. albiceps*, *G. psylloides* und *Mesostenopa* sp. [David 1978].

Die Mumie des Horemkenesi war, wie oben erwähnt, durch Insekten stark beschädigt worden. Sie enthielt Carabidae (möglicherweise *Calosoma* sp.), *Dermestes ater* und *D. frischii* [Strong 1981]. *D. ater* wurde von Adams [1990] als *Dermestes leechi* identifiziert, Taylor [1995] spricht weiterhin von *D. ater*. Die Mumie eines Amun-Priesters (21. Dyn.) enthielt ebenfalls *D. frischii* [Steffan

[4] *Dracunculus medinensis* (Medinawurm) gehört zur Klasse der *Nematoda* (Fadenwürmer).

1982], eine Mumie der Marro-Collection (Turin) Reste von Hymenoptera-Larven, die sich im Kopf der Mumie befanden [Fulcheri et al. 1986]. In einer in Belgrad aufbewahrten Mumie eines etwa 50 Jahre alten Mannes, der aus dem ersten Drittel der ptolemäischen Periode stammt, wurden ein Eigelege von *B. orientalis* und ein Fragment von *Anthrenus museorum,* das vermutlich nicht aus der altägyptischen Zeit stammt, entdeckt [Andelkovic et al. 1997]. Die Kopflaus *Pediculus humanus capitis* wurde bisher offenbar nicht an ägyptischen Mumien gefunden; daß diese jedoch schon zur damaligen Zeit vorhanden war, zeigten Funde an einem Kamm, der von der Ausgrabung einer Müllhalde in Antinoë (Unterägypten) stammt [Palma 1991].

Die zahlreichen, in den Köpfen der thebanischen Mumien gefundenen Insekten wurden wahrscheinlich durch die nach der Extraktion des Gehirns im Schädel verbliebenen Geweberestе angezogen und durch das Einbalsamieren im Schädel eingeschlossen [Levinson, Levinson 1994]. *C. albiceps*-Weibchen zum Beispiel legen ihre Eier in oder an Wunden von Tierkadavern, und die geschlüpften Larven dringen dann in die Eingeweide ein [Omar 1995]. Nach Vorstellungen von Lesne [1930] könnte es auch möglich gewesen sein, daß *D. frischii*-Larven während der Einbalsamierung in den Schädel der Verstorbenen gesetzt wurden, um die Hirnmasse zu verkleinern, wodurch die Entfernung des Gehirns erleichtert werden sollte. Hierbei wurden vermutlich auch auflösende Substanzen verwendet, die die *Dermestidae* getötet haben könnten, welche im Falle dieser Mumien aufgrund der Unachtsamkeit der Einbalsamierer in der Hirnschale verblieben waren. Da die Dermestidae-Larven kleinste Fleischreste von den Knochen entfernen, wurden sie zum Skelettieren eingesetzt [Harde, Severa 1984].

An Tiermumien wurden ebenfalls Insekten identifiziert. In einer Ibis-Mumie fand man *Akis reflexa* und *Trachyderma pilosum* [Hope 1840]. Zwei weitere Ibis-Mumien, die aus den Galerien von Tuna el-Gebel (griechisch-römische Periode) stammen, waren von *Anthrenus* sp. und *Dermestes* sp. bzw. *Bellamya unicolor*[5] und *Dermestes* sp. befallen worden [Boessneck 1988]. Die Mumie eines Fisches enthielt Häute von *Dermestidae*-Larven [Leek 1978] und *A. museorum* [Curry 1979], und in einer mumifizierten Katze (ptolemäische Periode, ca. 332-30 v. Chr.) wurden *D. frischii* gefunden [Kingsolver 1982].

[5] *B. unicolor* gehört zur Klasse *Gastropoda* (Schnecken).

Grabbeigaben

Den Verstorbenen wurden für das Leben im Jenseits Grabbeigaben wie Brot, Getreide, Früchte, Gewürze, Honig, Fleisch, Nüsse und Gemüse mitgegeben. Diese konnten ebenfalls von Insekten befallen werden. In einem aus Maadi stammenden Gefäß (prädynastische Zeit) waren fünf verschiedene *Tenebrinoidae*-Arten enthalten [Keimer 1938]. In einer Vase, die Reste einer organischen Substanz enthielt, identifizierte Alfieri *D. frischii* und *N. rufipes* [Keimer 1938]. An Beigaben aus dem Grab Tut-anch-Amuns fanden sich *L. serricorne, Sitoderpa panicea* und *G. psylloides* [Alfieri 1931]. Die Beigaben bestanden aus harz- oder ölhaltigem Material [Solomon 1965]. In einer Vase aus minoischer Zeit wurden *L. serricorne, Oryzaephilus surinamensis, Rhizopertha dominica, S. panicea* und *Tribolium castaneum* identifiziert [Zacher 1934, 1937, 1948]. Des weiteren wurden Samen gefunden, die durch verschiedene Insekten, hauptsächlich *Sitotroga cerealella*, angefressen waren [De Vartavan 1990]. In einer Tonvase aus einem Grab in Theben (Neues Reich), die eine harzartige Substanz enthielt, identifizierte Audouin [1835] *Gibbium* sp. Es kam damals die Frage auf, ob die Käfer, die in großer Zahl gefunden wurden, von selbst in das Gefäß gelangt oder in dieses gegeben worden waren [Zacher 1948]. Möglicherweise wurden sie sogar von Mumie und Beigaben abgesammelt um deren Beschädigung zu verhindern. In einem römischen Grab in Minija (150 bis 180 n. Chr.) wurde ein Glaskolben mit einem schwarzen Puder gefunden, der aus *D. frischii* Resten bestand [Lesne 1930]. Das Fehlen jeglicher larvaler Reste deutet darauf hin, daß die Käfer bei einer späteren Öffnung des Grabes gesammelt und in das Gefäß gegeben worden waren [Lesne 1930]. Weiterhin entdeckte man in einem Gefäß aus der 18. oder 19. Dyn. *N. rufipes* sowie in einem Terrakottagefäß derselben Zeit *N. rufipes* und *D. maculatus* [Hoffmann 1963].

An Feigen *(Ficus sycomorus)* aus einem Grab in Dra abu'l Nagga (20. Dyn., 25. Dyn. oder griechisch-römische Periode) wurde *Sycophaga* sp. und an Feigen aus dem Grab des Ani (Gebelen, 20. Dyn., ca. 1200-1085 v. Chr.) *Sycophaga* sp. sowie *Apocrypta* sp. gefunden [Galil 1967]. Linsen aus der ptolemäischen Periode waren von *Bruchidae* befallen [Burleigh, Southgate 1975].

In Getreide und den daraus folgenden Verarbeitungsprodukten fand man ebenfalls Befall durch Insekten. In einem pharaonischen Grab der 6. Dyn. (etwa 2500 v. Chr.) wurde an Getreide oder Mehl *T. castaneum* oder *Tribolium confusum* identifiziert [Alfieri, pers. Mitteilung, Andres 1931]. Eine genaue Bestimmung war nicht möglich, da den Käfern Beine und Fühler fehlten [Andres 1931]. Im Grab des Djoser (Sakkara, 3. Dyn.) wurde an Getreide *Sitophilus* sp. [Solomon 1965] und im Grab der Königin Ichetis (Sakkara, 6. Dyn.) *Sitophilus granarius* identifiziert [Howe 1972]. In Rückständen von Bier, das sich in den Gewölben der Stufenpyramide befunden haben soll, wurden Dermestidae-Larven gefunden, die von Grüss [zit. nach Keimer 1938] als *Anthrenus palaeoaegyptiacus* bezeichnet wurden. Dieser Terminus ist in der entomologischen Nomenklatur nicht bekannt, und Alfieri [pers. Mitteilung, Keimer 1938] nimmt an, daß es sich statt dessen um *D. frischii* oder *D. maculatus* handelt. Auch in und an Opferbroten, die einen wesentlichen Platz unter den Grabbeigaben einnahmen, wurden Insekten oder deren Spuren festgestellt [Levinson, Levinson 1988]. Im Grab des Oberaufsehers und Architekten Kah (Deir el-Medina, 18. Dyn.) entdeckte man Brot, das Löcher von *S. paniceum* und einer anderen Anobiidae-Art enthielt [Levinson, Levinson 1988; Levinson, Levinson 1994]. Weitere Untersuchungen von Brotproben wurden von Chaddick and Leek [1972] gemacht. Sie fanden in einer prädynastischen Probe aus Badari einen Mottenkokon, der möglicherweise von *Ephestia* sp. oder *Plodia interpunctella* stammt. In einer Probe aus Theben (11. Dyn.) wurde *S. paniceum* und in zwei weiteren aus Theben (18. Dyn.) *S. paniceum* bzw. *S. paniceum* und *Bracon hebetor* gefunden. Letztgenannter ist ein Parasit von Mottenlarven; eine Mottenpuppe wurde, wie oben erwähnt, in einer anderen Brotprobe entdeckt.

An Grabbeigaben, die im Liverpool Museum aufbewahrt werden, wurden ebenfalls verschiedene Insekten gefunden. Genaue Angaben zu den Funden fehlen teilweise. An Feigensamen, Linsen und Nüssen wurde *S. paniceum* identifiziert [Panagiotakopulu 1998]. Gerste (Kahun 12. Dyn.) war von *R. dominica* und Akaziensamen von *Bruchidius* sp. befallen. An Brot und Kuchen wurden *S. paniceum* und eine Diptera-Puppe gefunden [Panagiotakopulu 1998].

Gräber
In der Sargkammer des Grabes NE 28 auf der Insel Elephantine wurden *Trachyderma philistina* und *G. psylloides* identifiziert [Boessneck 1981, 1988]. Im Grab der Königin Nefertari (19. Dyn.), das sich im Tal der Königinnen (Biban el-Harem) befindet, traten *Lepisma saccharina*, *Attagenus* sp. und *Trogoderma* sp. auf [Arai 1988] und in Sakkara (3. Dyn.) *G. psylloides* [Hoffmann 1963]. Hope erwähnte *Copris scaraeus*, *C. midas*, *C. pithecius* und *Cantharis* sp. [Hope 1834; Pettigrew 1834]. Weitere Insekten wurden von Keimer [1938] zusammenfassend aufgelistet, wobei im folgenden nur die genannt werden, die bisher noch keine Erwähnung fanden: *Erodius costatus* (Medina, protohistorisch), *Zophosis* sp. (Merimde Benisalame, prädynastisch), *Mesostenopa picea* (Tuna el-Gebel, römische Periode), *A. reflexa*, *Scaurus puncticollis*, *P. coronata* (Minija, protohistorisch), *Ocnera philistina* (Minija, protohistorisch; Sakkara, 3. Dyn.; Deir el Medina, Neues Reich), *Blaps polychresta* (Maadi, protohistorisch; Deir el Medina, Neues Reich), *Steraspis* sp. (wahrscheinlich *squamosa*) (Armant, prähistorisch oder protohistorisch; Lischt 7. Dyn.; Deir el Medina, Neues Reich).

Tabellarische Übersicht über die Funde

Die beschriebenen Insektenfunde sind in Tabelle 2 zusammenfassend aufgelistet. Ist die Bestimmung der Art oder Gattung unsicher, wurden Klammern verwendet. Exakte Angaben zur Herkunft fehlen teilweise. Dies trifft v. a. auf Funde zu, die im 19. Jh. beschrieben wurden.

Mumie/Grab; Herkunft, Alter	Befallenes Material	Insekten
	Mumie	*Necrobia* sp.
	Mumie	(*Akis* sp.)
Theben	Mumie	*Dermestes vulpinus* *Necrobia violacea*
	Mumie	*Dermestes vulpinus* *Necrobia violacea*
Theben, ptolemäische Periode	Mumien	*Necrobia mumarium* *Dermestes* sp. 2 Diptera-Arten
Theben	Mumie	*Dermestes pollinctus*[6] *Dermestes roei* *Dermestes elongatus*
	oben genannte Mumien[7]	*Pimelia spinulosa* 3 Diptera-Arten
Gräberfeld bei Naga-ed-dêr, prädynastisch (3500 bis 4000 v. Chr.)	Mumien: Bauchhöhle Probe 7048, 7081	*Dermestes elongatus*[8]
Theben, Neues Reich	Mumie	*Corynetes rufipes*
Ramses II, Theben, 19. Dyn.	Mumie	*Dermestes frischii* *Thylodrias contractus* *Lasioderma serricorne* *Necrobia rufipes*
35-40 Jahre alter Mann, ptolemäische Periode (ca. 170 v. Chr.)	Mumie: PUM II	(*Atheta* sp.), (*Chrysomya* sp.) *Dermestes frischii*, *Piophila c* *Thylodrias contractus*
ca. 35 Jahre alte Frau, ca. 835 v. Chr.	Mumie: PUM III	*Chrysomya albiceps* (*N. rufipes*), *Thylodrias contr*
8-10 Jahre altes Kind 1. Jhd. n. Chr.	Mumie: PUM IV	*Stegobium paniceum*
Asru: Frau, möglicherweise Luxor, wahrscheinlich 25. Dyn.	Mumie "1777" der Manchester-Museum-Collection	(*Chrysomya albiceps*)
Frau wahrscheinlich Hawara, römische Periode	Mumie "1770" der Manchester-Museum-Collection	*Anobium museorum* *Anobium punctatum* Carbidae *Chrysomya albiceps* *Gibbium psylloides* *Musca domestica* *Necrobia rufipes* (*Piophila casei*)
Mann, Fayum, römische Periode	Mumie "1767" der Manchester-Museum-Collection	*Blatta orientalis*

Quelle

Latireille [1819]

Atkinson [1825]

Miller [1825]

Hope [pers. Mitteilung; Pettigrew 1834]; Hope [1834]

Netolitzky [1911a, b]

Keimer [1938]
Steffan [1982, 1985]

Lynn, Benitez [1974]; Cockburn et al. [1975];
Cockburn et al. [1980]

Riddle [1980]

Curry [1979]; David [1978]; David, Tapp [1992]

Curry [1979]; David [1978]; Harrison [1986]

David [1978]; David; Tapp [1992]

Tabelle 2.
Arthropoda, die an Mumien, Grabbeigaben oder
in Gräbern des alten Ägypten gefunden wurden

[6] *D. pollinctus* wurde von Erichson [1846] als
unvollständig sklerotisierte *D. frischii* identifiziert.

[7] Eine genaue Zuordnung zu einer der beiden
Mumien war nicht gegeben.

[8] Nach Hoffmann [1963] handelt es sich um
D. cadaverinus.

Mumie/Grab; Herkunft, Alter	Befallenes Material	Insekten
Brüder Nekht-Ankh und Khnum-Nakht, Rifeh, 12. Dyn.	Mumien "21470" und "21471" der Manchester -Museum-Collection	(Chrysomya albiceps) Gibbium psylloides Mesostenopa sp.
	Sarkophage der Manchester-Museum-Collection	Anobium punctatum
Horemkenesi: Mann Theben (Deir el-Bahari), 21. Dyn. (1040-1030 v. Chr.)	Mumie No 7386 des Bristol-Museum	(Calosoma sp.) Dermestes ater[9] Dermestes frischii
Amun-Priester, 21. Dyn.	Mumie	Dermestes frischii
	Mumie: Referenz 901, Marro-Collection (Turin)	Hymenoptera
50 Jahre alter Mann ptolemäischen Periode	Mumie	Anthrenus museorum[10] Blatta orientalis
Ibis	Mumie	Akis reflexa Trachyderma pilosum
Ibis, Galerien von Tuna el-Gebel, griechisch-römische Periode	Mumie	Anthrenus sp. Dermestes sp.
	Mumien	Dermestes sp.
Fisch (Eutropicus niloticus)	Mumie	Anthrenus museorum Dermestidae
Katze, ptolemäische Periode (332-30 v. Chr.)	Mumie	Dermestes frischii
	Vase	Coleoptera
Maadi, prädynastisch	Gefäß	5 Tenebrinoidae-Arten
	Vase: organische Substanz	Dermestes frischii Necrobia rufipes
Tut-anch-Amun, Tal der Könige, 18. Dyn. (1331 v. Chr.)	Grab Alabastervase Nr.16: harzartige Substanz Alabastervase Nr. 58: fettartige Substanz Alabastervase Nr. 60: trockene Substanz Alabastervase Nr. 61: fettart., aromat. Substanz Holzkästchen Nr. 115	Lasioderma serricorne Sitodrepa panicea Lasioderma serricorne Lasioderma serricorne Gibbium psylloides Lasioderma serricorne Lasioderma serricorne Sitodrepa panicea Gibbium psylloides
minoische Periode	Vase: wachsartige Substanz Museum Berlin	Lasioderma serricorne Oryzaephilus surinamensis Rhizopertha dominica Sitodrepa panicea Tribolium castaneum
	Samen	Ausgehöhlt durch Sitotroga cerealella
Theben, Neues Reich	Grab: Tonvase: harzartige Substanz	Gibbium sp.
Minija, römische Periode (150-180 n. Chr.)	Glaskolben	Dermestes frischii

Quelle
Curry [1979]; David [1978]
Curry [1979]; David [1978]; David, Tapp [1992]
Strong [1981]; Adams [1990]; Taylor [1995]
Steffan [1982]
Fulcheri et al. [1986]
Andelkovic et al. [1997]
Hope [1840]
Boessneck [1988]
—
Curry [1979]; Leek [1978]
Kingsolver [1982]
Latireille [1819]
Keimer [1938]
Alfieri [1931]
Zacher [1934, 1937, 1948]
De Vartavan [1990]
Audouin [1835]
Lesne [1930]

[9] *D. ater* wurde von Adams [1990] als *D. leechi* identifiziert; Taylor [1995] spricht weiterhin von *D. ater*.

[10] Diese Funde scheinen nicht aus der altägyptischen Zeit zu stammen [Andelkovic et al. 1997].

Mumie/Grab; Herkunft, Alter	Befallenes Material	Insekten
18. oder 19. Dyn.	Gefäß	*Necrobia rufipes*
	Terrakottagefäß	*Necrobia rufipes* *Dermestes maculatus*
Grab in Dra abu'l Nagga, 20. Dyn, 25. Dyn. od. griechisch-römische Periode	Feige (*Ficus sycomorus*)	*Sycophaga* sp.
Grab des Ani, Gebelen, 20. Dyn. (ca. 1200-1085 v. Chr.)	Feige (*Ficus sycomorus*)	*Sycophaga* sp. *Apocrypta* sp.
ptolemäische Periode (ca. 215 v. Chr.)	Linsen (*Lens culinaris*), British-Museum-Collection	Bruchidae
6. Dyn. (ca. 2500 v. Chr.)	Königliches Grab: Vase: Getreide oder Mehl	*Tribolium* (*castaneum* oder *confusum*)
Djoser, Sakkara, Stufenpyramide, 3. Dyn. (2900 v. Chr.)	Grab unter der Stufen- pyramide: Getreide	*Sitophilus* sp.
Ichetis, Sakkara, Stufenpyramide, 6. Dyn. (2300 v. Chr.)	Grab unter der Stufenpyramide	*Sitophilus granarius*
Sakkara, Stufenpyramide	Rückstände von Bier	*Dermestes* sp.
Kah, Deir el Medina, 18. Dyn.	Grab Brot (Ägyptisches Museum, Turin)	Angefressen durch *Sitodrepa panicea* und eine weitere Anobiidae-Art
Badari, prädynastisch (2999 v. Chr.)	Brot	(*Ephestia* sp.) oder (*Plodia interpunctella*)
Theben, 11. Dyn. (2049 v. Chr.)	Brot	*Stegobium paniceum*
Theben, 18. Dyn. (1399 v. Chr.)	Brot Brot	*Stegobium paniceum* *Stegobium paniceum* *Bracon hebetor*
	Feigen (Samen) Liverpool Museum	*Stegobium paniceum*
	Linsen, Liverpool Museum	*Stegobium paniceum*
Kahun	Nüsse, Liverpool Museum	*Stegobium paniceum*
Kahun, 12. Dyn.	Gerste, Liverpool Museum	*Rhyzopertha dominica*
Kahun, 12. Dyn.	Akazien-Samen Liverpool Museum	*Bruchidius* sp.
	Brot und Kuchen Liverpool Museum	*Stegobium paniceum* Diptera
Nekropole von Elephantine	Grab NE 28 Sargkammer	*Trachyderma philistina* *Gibbium psylloides*
Nefertai, Tal der Königinnen (Biban el-Harem), 19. Dyn.	Grab	*Lepisma saccharina* *Attagenus* sp. *Trogoderma* sp.
Sakkara 3. Dyn.		*Gibbium psylloides*
		Copris scaraeus *Copris midas* *Copris pithecius* *Cantharis* sp.
	Zusammenfassende Auflistung verschiedener Funde; siehe Insektenfunde aus Gräbern	

Quelle
Hoffmann [1963]
Galil [1967]
Burleigh, Southgate [1975]
Andres [1931]
Solomon [1965]
Howe [1972]
Grüss [zit. nach Keimer, 1938]
Levinson, Levinson [1988]; Levinson, Levinson [1994]
Chaddick, Leek [1972]
Panagiotakopulu [1998]
Boessneck [1981, 1988]; Hope [pers. Mitteilung; Pettigrew 1834]; Hope [1834]
Arai [1988]
Hoffmann [1963]
Hope [pers. Mitteilung; Pettigrew 1834]; Hope [1834]
Keimer [1938]

Insektenfunde im Zusammenhang mit der Mumie Aset-iri-khet-es

Aset-iri-khet-es

Die Mumie Aset-iri-khet-es stammt aus der ptolemäischen Nekropole in El-Gamhud und wird in das 3. bis 1. Jahrhundert datiert. Der Name Aset-iri-khet-es ("Rituale verrichtende Isis") läßt vermuten, daß die Verstorbene aus dem Gebiet von Abydos oder Assuan stammt [Babraj, Szymańska 1997]. Weiterhin wird angenommen, daß Aset-iri-khet-es eine Priesterin gewesen sein könnte.

Nach der Bestattung der Mumie wurde das Grab vermutlich noch zu antiker Zeit durch Grabräuber geöffnet und große Bereiche des Brustkorbs, der Oberarme und des Kopfes der Mumie zerstört [Babraj, Szymańska 1997]. Im Jahre 1907 wurde Aset-iri-khet-es erneut entdeckt. Sie befindet sich seitdem zusammen mit ihrem Sarkophag im Besitz des Nationalmuseums in Kraków. Die Mumie und der Sarkophag wurden während der Weltkriege im Keller des Museums aufbewahrt. Anfang 1995 wurde in einem interdisziplinären Projekt mit der Erforschung der Mumie begonnen [Babraj, Szymańska 1997]. Beschreibung und Identifizierung der Funde. Die Mumie Aset-iri-khet-es[11] erwies sich als relativ arm an Insekten. Diese fanden sich hauptsächlich in der Mumie und zwischen den Bandageschichten sowie in Kehricht aus Bandage- und Mumienfragmenten [Babraj, Szymańska 1998]. Es handelte sich bei den Funden vor allem um Fragmente wie Flügel, Flügeldecken und Beine sowie um Larven- und Puppenhüllen, die sich den Insektenordnungen der Coleoptera, Diptera und Plannipennia zuordnen ließen (Photo 1). Außerdem wurden die Reste einer Haut, die von einem Tier der Klasse Arachnida stammt, identifiziert.

Die Coleoptera-Funde bestanden aus Larven- und Puppenhäuten sowie Käferresten. Die Larven- und Puppenhäute gehörten zu den Dermestidae-Arten *Attagenus pellio* und *Trogoderma angustum*. Vollständig erhaltene Käfer wurden nicht gefunden. Bei den Käferfragmenten handelte es sich um Thoraxe, Flügeldecken und Beine sowie um ein Kopffragment. Ein Großteil der Funde stammt von Käfern der Familie Lathridiidae, die möglicherweise mehreren Arten dieser Familie zugeordnet werden können. Eine genauere Klassifizierung der Fragmente wurde nicht vorgenommen, da die Lathridiidae-Arten schwierig voneinander zu unterscheiden sind, und diese Fragmente vermutlich nicht aus altägyptischer Zeit stammen. Der zuletzt angesprochene Sachverhalt wird im folgenden noch weiter erörtert. Was das oben erwähnte Kopffragment anbetrifft, so kann davon ausgegangen werden, daß es zu einem Käfer der Familie Tenebrionidae gehört. Unter den gefundenen Flügeldecken befanden sich des weiteren zwei Fragmente von schimmernder blauschwarzer Farbe. Diese Flügeldecken könnten, wie oben erwähnt, im ursprünglichen Zustand metallischblau, grün oder rot gefärbt gewesen sein. Möglicherweise gehören sie zu einem Käfer der Familie Cleridae. In Frage kommen könnte zum Beispiel die Art *N. mumarium*. Käfer dieser Art wurden

[11] Die Mumie war, abgesehen von einer Füllung aus Zedernharz und Bitumen im Schädel, in der Bauchhöhle und in den Bandagen [Babraj, Szymańska 1997], auch mit Gräsern (Gramineae) gefüllt, und Reste davon befanden sich sowohl auf als auch zwischen den Bandageschichten [Babraj, Szymańska 1998].

bisher an sechs verschiedenen Mumien gefunden und sind im lebenden Zustand violett gefärbt. Weitere Flügeldecken, möglicherweise aus der Familie Dermestidae, waren mit Harz verklebt und in einem so schlechten Zustand, daß eine nähere Bestimmung nicht möglich war. Einige der Insektenfragmente wurden wahrscheinlich auch durch das Mitwirken anderer Insekten beschädigt. So fanden sich an Flügeldecken Spuren, die von Fraß herrühren können. Bei dem Diptera-Fund handelte es sich um einen Flügel, der der Familie Fanniidae und dort vermutlich der Art *Fannia canicularis* zuzuordnen ist. Die Plannipennia-Überreste waren zwei Flügel. Diese gehörten möglicherweise zu ein und demselben Individuum aus der Familie der Chrysopidae. Der Klasse der Arachnida konnte eine Haut zugeordnet werden. Diese stammt wahrscheinlich jedoch, ebenso wie die Lathridiidae-Fragmente, nicht aus der altägyptischen Zeit. Das Ergebnis der Identifizierungen wird in Tabelle 3 zusammengefaßt.

Fund	Anzahl	Klasse	Ordnung	Familie	Art
Flügeldecken	2	Insecta	Coleoptera	(Cleridae)	
Haut, z.T. Fragmente	7			Dermestidae	*Trogoderma angustum*
Haut, z.T. Fragmente	4				*Attagenus pellio*
Flügeldecken	4				
Beinfragmente	4				
Käferfragmente	57			Lathridiidae	
Kopf	1			(Tenebrionidae)	
Flügel	1		Diptera	Fanniidae	(*Fannia canicularis*)
Flügel	2		Plannipennia	Chrysopidae	
Hautfragment	1	Arachnida			
Sonstige Fragmente	8*				

Tabelle 3.
Funde an der Mumie Aset-iri-khet-es

Angaben in Klammern: Bestimmung unsicher.
*: Bruchstücke von Beinen, Flügeldecken, usw.

Diskussion der Funde

Ein Großteil der Insektenfunde an der Mumie Aset-iri-khet-es läßt sich wahrscheinlich nicht der altägyptischen Zeit zuordnen. Es handelt sich bei diesen um die Larven- und Puppenhüllen der Dermestidae, die Lathridiidae-Fragmente sowie die Arachnida-Haut. Diese Vermutung wird durch die Weichheit der Funde gestützt. Aus dem alten Ägypten stammen vermutlich die Cleridae-Fragmente, einige sehr schlecht erhaltene Dermestidae-Fragmente und der Tenebrionidae-Fund. Weitere Hinweise über das mögliche Alter der Fragmente und die Gefahr der lebenden Tiere für die Mumie können über deren Lebensweise und Verbreitung erhalten werden. Anhand dieser kommen Dermestidae, Cleridae und Fanniidae als mögliche Schädlinge der Mumie in Frage. Lathridiidae und Chrysopidae stellten dagegen keine Bedrohung dar.

Dermestidae, vornehmlich die Larven, ernähren sich von trockenen tierischen und pflanzlichen Rückständen. *Dermestes* sp. und *Attagenus* sp. werden an vollständig getrockneten Körpern gefunden [Smith 1986]. Dies läßt vermuten, daß der Befall entweder während der Mumifizierung, im Grab oder zu einem noch späteren Zeitpunkt der Lagerung der Mumie erfolgte. Aus letztgenannter Zeit stammen vermutlich die Larven- und Puppenhüllen von *T. angustum* und *A. pellio*. Die Larven von *A. pellio* ernähren sich von tierischem Material, die Käfer leben von Nektar und Pollen [Levinson, Levinson 1978]. Bei dem Cleridae-Fund handelt es sich höchstwahrscheinlich um Reste eines Insekts, das sich der Gattung Necrobia zuordnen läßt. Tiere dieser Gattung unterscheiden sich bezüglich Nahrung und Lebensraum von den anderen Mitgliedern der Familie [Smith 1986]. *N. rufipes*-Käfer ernähren sich bevorzugt von Aas, aber auch von Fliegenmaden, die sich im Aas befinden und die die Hauptnahrung der Necrobia-Larven sind. Die Tiere besiedeln einen toten Körper erst, nachdem Fetthydrolyse und -degradation abgelaufen sind. Die Tenebrionidae stellten genau wie die Dermestidae und Cleridae eine Bedrohung für die Mumie dar. Tenebrionidae-Larven leben hauptsächlich von pflanzlichen Stoffen, v.a. Getreide und Getreideprodukten, aber auch tierischen Substanzen [Weidner 1993]. So werden Tenebrionidae auch an trockenen toten Körpern gefunden [Smith 1986]. Fanniidae könnten ebenfalls mögliche Schädlinge der Mumie gewesen sein. Diese Fliegen pflanzen sich in Kot fort, können sich jedoch auch in Kadavern entwickeln, v.a. dann, wenn diese halbtrockene Gewebebereiche enthalten. Fanniidae-Arten zählen in Ägypten nicht zu den gewöhnlich an Leichen gefundenen Fliegen, die von forensischer Wichtigkeit sind [Tantawi, El-Kady 1997].

Lathridiidae und Chrysopidae ernährten sich nicht von der Mumie. Lathridiidae-Larven und -Käfer sind höchstwahrscheinlich alle mycetophag und ernähren sich vom Mycel und den Sporen niederer Pilze. Nach Studien von Attia und Kamel [1965] werden Lathridiidae in Ägypten an gespeicherten Produkten wie Mehl, Getreide und Kakao gefunden. Sie treten zwar an Leichen auf, haben jedoch keine Signifikanz im Sinne der Forensischen Entomologie [Smith 1986]. Hinzu kommt, daß die Lathridiidae bisher offenbar an keiner anderen Mumie gefunden wurden. Es existieren mehr als 500 Arten, die schwierig zu identifizieren sind [Hinton 1963]. Viele der Chrysopidae sind Prädatoren von Schädlingen [Aspöck et al. 1980]. Die Larven sind karnivor und ernähren sich von Blattläusen, Schildläusen und Insektenlarven. Die Imagines sind jedoch meist Honig- und Pollenfresser.

Weitere Hinweise zum Alter der Insektenfunde hätten vermutlich durch eine genaue Zuordnung der Funde in Bezug auf die Mumie gewonnen werden können. Möglicherweise könnte die Untersuchung der Lagerungsräumlichkeiten zu weiteren Erkenntnissen führen. Dies trifft auch für vergleichende grabstätten-archäoentomologische Untersuchungen der ebenfalls aus dem Sarkophag-Komplex von el-Gamhud stammenden Mumien zu[12].

Die Insektenfunde, die wahrscheinlich aus der altägyptischen Zeit stammten, sind von geringer Zahl, so daß ein starker Befall ausgeschlossen werden kann. Bedingt durch ihre Lebensweise, kommen Lathridiidae und Chrysopidae nicht

[12] Die weiteren Mumien befinden sich im Ägyptischen Museum in Kairo, dem Kunsthistorischen Museum in Wien und dem Museum für Bildende Künste in Budapest [Babraj, Szymańska 1997].

als Schädlinge der Mumie in Frage. So verbleiben Dermestidae, Cleridae, Tenebrionidae und Fanniidae als mögliche Schädlinge. Da jeweils nur Fragmente von einem oder wenigen Exemplaren gefunden wurden, kann davon ausgegangen werden, daß die Tiere eher zufällig an die Mumie gelangt waren oder daß ein stärkerer Befall rechtzeitig verhindert wurde. Auch wurde nach einer eingehenden Untersuchung der Mumie nicht von einer Beschädigung durch Insekten berichtet. Der geringe Insektenbefall deutet darauf hin, daß Aset-iri-khet-es mehr oder weniger sofort nach ihrem Tod mumifiziert worden ist. Ansonsten wäre aufgrund der klimatischen Verhältnisse mit einem starken Insektenbefall bzw. mit Schäden durch Insekten zu rechnen gewesen. Die Insektenarmut wurde vermutlich auch durch eine sorgfältige Mumifizierung bedingt. Aset-iri-khet-es war im Verlauf der Mumifizierung sogar rasiert worden [Babraj, Szymańska 1997], wodurch möglicherweise vorhandene Parasiten vermutlich entfernt wurden. Eine dicke Harzschicht, mit der Haut und Knochen überzogen waren [Babraj, Szymańska 1997], verhinderte das Vordringen von Insekten zum Mumienkörper. Höchstwahrscheinlich versuchten einige Dermestidae zu einem Zeitpunkt, als das Harz noch nicht vollständig getrocknet war, ins Innere der Mumie zu gelangen und kamen dadurch mit diesem in Kontakt.

Klassifikation, Auswertung und ergänzende Bemerkungen zu allen beschriebenen Funden

In Tabelle 4 wird die Zuordnung der Funde zu Insektenordnungen und -familien gegeben. Die Funde an Mumien entfallen zu 75% auf die Ordnung der Coleoptera. Diptera sind mit 20%, Blattodea mit 3%, Hymenoptera und Plannipennia mit jeweils 1% vertreten. Die am häufigsten gefundenen Coleoptera gehören zur Familie der Dermestidae (50%). Ebenfalls wurden Cleridae (15%), Tenebrionidae (13%), Anobiidae (10%), Carabidae (4%), Ptinidae (4%), Staphylinidae (2%) und Lathridiidae (2%) identifiziert. Auch die Ordnung der Diptera war, wie oben ersichtlich, verhältnismäßig häufig vertreten. Zahlreiche (36%) der an Mumien gefundenen Diptera waren nicht genauer bestimmt, auf die Familie der Calliphoridae entfielen 36% der Funde. 14% der Funde ließen sich den Piophilidae und jeweils 7% den Fanniidae bzw. Muscidae zuordnen.

Der Zeitpunkt des Befalls der Mumien mit Insekten ist unterschiedlich. Coleoptera wie Dermestidae treten bevorzugt an trockenen Geweben auf, d.h., daß sie einen Leichnam während der Mumifizierung sowie zu einem späterem Zeitpunkt im Grab oder im Museum befallen haben können. Viele der Coleoptera-Arten ernähren sich sowohl von pflanzlichen als auch von tierischen Produkten. Die Diptera konnten einen Leichnam vor oder während der Einbalsamierung befallen haben. Es war sogar möglich, daß Diptera in den lebenden Menschen eingedrungen sind und Madenfraßkrankheit hervorriefen [Curry 1979].

An Leichen der heutigen Zeit werden ähnliche Funde gemacht. Nach De Souza und Linhares [1997] gehören die Coleoptera-Funde hauptsächlich zu den Familien der Dermestidae, Silphidae und Cleridae und die Diptera zu den Calliphoridae, Sarcophagidae sowie Muscidae. Bei dem Vergleich der Insektenfauna an Mumien mit den heutzutage beobachteten Leichenfaunen ist zu beachten, daß die Toten im alten Ägypten nicht der natürlichen Verwesung überlassen waren. Durch die Natronbehandlung erfolgten Entwässerung und Entfettung schneller als bei einem Körper, der einer natürlichen Verwesung ausgesetzt war. So hat die Mumifizierung neben den bereits erwähnten Faktoren ebenfalls Einfluß auf die Fundzusammensetzung. Prinzipiell konnten der Mumienkörper, das Füllmaterial, die Mumienbinden sowie der Sarkophag von Insekten befallen werden, so daß auch Insekten gefunden werden, die sich nicht von tierischen Produkten ernähren. Des weiteren können Insekten identifiziert werden, die zufällig auftreten und sich zum Beispiel von den Grabbeigaben ernährten oder Insekten, deren Nahrung andere Insekten waren.

An Grabbeigaben wurden Coleoptera (86%), Hymenoptera (6%) und Lepidoptera (6%) sowie Diptera (1%) und Zygentoma (1%) gefunden. Die Coleoptera-Funde ließen sich 12 verschiedenen Familien zuordnen: Tenebrionidae (28%)[13], Anobiidae (23%), Dermestidae (11%) und Ptinidae (7%), Cleridae (5%), Buprestidae (5%), Scarabaeidae (5%), Bruchidae (4%), Bostrychidae (4%), Curculionidae (4%), Cantharidae (2%) und Cucujidae (2%). Die Hymenoptera-Funde gehörten zu den Familien der Chalcididae und der Braconidae, die Lepidoptera-Funde zu den Gelechiidae und Lymantriidae und der Zygentoma-Fund zur Familie der Lepismatidae.

Wie die Funde aus Gräbern beweisen (Tabelle 4), traten wie bereits angedeutet im alten Ägypten zum Teil dieselben Vorratsschädlinge auf, die heutzutage in den ägyptischen Speichern identifiziert werden [Zacher 1934; Chaddick, Leek 1972; Burleigh, Southgate 1975; Levinson, Levinson 1985]. *L. serricorne*, *R. dominica*, *O. surinamensis*, *S. granarius* und *T. castaneum*, die an Grabbeigaben gefunden wurden, zählen noch heute zu den Hauptschädlingen von gespeichertem Material [Kislev 1991]. Weitere Insekten an altägyptischen Grabbeigaben wurden in den Mühlen und Speichern Ägyptens [Zacher 1940] oder an gespeicherten Produkten in den Vereinigten Arabischen Emiraten identifiziert [Attia, Kamel 1965]. Da die Grabbeigaben im wesentlichen aus den Speichern der Familie des Toten stammten [Levinson, Levinson 1994], können somit Hinweise auf den Befall der Speicher erhalten werden. Die Nahrung zur damaligen Zeit konnte von Insekten befallen worden sein, die auch in der heutigen Zeit gefunden werden. Es wird angenommen, daß der Insektenbefall in der Antike niedriger als in neuerer Zeit war [Kislev 1991], da Spezies aus der Neuen Welt fehlten [Panagiotakopulu et al. 1995]. Von den wichtigsten Speicherschädlingen des heutigen Ägypten waren *Calandra granaria*, *C. oryzae* und *Trogoderma granarium* noch nicht vorhanden [Zacher 1937].

G. psylloides, ein Vertreter der Ptinidae, wurde an Mumien und Beigaben etwa gleich häufig gefunden. *G. psylloides* ist ein gefürchteter Schädling von pflanzlichen Produkten, und es ist wahrscheinlich, daß sich dieser von den

[13] In einer prädynastischen Probe aus Maadi wurden dabei von Keimer [1938] angeblich fünf verschiedene Tenebrionidae-Arten gefunden.

Bandagen ernährt [David, Tapp 1992]. Nach Smith [1986] leben die Ptinidae von Getreide, Mehl, getrockneten Früchten und anderen gespeicherten Produkten; die Käfer ernähren sich aber auch von getrocknetem Aas und menschlichen Körpern. Die Bestimmung der *G. psylloides* Funde ist umstritten. Zacher [1948] konnte im heutigen Ägypten nur *Gibbium aequinoctiale* finden. Die Verbreitung von *G. psylloides* soll auf Europa begrenzt sein, die von *G. aequinoctiale* auf tropische Regionen. So ist es nach Levinson und Levinson [1994] unsicher, ob es sich tatsächlich um *G. psylloides* handelt. Nach Attia und Kamel [1965] wurde *G. psylloides* jedoch auch in den Vereinigten Arabischen Emiraten gefunden.

Die meisten dieser Schädlinge ernähren sich nur von gespeicherten Stoffen. Ausnahmen bilden die Bruchidae, die die Samen noch an der Pflanze befallen. Nur wenige der Bruchidae-Arten können sich noch eine weitere Generation an den gespeicherten Samen entwickeln [Howe 1972]. Dementsprechend drangen die Bruchidae, die an Linsen aus der ptolemäischen Periode auftraten, noch auf dem Feld in diese ein. Eine weitere Bruchidae-Art wurde in Akaziensamen (Kahun, 12. Dyn.) gefunden [Panagiotakopulu 1998].

Das Eindringen von Apocrypta- und Sycophaga-Arten in Feigen, wahrscheinlich handelt es sich um *Apocrypta longitarsus* und *Sycophaga sycomori*, muß ebenfalls noch vor der Ernte der Feigen erfolgt sein. Diese Insektenfunde waren nicht wie von Chaddick und Leek [1972] angenommen wurde, zufällig. Vielmehr sind Wespen-Arten für die Bestäubung der Feigenblüte erforderlich, wozu sie zu verschiedenen Zeitpunkten in diese eindringen.

Durch einige Insektenfunde wurden Fragen in Bezug auf das Ursprungsland der betreffenden Schädlinge und auf die Handelsrouten zur damaligen Zeit aufgeworfen. Es handelte sich bei diesen Insekten um *L. serricorne* und *T. castenaeum*. Die Funde von *L. serricorne* an Grabbeigaben Tut-anch-Amuns [Alfieri 1931] sind nach Kislev [1991] durch eine Verunreinigung aus heutiger Zeit zu erklären. Es wurde jedoch auch in einer weiteren Grabbeigabe aus minoischer Zeit [Zacher 1934, 1937] sowie in der Mumie Ramses II [Steffan 1982, 1985] *L. serricorne* gefunden. Falls diese Insekten tatsächlich aus der damaligen Zeit stammen sollten, könnte dies bedeuten, daß *L. serricorne* Tiere möglicherweise nicht ihren Ursprung im tropischen Amerika haben oder daß schon zu dieser Zeit Handelsbeziehungen zu Amerika bestanden. Die Funde von Tabak in der Mumie Ramses II und in weiteren Mumien führte u.a. zu ähnlichen Hypothesen [Castello 1983]. Auch andere Funde werfen eine Vielzahl an Fragen in Bezug auf die Handelsrouten zur damaligen Zeit auf [Cockburn et al. 1980]. Von dem Käfer *T. castaneum*, der in einer Grabbeigabe aus minoischer Zeit [Zacher 1934, 1937] identifiziert wurde, wird angenommen, daß sein Ursprung in Indien liegt. Dies würde bedeuten, daß der Küstenhandel schon zu so früher Zeit in größerem Ausmaß stattgefunden hat [Buckland 1981]. Anderen Hypothesen zufolge soll Afrika das Ursprungsland von *T. canasteum* sein.

Die Fundzusammensetzung gibt wertvolle Einblicke in die Beziehung zwischen Mensch und Insekten zu damaliger Zeit. Ebenso können Informationen

Tabelle 4.
Zur Systematik der
beschriebenen
Insektenfunde:
Anzahlen zu
Ordnungen und
Familien;
zugehörige Gattungen
und Arten

Ordnung	Familie	Art	Anzahl Mumien	Funde Beigaben, Grab
Zygentoma			0	1
	Lepismatidae	*Lepisma saccharina*	0	1
Blattodea			2	0
	Blattidae	*Blatta orientalis*	2	0
Coleoptera			52	57
	Carabidae	*Calosoma* sp.	2	0
	Staphylinidae	*Atheta* sp.	1	0
	Scarabaeidae	*Copris midas*	0	3
		Copris pithecius		
		Copris scaraeus		
	Buprestidae	*Steraspis* sp.	0	3
	Cantharidae	*Cantharis* sp.	0	1
	Anobiidae	*Anobium museorum*	5	13
		Anobium punctatum		
		Lasioderma serricorne		
		Sitodrepa panicea		
		Stegobium paniceum		
	Bostrychidae	*Rhizopertha dominica*	0	2
	Dermestidae	*Anthrenus museorum*	26	6
		Anthrenus sp.		
		Attagenus pellio		
		Attagenus sp.		
		Corynetes rufipes		
		Dermestes ater		
		Dermestes frischii		
		Dermestes pollinctus		
		Dermestes roei		
		Dermestes leechi		
		Dermestes maculatus		
		Dermestes vulpinus		
		Dermestes elongatus		
		Dermestes sp.		
		Thylodrias contractus		
		Trogoderma sp.		
		Trogoderma angustum		
	Ptinidae	*Gibbium psylloides*	2	4
		Gibbium sp.		
	Bruchidae	*Bruchidius* sp.	0	2
	Cleridae	*Necrobia mumarium*	8	3
		Necrobia rufipes		
		Necrobia violacea		
		Necrobia sp.		
	Cucujidae	*Oryzaephilus surinamensis*	0	1
	Curculionidae	*Sitophilus granarius*		
		Calandra granaria		
		Sitophilus sp.	0	2
	Lathridiidae		1	0
	Tenebrionidae	*Akis reflexa*	6	16
		Akis sp.		

Ordnung	Familie	Art	Anzahl Funde Mumien	Beigaben, Grab
		Blaps polychestra		
		Erodius costatus		
		Mesostenopa picea		
		Mesostenopa sp.		
		Pimelia spinulosa		
		Prionotheca coronata		
		Scaurus punctiollis		
		Trachyderma pilosum		
		Trachyderma philistina		
		Tribolium castaneum		
		Tribolium sp.		
		Zophosis sp.		
Diptera			14	1
	Piophilidae	Piophila casei	2	0
	Muscidae	Musca domestica	1	0
	Fanniidae	Fannia canicularis	1	0
	Calliphoridae	Chrysomya albiceps	5	0
		Chrysomya sp.		
Plannipennia			1	0
	Chrysopidae		1	0
Hymenoptera			1	4
	Chalcididae	Apocrypta sp.	0	3
		Sycophaga sp.		
	Braconidae	Bracon hebetor	0	1
Lepidoptera			0	4
	Gelechiidae	Sitotroga cerealella	0	1
	Lymantriidae	Ocnera philistina	0	3

über die Herkunft der Insekten und deren Verbreitung erhalten werden. Um weitere Aussagen über die Verteilung der Arten im alten Ägypten treffen zu können, ist die Analyse zusätzlicher Insektenfunde erforderlich. Auch die Untersuchung von Insekten, die nicht an Mumien, Grabbeigaben und Gräbern, sondern aus Ausgrabungen im allgemeinen stammen [Kenward 1974, 1978], könnte weitere interessante Hinweise geben.

Danksagung

Für die Anregung zu dieser Arbeit und die Zurverfügungstellung der Insektenfragmente von der Mumie Aset-iri-khet-es gilt der besondere Dank der Verfasserin Frau Dr. H. Szymańska und Herrn K. Babraj, Muzeum Archeologiczne, Kraków. Für das Interesse an dieser Arbeit und deren beratende Förderung von Seiten der Entomologie her dankt die Verfasserin weiterhin Herrn Prof. Dr. E. Wachmann, Institut für Zoologie der Freien Universität Berlin, Herrn Dr. J. Haupt, Institut für Ökologie und Biologie der Technischen Universität Berlin sowie Herrn Priv.-Doz. Dr. S. Scheurer, Institut für Tropenmedizin, Berlin.

Literaturverzeichnis

R. G. Adams, *Dermestes leechi Kalik (Coleoptera: Dermestidae) from an Egyptian mummy*, Entomologist's Gazette 41(1990), 119-120

A. Alfieri, *Les insectes de la tombe de Toutankhamon*, Bulletin de la Société Royale Entomologique d'Egypte 24 (1931), 188-189

C. Alluaud, *Note sur les Coléoptères trouvés dans les Momies d'Egypte*, Bulletin de la Société Royale Entomologique d'Egypte 1(1908), 29-36

B. Andelkovic, L. Andus, S. Stankovic, *The entomological and bacteriological analyses of the Belgrade mummy*, Journal of the Serbian Archaeological Society (Belgrade) 13 (1997), 379-384

A. Andres, *Catalogue of the Egyptian Tenebrionidae*, Bulletin de la Société Royale Entomologique d'Egypte 15 (1931), 74-125

Anonymus, *UIUC mummy project: The University of Illinois Mummy Project*, Internet: uiuc mummy project (1997)

Anonymus, *Forensic entomology. Insects in legal investigations*, (2000), Internet: Forensic entomology literature.

H. Arai, *On microorganisms in the tomb of Nefertari, Egypt*, Hozon Kagaku 27 (1988), 13-20

H. Aspöck, U. Aspöck, H. Hölzel, *Die Neuropteren Europas 1, 2*, Krefeld 1980

J. Atkinson, *Extracts from the minute-book*, 16. Nov. Transactions of the Linnean Society of London 14 (3) (1825), 585-586

R. Attia, A. H. Kamel, *The fauna of stored products in U.A.R.*, Bulletin de la Société Royale Entomologique d'Egypte 49 (1965), 221-232

J. V. Audouin, *Observation sur la découverte de Gibbium scotias dans un ancient tombeau à Thébes*, Bulletin de la Société Entomologique de France 5 (1835), 5-6

K. Babraj, H. Szymańska, *Eine Mumie unter dem Mikroskop*, Antike Welt 28/5 (1997), 369-374

K. Babraj, H. Szymańska, Persönliche Mitteilung vom 20.11.1998

M. Benecke, *Zur insektenkundlichen Begutachtung in Faulleichenfällen*, Archiv für Kriminologie 198 (1996), 99-109

J. Boessneck, *Gemeinsame Anliegen von Ägyptologie und Zoologie aus der Sicht des Zooarchäologen*, München 1981

J. Boessneck, *Die Tierwelt des Alten Ägypten, untersucht anhand kulturge-schichtlicher und zoologischer Quellen*, München 1988

H.N. Bourel-Benoit, Hedouin V. et Gosset D., *Entomologie médico-légale appliquée à un cas de momification.* Annales de la Societé Entomologique de France 36(3), (2000), 287-290.

B. Brier, R. S. Wade, *The use of natron in human mummification: a modern experiment,* Zeitschrift für Ägyptische Sprache und Altertumskunde 124 (1997), 89-100

P. C. Buckland, *The early dispersal of insect pests of stored products as indicated by archaeological records*, Journal of Stored Product Research 17 (1981), 1-12

E.A.W. Budge, *The mummy. A handbook of Egyptian funerary archaeology*[2], Cambridge 1925.

R. Burleigh, J. B. Southgate, *Insect infestation of stored Egyptian lentils in antiquity*, Journal of Archaeological Science 2 (1975), 391-392

M. Castello, *L'affaire Ramsès II*, Sciences et Avenir (Paris) 441(1983), 38-42

F. Celoria, *Insects and archaeology*, Science and Archaeology 1(1970), 15-19

P. R. Chaddick, F. F. Leek, *Further specimens of stored products insects found in Ancient Egyptian tombs*, Journal of Stored Product Research 8 (1972), 83-86

A. Cockburn, R. A. Barraco, T. A. Reyman, W. H. Peck, *Autopsy of an Egyptian mummy*, Science 187 (1975), 1155-1160

A. Cockburn, W. H. Peck, R. A. Barraco, T. A. Reyman, *A classic mummy: PUM II.*, in: A. Cockburn, E. Cockburn (eds.), *Mummies, Disease, and Ancient Cultures*, Cambridge 1980, 52-70

J. Connan, A. Macke und C. Macke-Ribet, *Das Geheimnis der Mumien*, Spektrum der Wissenschaft 8/2001, 34-41.

G. R. Coope, *Interpretations of quaternary insect fossils*, Annual Review of Entomology 15 (1970), 97-120

A. R. Curry, *The Insects associated with the Manchester Mummies*, in: A. R. David (ed.), *Manchester Museum Mummy Project*, Manchester 1979, 113-117

A. R. David, E. Tapp (eds.), *The Mummy's Tale. The Scientific and Medical Investigation of Natsef-Amun, Priest in the Temple of Karnak*, London 1992

R. David (ed.), *Mysteries of the Mummies. The Story of the Manchester University Investigation*, New York 1978

W. R. Dawson, G. E. Smith, *Egyptian Mummies*, London 1924

A. M. De Souza, A. X. Linhares, *Diptera and coleoptera of potential forensic importance in southeastern Brazil: relative abundance and seasonality*, Medical and Veterenary Entomology 11 (1997), 8-12

C. De Vartavan, *Contaminated plant-foods from the tomb of Toutankhamun: A new interpretive system*, Journal of Archaeological Science 17 (1990), 473-494

S. Dibs, F. Klingauf, *Laborversuche zur Wirkung des Weihrauches auf einige Vorratsschädlinge*, Zeitschrift für angewandte Entomologie 96 (1983), 448-451

W. F. Erichson, *Naturgeschichte der Insekten Deutschlands*, 1. Abt. *Coleoptera* Vol III, 3. *Lieferung*, Berlin 1846, 321-480

L. Evans, *The depiction of animal behaviour in Egyptian art*, MA thesis, Sydney, (2001), Internet.Unspecified document.

G. Fischhaber, *Mumifizierung im koptischen Ägypten*, in: M. Görg (Hrsg.), *Ägypten und Altes Testament*, Wiesbaden 1997

E. Fulcheri, E. R. Massa, T. D. Garetto, *Differential diagnosis between palaeo-pathological and non-pathological post-mortem environmental factors in ancient human remains*, Journal of Human Evolution 15 (1986), 71-75

J. Galil, *Sycomore wasps from Ancient Egyptian tombs*, Israel Journal of Entomology 2 (1967), 1-10

R. C. Garner, *Insects and mummification*, in: A. R. David (ed.), *Science in Egyptology*, Manchester 1986, 97-100

B. Gerisch, *Entomologische Untersuchungen an der Mumie Ramses' II. und anderen Mumien*, Kemet 6/1 (1997), 39-41

R. Germer, *Das Geheimnis der Mumien* [2], Reinbek 1994

L. Gozmany, *Seven-language Thesaurus of European Animals I*, London–New York–Tokyo 1978

B. Greenberg, *Flies as forensic indicators*, Journal of Medical Entomology 28/5 (1991), 565-577

K. Günther, H.-J. Hannemann, F. Hieke, E. Königsmann, F. Koch, H. Schumann, *Urania - Tierreich in sechs Bänden, 3, Insekten*, Leipzig–Jena–Berlin 1994

P. J. Gullan, P. S. Cranston, *The insects: an Outline of Entomology*, Madras 1995, 392

H.-J. Hannemann, B. Klausnitzer, K. Senglaub, *Exkursionsfauna für die Gebiete der DDR und der BRD, 2/1: Wirbellose, Insekten* (1. Teil) [7], Berlin 1986

H.-J. Hannemann, B. Klausnitzer, K. Senglaub, *Exkursionsfauna für die Gebiete der DDR und der BRD, 2/2: Wirbellose, Insekten* (2. Teil) [6], Berlin 1988

K. W. Harde, F. Severa, *Der Kosmos-Käferführer* [2], Stuttgart 1984

I. R. Harrison, *Arthropod parasites associated with Egyptian mummies with special reference to 1770 (Manchester Museum)*, in: A. R. David (ed.), *Science in Egyptology*, Manchester 1986, 171-174

W. Helck, W. Westendorf (Hrsg.), *Lexikon der Ägyptologie*, II, Wiesbaden 1977

H. E. Hinton, *A Monograph of the Beetles Associated with Stored Products*, First reprint, New York 1963

H. Hoffmann, *Käfer und Motten als Vorratsschädlinge bei den alten Kulturvölkern des Nahen Ostens*, Abhandlungen und Verhandlungen des Naturwissenschaftlichen Vereins in Hamburg, 8 (1963), 73-91

F. W. Hope, Transactions of the Entomological Society of London 1(1834), Journal of Proceedings XI-XIII

F. W. Hope, *Observations on some mummied beetles taken from the inside of a mummied ibis*, Transactions of the Entomological Society of London 3 (1840), 191-193

E. Hornung, *Die Bedeutung des Tieres im alten Ägypten*, Studium Generale (Berlin) 20/2 (1967), 69-84

R. W. Howe, *Insects attacking seeds during storage*, in: T. T. Kozlowski (ed.), *Seed Biology* III, London 1972, 247-300

J.-B. Huchet, *Insectes et momies égyptiennes*, Bulletin de la Société Linnéenne de Bordeaux 23/1, (1995), 29-39

J.-B. Huchet, *L'archéoentomologie funéraire: une approche originale dans l'interprétation des sépultures*, Bulletin et Mémoirs de la Société d'Anthropologie de Paris n.s. 8/3-4 (1996), 299-311

S. Ikram and A. Dodson, *The mummy in Ancient Egypt: Equipping the dead for eternity*, London 1998.

L. Keimer, *Insectes de l'Égypte ancienne. Études éntomologique publiées de 1931 à 1937 dans les annales du service des antiquités de l'Égypte,* Le Caire 1938

H. K. Kenward, *Methods for palaeo-entomology on site and in the laboratory,* Science and Archaeology 13 (1974), 16-24

H. K. Kenward, *The value of insect remains as evidence of ecological conditions on archaeological sites,* in: D. R. Brothwell, K. D. Thomas, J. Clutton-Brock (eds.), *Research problems in zooarchaeology,* Institute of Archaeology, University of London, Occasional publication 3 (1978), 25-38

S. von Kiler, *Entomologisches Wörterbuch* 3, Berlin 1963

J. M. Kingsolver, *A 2000+-year-old beetle (Coleoptera: Dermestidae),* Proceedings of the Entomological Society of Washington 84/2 (1982), 390

M. E. Kislev, *Archaeobotany and storage archaeoentomology,* in: J. M. Renfrew (ed.), *New light on the early farming,* Edinburgh 1991, 121-136

B. Klausnitzer, *Aussage- und Bestimmungsmöglichkeiten von Insektenbruchstükken aus vor- und frühgeschichtlichen Fundzusammenhängen,* Ausgrabungen und Funde 9 (1964), 123-125.

F. Klingauf, H. J. Bestmann, O. Vostrowsky, K. Michaelis, *Wirkung von ätherischen Ölen auf Schadinsekten,* Mitteilungen der deutschen Gesellschaft für allgemeine und angewandte Entomologie 4 (1983), 123-126

A. Krajewski, *Uszkodzenia zabytków w Egipcie powodowane przez owady* (Insect-produced damage of Egyptian monuments). Ochrona Zabytków (Denkmalschutz), ISSN 0029-8247, 1/1999, 45-53.

P. A. Latireille, *Des insect peints ou sculptés sur les monuments antiques de l'Égypte,* Mémoirs du Muséum d'Histoire naturelle (Paris) 5 (1819), 249-270

F. F. Leek, *Eutropius niloticus,* Journal of Egyptian Archaeology 64 (1978), 121-122

P. Lesne, *Le Dermeste des cadavres (Dermestes Frischi Kug.) dans les tombes de l'Egypte ancienne,* Bulletin de la Société Royale Entomologique d'Egypte n. s. 14 (1930), 21-24

H. Levinson, A. Levinson, *Dried seeds, plant and animal tissues as food favoured by storage insect species,* Entomologia Eexperimentalis et Applicata: Proceedings 4th insect/host plant symposium (1978), 305-317

H. Levinson, A. Levinson, *Storage and insect species of stored grain and tombs in ancient Egypt,* Zeitschrift für angewandte Entomologie 100 (1985), 321-339

H. Levinson, A. Levinson, *Hungersnot und Nahrungsspeicherung im alten Ägypten,* Spektrum der Wissenschaft 3 (1988), 40-47

H. Levinson, A. Levinson, *Die Ungezieferplagen und Anfänge der Schädlingsbekämpfung im Alten Orient,* Anzeiger für Schädlingskunde, Pflanzenschutz, Umweltschutz 63 (1990), 81-96

H. Levinson, A. Levinson, *Origin of grain storage and insect species consuming desiccated food,* Anzeiger für Schädlingskunde, Pflanzenschutz, Umweltschutz 67 (1994), 47-59

H. Levinson, A. Levinson, *Prionotheca coronata Olivier (Pimeliinae, Tenebrionidae) recognized as a new species of venerated beetles in the funerary cult of predynastic and archaic Egypt,* Journal of Applied Entomology 120 (1996), 577-585

H. Levinson, A. Levinson, *Control of stored food pests in the ancient Orient and classical antiquity,* Journal of Applied Entomology 122 (1998), 137-144

G. E. Lynn, J. T. Benitez, *Temporal bone preservation in a 2600-year-old Egyptian mummy,* Science 183 (1974), 200-202

Miller, *Extracts from the minute-book*, 16. Nov. Transactions of the Linnean Society of London 14/3 (1825), 586

R. Miller, *Appendix: ash as an insecticide*, in: B. J. Kemp (ed.), Amarna Reports 4 (1987), 14-16

F. Netolitzky (a), *Ein Dermestes aus ägyptischen Gräbern,* Deutsche entomologische National-Bibliothek II 14 (1911), 111-112

F. Netolitzky (b), *Nahrungs- und Heilmittel der Urägypter,* Zeitschrift für Untersuchung der Nahrungs- und Genußmittel 21 (1911), 607-613

A. H. Omar, *Studies on Chrysomyia albiceps (Weidemann) one of the most important carrion flies in Egypt*, Journal of the Egyptian Society of Parasitology 25/3 (1995), 607-624

R. L. Palma, *Ancient head lice on a wooden comb from Antinoë, Egypt*, Journal of Egyptian Archaeology 77 (1991), 194

E. Panagiotakopulu, P. C. Buckland, P. M. Day, A. A. Sarpaki, C. Doumas, *Natural insecticides and insect repellents in antiquity: a review of the evidence*, Journal of Archaeological Science 22 (1995), 705-710

E. Panagiotakopulu, *An insect study from Egyptian stored products in the Liverpool Museum*, Journal of Egyptian Archaeology 84 (1998), 231-234

T. J. Pettigrew, *A History of Egyptian Mummies*, London 1834

J. M. Riddle, *A survey of ancient specimens by electron microscopy*, in: A. Cockburn, E. Cockburn (eds.), *Mummies, Disease, and Ancient Cultures*, Cambridge 1980, 274-286

M. S. Schenkling, *Clérides nouveaux du Muséum d'Histoire Naturelle de Paris*, Bulletin du Muséum d'Histoire Naturelle 5 (1902), 317-333

K. Sethe, *Zur Geschichte der Einbalsamierung bei den Ägyptern und einiger damit verbundener Bräuche,* Sitzungsberichte der Preußischen Akademie der Wissenschaften, Philosophisch-historische Klasse 1934, 211-239, Anhang 1-16

N. F. Shaumar, M. M. El-Agoze, S. K. Mohammed, *Parasites and predators associated with blow flies and flesh flies in Cairo region*, Journal of the Egyptian Society of Parasitology 20/1 (1990), 123-132

K. G. V. Smith, *A Manual of Forensic Entomology,* London 1986

M. E. Solomon, *Archaeological records of storage pests: Sitophilus granarius (L.) (Coleoptera, Curculionidae) from an Egyptian pyramid tomb*, Journal of Stored Product Research 1 (1965), 105-107

J.-R. Steffan, *L'entomofaune de la momie de Ramsès II,* Annales de la Société entomologique de France n. s. 18/4 (1982), 531-537

J.-R. Steffan, *L'entomofaune de la momie*, in: L. Balout, C. Roubert (éds.), *La momie de Ramsès II*, Contribution Scientifique à l'Egyptologie, Paris 1985, 108-115

L. Strong, *Dermestids - An enbalmer's dilemma*, Antenna 5 (1981), 136-139

T. I. Tantawi, E. M. El-Kady, *Identification of third larvae of forensically important flies (Diptera: Calliphoridae, Sarcophagidae and Muscidae) in Alexandria*, Journal of the Egyptian-German Society of Zoology 23 E (1997), 1-19

J. H. Taylor, *Unwrapping a mummy. The life, death and embalming of Horemkenesi*, London 1995

H. Weber, H. Weidner, *Grundriß der Insektenkunde*[5], Stuttgart 1974

H. Weidner, *Bestimmungstabellen der Vorratsschädlinge und des Hausungeziefers Mitteleuropas* [5], New York 1993

F. Zacher, *Vorratsschädlinge und Speicherwirtschaft im alten und neuen Ägypten*, Forschungen und Fortschritte 26 (1934), 347-348

F. Zacher, *Vorratsschädlinge und Vorratsschutz, ihre Bedeutung für Volksernährung und Weltwirtschaft*, Zeitschrift für hygienische Zoologie 29 (1937), 193-202

F. Zacher, *Die Fauna der Mühlen und Speicher in Aegypten*, Zoologischer Bericht 52 (1940), 353-368

F. Zacher, *Mitteilungen über Diebkäfer (Ptinidae) von wirtschaftlicher Bedeutung*, Anzeiger für Schädlingskunde 21/7 (1948), 97-102

Photo 1.
Ausgewählte Insektenfunde an der Mumie
Aset-iri-khet-es
(a) Käferreste, Lathridiidae;
(b) Käferfragment, Lathridiidae;
(c) Haut, Dermestidae, *Trogoderma angustum;*
(d) Haut, Dermestidae, *Attagenus pellio;*
(e) Flügeldecken, Dermestidae;
(f) Flügeldecken, Cleridae;
(g) Kopffragment, Tenebrionidae;
(h) Flügel, Fanniidae;
(i) Flügel, Chrysopidae;
– Maßstab 1 mm

Marian Paciorek

Conservation of a wooden painted coffin from Ancient Egypt in the collection of the Archaeological Museum in Cracow

Introduction

The Ancient Egyptian coffin of the priestess Aset-iri-khet-es arrived in Cracow (with some other objects) after Polish archaeologist Tadeusz Smoleński completed excavations at the locality of el-Gamhud in Middle Egypt in 1907.[1] Dated to the thirties of the 4th century B.C. (Ptolemaic cemetery), the coffin with its contents, that is, the mummy and cartonnage, was loaned to the National Museum and displayed at the Czapski Museum until the outbreak of the war in 1939. Hidden in the boiler room and the cellars of the museum for the duration of the hostilities, it was not returned to the Archaeological Museum before 1958. It was exhibited first at the halls in 22 Św. Jana street, from where it was removed along with the entire collection to the new seat of the museum on 3 Poselska street and placed on permanent display.

This brief review of the coffin history after its discovery reveals how after surviving practically 2000 years almost untouched, the coffin was quite suddenly subjected to a variety of destructive processes that have affected it in varying degrees. The varied and changeable conditions of its storage and display have had a strongly unfavorable effect on its overall condition. Generally considered as poor for all parts of the object, it required the undertaking of comprehensive research and conservation treatment to stop the processes of deterioration and to restore in full the display value, while assuring safe conditions for the future.

[1] H. Szymańska, *Tadeusz Smoleński. Excavations at el-Gamhud* (in present volume).

The present article is devoted to describing the nature and scope of conservation work carried out on the painted wooden coffin (inv. no. MAK/AS/2438). The damages to the coffin were such that it was necessary to fix and re-attach to the structure the layers of ground, polychromy and clay, reinforce the structure, clean and impregnate the damaged wood, remove traces of previous restorations and elaborate principles for safe display.

Coffin execution techniques and material

The coffin was executed basically of a single piece of sycamore wood[2] (*Ficus sycomorus* L.),[3] which is a local species that is quite common in Egypt. Trees grow to a height of 15 m with trunk reaching a diameter of 1 m across; the wood encompasses many faults of anatomic and morphological structure[4] (Photo 1).

The outer form of the coffin was initially carved as a whole and was later cut into two at one-fourth of the height. It is made up of two main elements: a shallow bottom and a convex lid.[5] Both parts were then hollowed to make space for the mummy. The places of the more serious defects and faults of the anatomic structure of the wood were either patched or reinforced structurally. These faults, which are observed on both parts, are much more frequent on the sides of the lid, the shoulders and the more spatially developed foot part of the coffin. Here, the pieces of wood that had splintered off or cracked during the carving process were re-attached and structurally reinforced. Particular sections of the wood were joined using a gluten glue and structural reinforcement in the form of wooden tenons and pegs. These parts were worked very precisely and reveal traces of the tools that were used in the carving process.[6]

The upper part of the coffin was given the overall shape of a human figure with a carved mask, the face of a young woman. It was joined to the bottom part with three pairs of heterogeneous tenons fixed with the aid of pegs in deeply cut sockets found in both parts. The tenons had been inserted into the lid first most probably and after the mummy had been placed inside the coffin, they were inserted into the sockets in the bottom part and fixed there with pegs for good (Photo 7).

The wood surface with its numerous flaws (bark growth, knots, cracking from the core), as well as the points of connection and general unevenness were all covered with a layer of clay and sand[7] fixed with a gluten glue.[8] A layer of

[2] The examination was carried out by J. Ptak, M.A., from the Department of Artwork Conservation and Restoration of the Fine Arts Academy in Cracow.

[3] Crosswise section: the wood is characterized by scattered vessels, the vessels are very big (diameter of c. 350 μ), few, arranged in radiate manner or in small groups. The fibers and soft tissue form highly obvious, adjacent bands. Lengthwise section: core rays wide, up to a dozen and more rows, mostly 8-row, heterogeneous. Straight vessel perforation. The sample studied represents sycamore wood (*Ficus sycomorus* L.).

[4] J. Lipińska, *Historia rzeźby, reliefu i malarstwa starożytnego Egiptu*, Warszawa 1978, 108; J. Śliwa, *Ancient Egyptian Handicraft Woodworking*, Zeszyty Naukowe UJ 304 (21), 1975, 20-30.

[5] The evidence for the coffin being made from a single piece of wood includes anatomical characteristics of its structure, a continuation of tree-growth rings, flaws in the wood, overgrowth of bark, which are visible in the crosswise sections of the foot and head part of the coffin.

[6] Woodworking tools included axes, picks, saws, chisels of all kinds, burins and drills, also the so-called bow drill, Śliwa, op. cit., 20-30. Traces of saws being used are visible in a few places on the inside surfaces of the connection between the lid and bottom of the coffin.

[7] The elements in this layer were determined using nuclear methods (non-destructive activation and X-ray fluorescence analyses) applied for the identification of works of art, M. Ligęza, E. Pańczyk, L. Waliś, *Zastosowanie metod jądrowych do identyfikacji dzieł sztuki*, Nationwide symposium entitled „Radiation and isotope techniques in artwork conservation", Łódź, 23-24 IV 1996, 57-59. The chief components of the clay were identified: O, Si, Al, Ca, K, Mg. Apart from quartz, calcite and dolomite, numerous feldspars and pyroxenes were also noted.

[8] The IR spectrum reveals bands with a frequency like in note 9. There also occur bands with frequencies of 1540, 1640 and 1730 cm^{-1}, resulting from peptides group oscillation. The conclusion is that the binder used here for the chalk mortar with some clay added was an adhesive of protein origin.

clay[9] was used for both the inside and outside of the coffin, for filling the cracks, flaws in the wood, uncovered bark growth and inexact connections.

Thus prepared, the surface of the coffin was covered with a white ground made of calcium carbonate[10] and gluten glue.[11] On a thick layer of ground and a red bolus in the facial part of the coffin mask, the gilding is of polished gold foil (Photo 6). The rest of the coffin surface, including the bottom of the lower part, was covered with polychromy and hieroglyphic writing (Photo 9) applied with a characteristic set of colors and pigments[12] and using Arabic gum as binder.[13]

On the inside surface of the coffin bottom traces of a dark resinous substance have been preserved, presumably evidence for how the mummy was settled inside the coffin.

The polychromy, which was initially probably less damaged than at present, was in the early years of the 20th century fixed with adhesives wherever intervention was required, locally restored with gypsum putties[14] and retouched.[15] These restorations, made in a few places on the coffin lid, included most often the interrupted lines dividing the composition, repetitive ornaments and the background. Their immediate character and the patina of the coloring corresponded with the already considerably dirtied coloring of the original polychromy.

Description of the coloring and formal style attributes

Initially, the painted anthropoid coffin was not covered with polychromy all over nor had it a layer of plaster on the bottom part of the feet. In the section with the mask it had a tripartite wig painted blue[16] and framed with a broad red[17] band at the sides and bottom. The face is gilded, the eyeballs white with black pupils. The decoration of the lid was divided into many vertical and horizontal bands. The breast is covered entirely with an ornamental necklace consisting of thirteen rows of beads and lotus flowers, terminating in falcon's heads. Also present is a motif of olive-tree and willow leaves, white lotus petals and field bluebottles. Bands of a cubic ornament separate the plant motifs. A frequent ornamental motif is the eye of Horus symbolizing all offerings, as well as triumph over the enemy.[18] Below the necklace Isis is shown kneeling, spreading her wings in a gesture of protection over the deceased. Hieroglyphic inscriptions run above the wings. The next ornamental band is taken up by the embalming table with the head, paws and tail of a lion, on

[9] The IR spectrum reveals bands with a frequency of 465, 700 and 1200 cm[-1], resulting from the presence of SiO_2. Also particles of black visible. Conclusion: $[Al_2Si_2O_5(OH)_4]_2$, hydrated aluminum silicate, called clay with coal black intermixed.

[10] Microscope examination reveals small particles of white, in compact groups, birefringent. The sample is dissolved with 2n HCl with CO_2 gas emitted. Conclusion: calcium carbonate $CaCO_3$.

[11] See note 8.

[12] Examinations by M. Rogóż, M.A., from the Applied Chemistry Laboratory of the Artwork Conservation and Restoration Department of the Fine Arts Academy in Cracow.

[13] The IR spectrum of sample no. 1 reveals bands of the frequency: 1070, 1220, 1385, 1440, 1620 and 2930 cm[-1] that are characteristic of carbonates and tannins. Conclusion: gum is the binder of the painted layer. It may be Arabic gum, a product that is commonly made of acacia wood, which is widespread in Egypt.

[14] In places where the outer polychromy layer, plaster and detached clay are missing evidence of modern adhesives, gypsum putties and retouching have been observed. This confirms that before being displayed for the first time the coffin was restored on the spot in order to lessen the effects of the various damages. Executed probably in the early years of the 20th century, this work had little effect on the original appearance and coloring of the object. More serious damages to the structure of the object, especially the layer of plaster and polychromy, occurred at a later date, often in drastically changing conditions and storage areas.

[15] Black particles recalling splintered forms, mat in color, are visible under the microscope. The pigment was dissolved in 2n HCl, carrying out a microcrystaloscopic reaction with $Cu(CH_3COO)_2$. $PbCl_2$ and Na NO_2, confirming the presence of K[+] ions. Conclusion: vegetable black – C + K_2CO_3.

[16] The crystals visible under the microscope are characterized by pleochroism, birefringent, also visible are calcite and quartz crystals. The pigment is not acid-soluble. A drop reaction was carried out with an alcohol solution of rubeanic acid, confirming the presence of Cu[+2] ions. Conclusion: $CuOCaO_4SiO_2$ – Egyptian blue.

[17] Heterogeneous crystals of an intense red observed under the microscope, birefringent of various shapes and sizes. Also visible a few pale yellow crystals of irregular size and shape, transparent, characterized by birefringence. Pigment partially soluble in 2n HCl. Drop reaction with 2n $K_4[Fe(CN)_6]$, confirming the presence of Fe[+3] ions. Conclusion: red ochre with yellow mixed in.

[18] A. Niwiński, *Mity i symbole starożytnego Egiptu*, Warszawa 1995.

which the mummy is depicted. Below the table there are four Canopic jars for the internal organs removed during the mummification process; the jars are covered with lids in the shape of the heads of the sons of Horus. Closing the composition at the bottom is a band of geometric decoration. Below runs a hieroglyphic inscription of seven vertical columns reaching the base of the feet, limited on the sides with bands of cubic ornament. The middle column is longer, extending onto the feet of the coffin. Flanking it are antithetical figures of Anubis lying on the naos. On the side walls of the feet of the coffin a gate for the *ka* soul was shown; the *ka* was supposed to be able to leave the coffin through here. The side walls of the coffin are taken up by figures of six (three on each side) deities protecting the tomb and inscriptions. On either side of the wig falcon heads are shown in profile on the right and left, crowned with solar discs (Photo 8). The entire back part of the coffin is taken up by a representation of Isis. The painted decoration of the coffin is characterized by the typically Egyptian broad palette of the principal basic colors. The predominant colors overall include white, yellow covered in places with orpiment,[19] Egyptian blue, greens, red and black. The background for the figural scenes is alternately white or yellow. The skin of the figures is mostly green,[20] of an olive shade and the color of ocher.[21] Robes are blue, green and red. The face profiles, hieroglyphic inscriptions and other outlines are marked with a vivid black line. Considerable color variation is evident on the necklace part and the bottom section of the wig. The plant motifs, cubes and other ornaments of a graphic character are painted with blue, green and red using the white and yellow of the background. The face of the coffin mask is gilded with gold leaf[22], the eye outlined in black[23] and with white eyeballs (Photo 6).

Condition of the coffin and painted decoration before conservation

The original polychromy with gilding superimposed on the white plaster in the face part of the mask covered the entire surface of the lid and bottom of the coffin, except for the bottom part of the feet. This would suggest that the coffin had probably stood upright in the tomb. Losses of the polychromy on both sides, the foot and the wig are presently considerable with smaller parts missing from the rest of the front, the gilded mask, necklace and the coffin bottom (Photos 2, 8, 9).

[19] Particles of a coarse-grained pale golden-yellow pigment visible under the microscope. Reaction was achieved with concentrated HCl, zinc filings and 2n $AgNO_3$, confirming the presence of As^{+3} ions. Conclusion: orpiment – As_2S_3.

[20] H. James, *Painting techniques on stone and wood*, Conservation of Ancient Egyptian materials, UKIC Archaeology section 1988.

[21] Minor particles of white in bigger concentrations, birefringent, visible under the microscope. The pigment is dissolved in 2n HCl emitting CO_2. Observable heterogeneous red crystals of various shapes and sizes. Conclusion: mixture of red and yellow ocher whitened with lime white.

[22] In studies on the subject there is frequently a difference noted between leaf and film depending on the thickness, T. G. H. James. *Gold technology in Ancient Egypt*, Gold Bulletin 5 (2), 1972, 38-42; A. Lucas, *Ancient Egyptian Materials and Industries*, 4th ed. revised and enlarged by J. R. Harris, London 1962.

[23] Tiny black particles, mat, observed under the microscope. The pigment burns completely. Conclusion: carbon black.

Particularly heavy losses are visible on the side surfaces and all the joinery, faults and cracks in the wood, where the polychromy has become completely detached along with the plaster and layer of clay that smoothed the rough wood surface. The loosening of the wooden joinery elements and damage to particular sections of the structural reinforcements has led to the parts once attached on either side of the coffin lid and base to slide apart. Made practically of a single piece of wood, the coffin, both lid and bottom, reveals varied changes of size and rheological deformation that is due to the changing places and conditions of display. The wood, which continues to have a considerable mechanical durability, has undergone destruction over time, having been weakened by existing flaws in its anatomical and morphological structure. The wooden surface coming in contact with the elements has become dark, coarse and brittle. The coffin, exhibited in variously heated rooms and stored during the war in a boiler room, was especially threatened by the harmful influence of gas in the air, as well as light, especially ultraviolet radiation, which results in the cellulose chain being broken and lignin undergoing chemical changes. Changes in the humidity of the hygroscopic properties of the wood constituted one of the principal reasons for its aging, damage to the ground layers and the polychromy. Repeated periods of increased and lowered humidity have weakened the fibrous structure of the wood, causing all kind of cracks, gaps and loosening of the structural joints (Photo 3). The carving of the coffin from the inside and the removal of the core has largely prevented the cracking of the wood. Cracks have not appeared near the carved places, but in the thickest uncarved parts of the foot of the coffin, at all the joinings and wherever the numerous anatomical faults in the wood structure occur. Low humidity has caused an uneven shrinking of the wood in these places, tension in certain areas, deformation and loosening of the ground layers, the thickness of which varies. This has triggered a process of peeling and detaching of the clay, plaster and painted layers from the wooden substance, which has cracked and fallen away in the outcome. In the present state, considering the simple technology of coffin execution, the wood also reveals considerable mechanical weakening caused by insects and lichen, especially in the lower parts of the object. The losses of the wood from the edges of the coffin lid and bottom are also largely a consequence of anatomical faults and biological damages referring to the period of tree growth. The wood weakened in these places and with widely differing properties was much more susceptible (together with the painted layer) to mechanical damages resulting from transport and changes of exhibition. At the same time, frequent and considerable changes in humidity have led to radial cracking and an almost complete loosening of wood connections, both those where an adhesive had been used, and those that constituted structural reinforcement. The consequence were losses of the wooden substance, detaching fragments and falling out of parts fitted in already in antiquity. The destruction processes in the wood itself and in the coffin structure have resulted in considerable losses of the plaster and painted layer, especially on the sides of the coffin elements, up to 70% of the surface in all. The plaster and painted layer reveals a network of cracks resulting from the changes in wood size; they have also become more brittle and detached from the wooden substance. The painted layer, which is best preserved on the top part of the lid and on the underside of the coffin bottom, also revealed many minor losses and cracking, exhibiting at the same time a tendency to peel away together with the plaster. Overall, the polychromy was in a deteriorating condition, damaged and poorly adhering in some areas, detaching in others. The thin and deformed plaster layer, the edges of which are turning up, was brittle and fragile, and like the painted layer had a tendency to detach along vertical planes. The polychromy on the underside of the coffin bottom, most endangered mechanically, showed less signs of detaching. However, other damages were more plentiful here, like cracking, stains left by resinous substances,[24] uneven discoloring of pigments, rubbing off. Dark stains combined with loss of transparency are observed locally on the outer surfaces of the coffin head and shoulders. It may be the outcome of wood discoloration caused by humidity or reattachment made during an earlier renovation, when cracked parts of the wood were fixed locally with a strong animal glue, while some losses of the wood, clay and plaster were filled with gypsum. In the middle part of the coffin lid missing plaster was restored with gypsum and a fragment of the decoration was reconstructed on it. A few of the surviving fillings had spread over the original painted surface. The coffin

[24] The stains are quite clearly due to the substance used to make the mummy bandages stick and applied locally to the coffin bottom to attach the mummy, A. Kłosowska, *The conservation and technical examination of three corn-mumies at the Archaeological Museum in Cracow*, Materiały Archeologiczne 30 (1997), 19.

including the preserved polychromy and gilded mask, as well as the wooden surface revealed at one time or another, was covered with a layer of dust and more permanent dirt deposited clearly more extensively on the horizontal parts of the coffin lid.

Conservation

The coffin conservation program required a full treatment combined with preparing the object for safe museum display in the future. Understanding the execution techniques and the condition of the object before conservation permitted the chief objectives of the work to be determined. Foremost, it was essential for later superimposed layers that were technically harmful and aesthetically displeasing to be removed. This had to be followed by a full range of technical sustaining conservation steps in order to stop the destruction processes working on the substance and the technology. This form of conservation without interfering with the preserved substance and aesthetics of the object, was dictated mainly by the desire to retain the specificity of the archaeological and historical character of the object and its function and importance as a museum exhibit.

The state of preservation of the object, overall considered as poor, although highly differentiated for the different parts, determined the stages of the work and their extent, consequently also the choice of material, technical means and methods necessary for proper execution.

After separating the coffin pieces and taking out the mummy and cartonnage, the first stage consisted of cleaning the surface of the wood and the painted layer of as much of the dust and other dirt as possible (Photos 2, 4). After preliminary fixing with Paraloid B-72 and protection of the loosened polychromy and plaster with Japanese tissue paper, the coffin could be cleaned successively, both on the outside and on the insignificantly dirtied carved interior. The loose surface deposits of dust and dirt were removed by delicate brushing with a soft brush and vacuuming with a weak vacuum cleaner equipped with a flexible rubber ending. Thicker deposits of dirt in the unevenness of the exposed wood surface were removed with a wooden probe. Under fourfold magnification, cotton tampons soaked in a 0.5% solution of a non-ionic detergent mixed with ethylene oxide in distilled water or a mixture of methanol and mineral spirits (1:2) were used to clean the surface of accumulated dirt. This also served as a mild anti-fungus treatment for the weakened wood. In similar fashion, using the same agents but applying compresses, modern stains and spots left by glue on the wood surface were swollen and removed from the wood surface together with the dirt. Applying a 10% solution of an acid ammonium carbonate dispersed in polyvinyl alcohol in gel form in distilled water helped soften the gypsum putties and fillings that were introduced in the early 20th century restoration; these were later removed using scalpels and dentistry tools, revealing in the process fragments of the original polychromy that had thus been partly concealed. Their surface covered in these places with a white gypsum tarnish was cleaned delicately with glass fiber brushes, followed by trichloroethane and acetone. Applying different chemical agents and methods to the various parts of the object was dictated by the condition of these elements, as well as the technique of execution of the polychromy, which is generally not resistant to damp and water. To clean the gilding made in the adhesive technique on a red bole acetone-saturated swabs were used. For the painted parts, which were mat in texture, using bread erasers turned out to be completely satisfactory; for the especially persistent dirt and stains organic solvents were used, such as dimethylformamide acetone and petrol. Using solvents while mechanically brushing and drying with cotton and wool tampons permitted the dirt to be removed from various unevenness of the surface, both of the wood and the painted parts. Stains and discoloration caused by resinous substances on the polychromy of the coffin bottom were removed by extraction to lignin compresses saturated with chloroform, then washed with extraction naphtha. The mostly mechanical character of the cleaning of the polychromy and the layers of clay and wood forced the simultaneous undertaking of treatment required to protect the surfaces that were to be cleaned from further damage and deterioration. Particular fragments of the weakened wood surface, brittle clay and plaster were reinforced and fixed with repeated saturation with a 5% solution of Paraloid B-72 in acetone. Numerous tests were made and the decision was made to use a 4-8% water solution of gluten adhesive (*isinglass*) modified by a 10% addition of polyethylene glycol 1500 for the principal reattachment and consolidation work. The application of polyethylene glycol facilitated glue penetration and made it more flexible. Prior to introducing the adhesive the detached places were wetted with methyl alcohol, again in an effort to facilitate glue penetration into cracks and peeling elements. The reattached surfaces were pressed with filtering tissue paper in order to remove excess adhesive and to press down the layers of plaster and polychromy. The partly loosened fragments of the clay and bark growth were reattached. Wherever the detached layer had to be pressed down, it was weighed down with bags of sand until dry. Using an 8% solution for the reattachment procedure gave the best results, resulting in the least discoloration of the original material and good adherence to the ground of the detached surfaces. The poor condition of the wood in many places that were particularly endangered and damaged by biological factors pointed to the need for preserving, reinforcing and hardening the weakened structure of the wood by means of impregnation and disinfestation. Impregnation was carried out by repeatedly coating the surface with an impregnate under conditions of a delayed evaporation of solvents (in a chamber of polyester film). The substance used to impregnate was a 10% solution of Paraloid B-72 in xylene and acetone (3:1) or dissolved only in carbon tetrachloride for the inner surfaces of the coffin, where spots of resinous substance could be dissolved with commonly used solvents. The action of structurally reinforcing the wood was combined with disinfecting and disinfestation by adding a mixture of ethylene oxide and thymol to the impregnating substance. In order for the substance to be deposited evenly in the wood structure solvent evaporation was delayed by covering the coffin with film and keeping it for a few days in an atmosphere consisting of the vapor of a non-solvent, extraction naphtha in this case. The treatment fully reinforced and protected the structure of the wood and allowed for the structural reinforcement and reconnection of loosened parts of the coffin. This work demanded first of all that the detached or loosened elements be fixed and structurally reinforced, and remounted to form a whole defined by the coffin-execution technology. All the points of joining, that is, fragments closely fitted together, were glued together with gluten glue (*isinglass*). On the other hand, elements which did not have the joining surface preserved, where bigger gaps or even losses were revealed, were set in a special sawdust putty (Photo 2). The putty was prepared of different-sized sawdust granules and a 30% solution of Paraloid B-72 in acetone, which was introduced into the bigger voids in layers. These fillings and joinings were for reasons of display, to emphasize their solely structural nature, slightly depressed with regard to the surface and are lighter in color than the wood of the coffin. All the original tenons and pegs were preserved and reused when reattaching and remounting the loosened fragments. In a few cases when original pegs were missing, new ones were made of mahogany.

The original coloring of the coffin polychromy became more obvious after conservation and the chiefly technical-sustaining conservation treatment served its role in stopping the processes of destruction of the wooden structure, the layers of plaster and polychromy. The durability of the treatment and the protection of the original coffin execution technology is dependent, however, mainly on the conditions of use and display of the object. The issue of the damages is complex as it depends on many factors. An important factor affecting the stability of the wood in terms of its size and by the same its safety and that of the materials connected with it is maintaining constant relative humidity of the air (55-60%) and constant temperature (16-18°C), and to keep potential changes within acceptable limits. A new form of prophylactics in protecting the coffin is placing it inside a glass case where humidity (set at 55%) is stabilized with silica gel. Furthermore, placing the coffin at a certain height above a mirror permits the outer polychromy of the coffin bottom to be viewed as a reflection in it (Photo 5).

Appendix

The Research

Examination in daylight (white light). Daylight examination of the coffin led to a preliminary description of its condition. An assessment was made of the extent of the damages and the scope of the restoration work carried out after the coffin had been brought to Cracow following its uncovery in Egypt. In the voids where layers of the polychromy, plaster and detached clay were missing, traces of modern adhesive layers were observed, as well as gypsum putties and retouching of the missing parts of the polychromy. This confirmed the belief that the coffin had undergone some repairs before its first public display in order to lessen the effects of the damages and deterioration it had sustained. Presumably carried out at the beginning of the 20th century, these restorations did not change the initial appearance and coloring of the coffin. More serious damages to the structure, and primarily the plaster and polychromy occurred at a later date, often in drastically changed conditions and storage places. Considerable damages to the coffin structure were observed as well as a weakening of the mechanical properties of the wood. Furthermore, considerable losses of the clay ground layer evening out the wooden surface were noted, also a loosening of the structure, losses of the plaster and polychromy, as well as the presence of later deposits of dirt, locally applied gypsum putties, reattaching and stains left by a strong skin glue, all having a negative effect on the technical condition and the aesthetic appearance of the object.

Identifying trace elements in the fillings on the Egyptian coffins from el-Gamhud and the cartonnage coffin from el-Hiba[25]. A preliminary analysis of the element composition in the fillings was carried out with the aid of X-ray fluorescence with energy dispersion. The method chosen for trace element identification was the model non-destruction activation analysis. Based on the results obtained in the X-ray fluorescence analysis a set of model readings was prepared. Seven samples, each 50 mg, were taken from four coffins. In the samples, 27 elements were traced and identified. The results are shown in Table 1 below.

[25] Research carried out by Dr. M. Ligęza of the Nuclear Chemistry and Technology Institute in Warsaw.

Sample no Element	1	2	3	4	5	6	7
Na	4860	7350	3370	4600	4420	1020	2600
K	50300	77700	55000	50000	40000	-	-
Sc	43.8	6.9	4.9	5.9	5.4	2.9	3.2
Cr	11.0	31.7	17.6	18.0	14.0	16.0	9.0
Fe	2120	2270	1600	1900	1650	870	1170
Ni	-	470	320	-	-	1300	-
Co	134	177	74.7	110	88	39	85
Zn	3.1	7.7	5.2	5.1	1.2	2.0	4.1
Ga	-	-	93.5	-	-	100	-
As	1.8	0.22	8.0	3.1	1.6	140	2.9
Br	30.5	60.2	25.7	23	35	17.3	7.0
Mo	0.5	0.54	0.33	0.43	0.46	1.9	0.3
Cd	3.37	2.8	-	-	-	-	-
Sb	16.0	24.2	26.0	26.0	27.4	30	34
Cs	0.35	0.22	0.35	0.39	0.31	0.05	0.02
Ba	29.4	37	41	42	48	14	2.3
La	7.4	5.2	5.5	6.3	6.3	2.4	8.6
Ce	7.2	5.2	6.1	6.0	6.9	3.5	9.2
Nd	2.4	12.3	8.6	7.5	16.4	2.45	19.7
Eu	0.3	0.24	0.21	0.25	0.25	0.04	0.04
Yb	0.7	0.38	0.65	0.31	0.33	0.28	0.5
Tb	0.4	0.17	0.28	0.49	0.17	0.03	0.12
Hf	3.9	3.3	4.5	4.1	2.5	0.31	0.6
Ta	41.8	41.2	36.0	44	32.4	13.0	42
W	4.1	4.32	7.2	4.5	4.1	7.4	0.4
Au	0.004	0.03	0.19	0.03	0.009	1.1	0.7
Th	0	0.3	0.24	0.22	0.2	0.11	0.7
U^{238}	0.34	0.45	0.34	0.33	0.26	2.6	0.55

Table 1.
Concentration of trace elements in the coffin clay [ppm]

Samples designated as nos. 1, 2, 4 and 7 – two coffins of the Ptolemaic period from el-Gamhud, samples nos. 3 and 5 – coffin of the Twenty-Second Dynasty, sample no. 6 – coffin from the Late Ptolemaic period, from el-Hiba.

Sample no Element	1	2	3	4	5	6	7
Na	4560	8760	4330	1160	5580	5460	3370
K	55400	82400	51400	57200	39500	63200	39800
Sc	4.26	5.51	4.55	4.21	4.46	13.2	2.51
Cr	10.1	45.9	15.4	17.9	17.3	75.2	20.6
Mn	560	672	460	380	458	1200	540
Fe	1780	2350	1390	1690	1680	5040	995
Co	98	165	87.6	107	93.4	246	79.1
Ni	283	335	380	268	211	499	142
Cu	12100	4490	28900	40800	7800	85400	16200
Zn	2.08	6.65	4	3.37	2.29	7.64	2.52
Ga	138	57.5	35.8	107	-	788	501
As	1.51	1.59	3.22	3.56	1.09	570	2.67
Br	30.3	94.6	28.9	30.6	42.7	118	54.8
Mo	0.7	1.96	0.76	0.65	1.03	7.87	1.8
Ag	0.43	0.85	1.96	1.08	0.65	8.97	0.62
Cd	5.75	1.66	5.26	1.75	4.01	14.8	2.94
Sn	0.31	0.18	0.13	0.11	0.17	0.31	0.13
Sb	14.2	25.5	26.7	23.4	21.4	110	23.7
Cs	0.28	0.29	0.27	0.29	0.34	1.09	0.25
Ba	38.6	36.2	41.1	39.4	39.7	211	31.8
La	10.6	6.44	6.81	6.48	5.86	12.9	8.84
Ce	5.45	4.27	4.52	4.79	4.58	9.91	4.69
Nd	2.92	5.61	5.66	4.39	4.38	4.8	5.43
Eu	0.26	0.19	0.23	0.21	0.19	0.30	0.12
Tb	0.16	0.16	0.19	0.18	0.12	0.19	0.12
Yb	0.87	0.67	0.69	1.21	0.95	1.15	0.46
Hf	4.52	9.42	3.72	7.38	5.26	0.41	1.63
Ta	32.3	37.6	25.3	42.2	33	58	26.6
W	4.29	6.26	6.8	6.88	4.57	28.4	7.34
Ir	0.0003	0.0002	0.0002	0.0003	0.0004	0.0002	0.0001
Au	0.0037	0.023	0.11	0.03	0.01	0.006	0.05
Hg	0.029	0.022	0.036	0.011	0.002	0.028	0.028
Th	0.37	0.16	0.18	0.29	0.22	0.55	0.22
^{238}U	0.34	0.45	0.34	0.33	0.26	2.68	0.55

Table 2.
Chemical composition of the clay constituting the filling in %

The observed model of trace element distribution for three of the coffins (Twenty-Second Dynasty, coffins of the Ptolemaic period) is similar, while the coffin from el-Hiba shows obvious differences in the content of iron, arsenic, cobalt, nickel, terbium, hafnium and gold. The same kind of dependency was confirmed by the results of the X-ray fluorescence analysis. Data processed with AXIL-QXAS software, achieved concentration of line X 32 of the elements and dispersed radiation, is presented in Table 2.

Similarly, the X-ray phase analysis permitted numerous feldspars and pyroxenes to be identified beside quartz, calcite and dolomite. In sample no. 6 taken from the el-Hiba coffin, which was different from the other samples, the concentrations of some of the elements revealed an important difference in the crystal structure as well. This sample contains, apart from aragonite and magnesite, also hutite, which is a mineral used in Ancient Egypt as a white pigment for decorating pottery.

Analysis of the binders using the infrared absorption spectrophotometry method. The samples for analysis were taken of the binder of the polychromy (no. 1) and of the plaster (no. 2). In the IR spectrum of sample no. 1 bands of 1070, 1220, 1385, 1440, 1620 and 2930 cm^{-1} frequency appear. These are characteristic for carbohydrates and tannins.

Conclusions
1. The binder of the painted layer is gum.

In the IR spectrum of sample no. 2 bands of 695, 715, 880, 1480 and 1800 cm^{-1} appear. These originate from the oscillations of the carbonate group in calcium carbonate. Also occurring frequency bands include 465, 750, 1100 and 1200 cm^{-1}, these originating from the presence of SiO_2, and 1540, 1640 and 1730 cm^{-1}, these being the outcome of peptides group oscillation.
2. The binder of the chalk ground with clay added is an adhesive of protein origin.

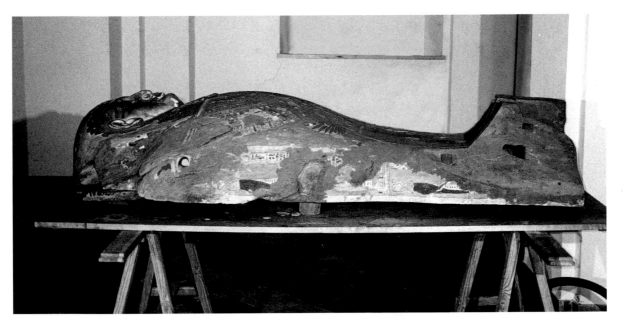

Photo 1.
The coffin lid before conservation

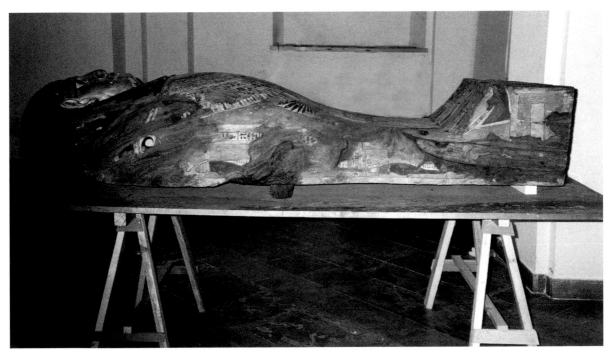

Photo 2.
The coffin lid after conservation

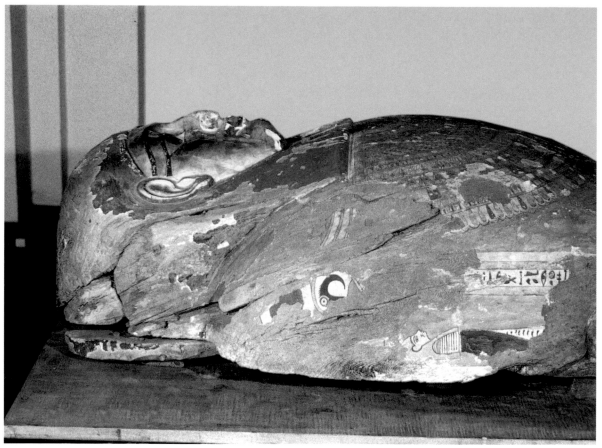

Photo 3.
Fragment of the coffin lid before conservation
with cracks in the wood and polichromy

Photo 4.
Fragment of the coffin lid after conservation

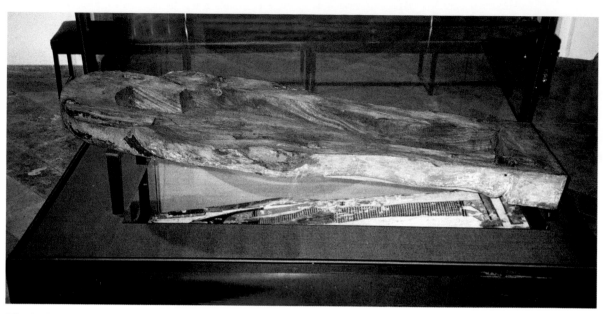

Photo 5.
Bottom part of the coffin after conservation

Photo 6.
Gilded mask of the sarcophagus after conservation

Photo 7.
Bottom part of the coffin with the image of Isis

Photo 8.
Fragment of the image of Isis from the bottom
part of the coffin

Photo 9.
Foot of the coffin

Barbara Aleksiejew-Wantuch

Conservation of a cartonnage piece of the mummy of Aset-iri-khet-es

Conservation treatment began in 1995.[1] The cartonnage had a form of an inner coat placed immediately on the mummified and shrouded body. Initially it comprised three pieces: a head dress with a face mask, a chest and leg plate and boot cartonnage that represented sandals. It was constructed from several layers of adhered bandages. After cutting out the openworks, the ground, gilding and polychrome were applied to the cartonnage.

Prior to conservation treatment the cartonnage was in an extremely poor condition. It was torn into tens of separate fragments and series of minute pieces. The head dress was in the worst state. Initially three-dimensional, before conservation it resembled a scattered puzzle.

The history of the cartonnage dates back several thousands of years. In favourable Egyptian climate, placed in a sarcophagus, it was exposed to the natural ageing processes. Then the tomb was plundered and the sarcophagus and the wooden coffin devastated. At that time the cartonnage was torn into pieces. Many of them were broken down completely, other got lost; those which remained underwent considerable deformation. The fact that the coffin was stored in a boiler room of the National Museum in Kraków was a key factor exacerbating the damage and degradation of the materials.

Considering preservation of particular technological strata of the cartonnage, the polychrome was in the best state. The extreme vividness of its colours and good condition of grounds is striking. The gold leaf used for gilding of the mask and the head dress was also in excellent state; the reddish discolouring surely came from alloys of iron in the gold deposit.[2] It needs to be stressed that no protective layer (varnish) was found neither on the polychrome nor the gilding.

[1] Conservation was carried out under the supervision of Professor Marian Paciorek from the Faculty of Art Conservation of the Jan Matejko Academy of Fine Arts in Kraków.

[2] The fusion temperatures of these metals are almost the same thus extracting iron from the alloy proved difficult at times.

At the bottom layer of the head dress the ground adhesive degraded. Also the bandages, which initially formed the cartonnage support, underwent considerable damage; they created the most serious conservation problems during the treatment. (Photo 1 shows the cartonnage before conservation).

Prior to examination and conservation procedures the cartonnage had to be placed on a suitable support. Before it was removed from the coffin a custom "working mummy" mount was made (after the measuring of the original one). The chest and leg plate was placed on the mount, and then smaller and bigger pieces of the head dress and gilded face mask were gradually drawn out of the bandages and the bottom of the coffin. The working mummy mount was made of polyurethane foam. For the main cartonnage plate required treatment on its outside and inside, both the negative and positive mounts were prepared.

The initially three-dimensional head dress was torn into series of fragments and many tiny pieces. To put them together another working mount was needed; this time a human head served as a model.

Because of a specific character of the cartonnage, microbiological tests preceded all conservation procedures.[3] The purpose of the tests was to identify the micro-organisms and their impact on preservation of the cartonnage materials (textiles, pigments, binding media and grounds).

In several samples taken from the cartonnage seven types of bacteria and actinomycetates, as well as seven species of fungi were identified. All recognised micro-organisms, through their biochemical activity and metabolic products such as: organic acids, pigments and chelation compounds, had a damaging effect on both the organic (polychrome) and mineral (ground) support.

The following examples illustrate the effects of micro-organism activity:

Streptomyces albidoflavus Waksman et Henrici causes degradation of cellulose and lignin, and produces a yellow pigment that changes into the brown one with time.

Streptomyces cinereochromogens Miyari et al. causes degradation of cellulose, pectins and lignin, and produces a brown pigment.

Probably the slight yellowing and darkening of the cartonnage bandages, the polychrome and the ground was not only due to the effect of ultraviolet rays but also to the activity of micro-organisms.

The loss of the initial properties of ground could have been the effect of *Bacillus circulans* Jordan, bacteria causing dissolution of silicate, aluminosilicate and calcium carbonate.

Additionally, in sample material taken from the polychrome, a toxinogenic species of fungi *Myrothecium Roridum* Tode ex Fr. was identified; it produces mycotoxins with cytotoxic, mutagenous and cancerogenic effects.

The results of the tests proved the need of disinfection.[4] It was carried out in a climatic chamber using ethylene oxide (C_2H_4O) cooled to the temperature below 0°C. The cartonnage was kept in the chamber filled with ethylene oxide gas for several days.

[3] Microbiological tests were carried out at the Chair of Microbiology of the University of Agriculture in Kraków by a team of researchers headed by Professor Bolesław Smyk.

[4] Not only the safety of conservators and visitors to the exhibition was taken into account but also the fact that during the treatment various materials (adhesives and solvents) would be insert into the object, and they might become a perfect culture medium for the identified micro-organisms.

Technological structure of the cartonnage

To examine the make-up of the cartonnage all materials underwent chemical laboratory tests.[5] A dozen samples were taken from the cartonnage bindings, pigments and grounds.

In the analysis of pigments microscopical and microchemical methods were employed. Pigment samples were observed in polarised light through a mineralogical microscope with a magnification range of up to 800× to determine the pigments' colour, shape, optical properties of the crystals and chemical reactions (microcrystaloscopic and guttulateous).

The analyses of binding media and grounds were performed with the use of absorption spectrophotometry in infra-red light. The technique of spectrally clean KBr was chosen for the purpose, and IR. spectra of the tested samples were examined with an Acculab 6 spectrophotometer within the range of 4000 – 250 cm/-1.

According to the tests the cartonnage pigments were as follows: white – calcium carbonate ($CaCO_3$), yellow – yellow ochre ($Fe_2O_3 + H_2O$), red – red ochre (Fe_2O_3), blue – Egyptian blue ($CuOCaO_4SiO_2$), green – a mixture of Egyptian blue and ochre, brown – umber ($Fe_2O_3 + MnO_2$ with a trace amount of red ochre Fe_2O_3), black – carbon black. White was also used for the ground – a white chalk mixed with proteinaceous adhesive, gluten glue. Moreover, the ground paste contained clay – hydrated aluminosilicate often mixed with carbon black pigment.

Ancient Egyptian palette[6] comprised naturally occurring and artificially created pigments. The natural ones were: chalk, gypsum (not found in the examined samples) and natural earth pigments, like yellow and red ochres, and umbers. Yellow ochres mixed with sand produced warmer colours, similar to sienna. Red ones derived from the burning of raw ochres, umber and sienna. Egyptian blue was produced through the heating of sand, silica, copper compounds and calcium carbonate. Mixing Egyptian blue with yellow ochre created the green pigment identified in the tested samples. Moreover, the sample taken from the cartonnage face mask contained gold.

Adhesive with which the cartonnage was attached to the mummy was identified as a mixture of organic resins with an alloy of oil and bituminous substances.[7]

The cartonnage bandages and the shroud were made of flax, a fibre widely grown in Egypt and commonly used for mummification.

Initially the cartonnage consisted of three pieces: a head dress with a face mask, a chest and leg plate and boot cartonnage that represented sandals. Investigations into its technology revealed how the cartonnage was constructed.

On average three layers of bandages were sized with gluten glue and then moulded to the shape of a mummy. When moulded and dried, the cartonnage designs were outlined in carbon black. The openworks were outlined as well and cut out with a sharp tool. Then the cartonnage was covered with a layer of chalk-and-glue ground, which was later polished or smoothed while it was still wet. A drawing in umber was then applied to the

[5] The test were conducted by Maria Rogoż from the Chemical Laboratory of the Faculty of Art Conservation of the Jan Matejko Academy of Fine Arts in Kraków.

[6] A. Lucas, *Ancient Egyptian Materials and Industries*, 4th ed. revised and enlarged by J. R. Harris, London 1962, 338-361.

[7] Detailed descriptions of chemical analyses are to be found in the conservation report kept in the Archives of the Archaeological Museum in Kraków.

ground, and later each of the particular areas of the design was painted with pigments in a gluten medium.

The head dress comprised more technological strata, possibly because of its function. Since it had to be more rigid, the head dress was constructed from four to five layers of flax fabric coated from the inside with a layer of a chalk ground. The inside was not polished; there were brush strokes clearly visible. A warm tone to the ground colour showed it contained a large amount of clay. Gold leaves on the cartonnage face mask were applied using proteinaceous technique.

The chest and leg plate of the cartonnage consisted of three pieces. Some parts of the design were not visible because the cartonnage pieces overlapped. Therefore it is assumed that in ancient Egypt cartonnage plates had been prepared beforehand or even manufactured on a large scale, and after mummification had been completed they were adjusted to the height of the mummy and provided with the appropriate hieroglyphs.

To prevent the cartonnage from slipping of the mummy, its bottom was adhered to the wrappings with a mixture of organic resinous substances modified with oil and bitumen. Additionally around the edges of the cartonnage there were deliberate holes (made before the application of the ground) through which a fine linen string was threaded and the cartonnage stitched to the shroud and the bandages. The same method was employed to attach the boot and the head dress.

[8] So far I have not found any account of treating cartonnages with openworks. Description of a treatment of a comparably manufactured Egyptian cartonnage was published in 1988 by Gina Laurin in the article *Conservation of Egyptian mummy from Swindon* (cf. Conservation of Ancient Egyptian Materials, Archaeology Section 85-95). A treatment of a cartonnage fragment in Hamburg *Kunst und Gewerbe* Art Museum in 1993 represented similar conservation issues (cf. J. Klocke, in: *Das Geheimnis der Mumien. Ewiges Leben am Nil. Hamburg 24. January – 20. April 1997*, München-New York 1997, 133-135). However, those treatments differ from that of mine because both artefacts did not suffer such devastation and despite deformations they maintained the original appearance.

Conservation assumptions

Since the cartonnage was an object of display, a typically preservative treatment was planned. Nevertheless, those preservative procedures resulted in restoration of the three-dimensional structure of the cartonnage and outlining its original appearance, as well as that of the mummy.

Also it should be stressed that all the proposed methods of treatment were in fact an innovation due to the unique character of this Egyptian artefact.[8]

Conservation treatment involved several steps:
- preservation of the paint layer,
- sizing of the grounds,
- sizing of the fabrics,
- consolidation of delaminated fabrics and grounds,
- repairing deformations of the cartonnage pieces,
- adhesion of torn cartonnage fragments,
- identifying the relationship of tiny monochromatic pieces of the head dress that finally created a three-dimensional structure,
- devising and manufacturing a display mount.

Conservation procedures

After all cartonnage pieces were removed from the coffin their surface was carefully brushed with small soft brushes from outside and inside. The dirt on polychrome and gilding was thoroughly cleaned with bread gum. Both layers were in a good condition so no chemical treatment was necessary. The polychrome was protected and the grounds impregnated by brushing a 7% solution of Paraloid B72 in xylene.

An important step in the treatment was restoration of technological properties of the bandages supporting the cartonnage. The weakened linen required an appropriate seizing material to strengthen the textile structure, yet to retain its flexibility.[9] A 15% solution of Paraloid B72 in acetone with 10% solution of polyglycol in methanol mixed in proportion of 1:2 proved to have the best properties. The cartonnage fabrics were seized by brushing but the shroud was sprayed to avoid stains. After the textile had been strengthened attempts were made to eradicate creases and deformation. Then it was immersed in a 10% solution of polyglycol in water with methanol[10] and relaxed under the weight of small pouches of sand.

Consolidation of delaminated linen and grounds was conducted by injecting a 10% solution of fish glue with glycol ethylene. Connecting torn cartonnage fragments was extremely time-consuming, and it proceeded parallel to eradication of creases and deformation. Edge to edge adhesion was done using a mixture of 30% gluten glue and a 20% solution of polyglycol in water in proportion of 3:1. The task was difficult, especially with the head dress, where only after the relationship of separate pieces had been established and the pieces stuck together a three-dimensional structure was revealed. The edge-to-edge joints were reinforced from the inside with decatized linen stripes masked with fragments of original bandages.[11] In parts of the head dress there were many losses in the pain layer. They were also filled in with original bandages.

The chest and leg plate and the boot cartonnage did not need additional reinforcement as after being treated they showed a good mechanical resistance. However, a reinforcement was necessary for the three-dimensional head dress structure. An additional support was created using fragments of decatized linen fabric gradually stuck with an acetone solution of Paraloid B72 modified with polyglycol ethylene. The utilised method was a kind of lining with a totally reversible adhesive that would not interfere with original layers of the cartonnage. (Photos 2 and 3 show stages of adhesion of the cartonnage pieces).

After conservation of the cartonnage had been completed, there was a time for devising a suitable display mount. It was thought that the best mount would be a form close to the original one, in this case – a kind of a mock mummy. The length, width and shape of the cartonnage determined the mount form. The fact that the cartonnage was brittle and built of three separate pieces and that the shroud was limp, made it impossible to create a negative of the mount. Therefore a positive of the mount had to be manufactured. Material chosen for the mount had to be inert, sturdy, light and easily processed to create the possibility of gradually building-up the form. Various materials used in conservation were taken into consideration for the purpose. The chosen one was an air-setting modeling paste that does

[9] Several textile samples were used to test various combinations of consolidants.

[10] For better agent penetration.

[11] They were bandages taken from the bottom of the coffin which were sufficiently well preserved.

not need firing in a kiln. Besides having all the desired properties the modeling paste was dough-like before hardening that eased the moulding of the mount and gave extra protection to the cartonnage during the work. When hardened and dry the mount was seized with a solution of Paraloid B72 in xylene and filled with polyurethane foam.

Previously prepared bandages, in the form of linen stripes, were mounted onto the "mummy" and point-stuck with vinyl polyacetate at the back and in places difficult to wrap. Then the cartonnage was replaced on the "mummy" and attached to the mount by close-to-the-original mounting method, e.g. by fastening with twisted linen threads through the existing mounting holes around the edges of the cartonnage. The bandages were dyed so their colour resembled that of the original one and yet it tone-differed from that of the original shroud. (Photos 4 and 5 show the cartonnage after conservation).

I hope that conservation of the cartonnage restored the original properties of this exceptional piece of art.[12]

[12] I would like to acknowledge the help of Professor Marian Paciorek; without his knowledge and expertise this treatment would not have been successful.

Photo 1.
Cartonnage of the mummy of priestess Aset-iri-khet-es. Property of the Archaeological Museum, Kraków. Cartonnage before conservation (phot. Tomasz Kalarus)

Photo 2.
Cartonnage of the mummy of priestess Aset-iri-khet-es. Property of the Archaeological Museum, Kraków. Main cartonnage plate during the treatment. The cartonnage placed on the "working mummy" mount, after cleaning, seizing of linen and grounds, and consolidation of the polychrome; during adhesion of separate pieces (phot. T. Kalarus)

Photo 3.
Cartonnage of the mummy of priestess Aset-iri-khet-es. Property of the Archaeological Museum, Kraków. Head dress with gilded face mask during the treatment; adhesion of separate pieces (phot. T. Kalarus)

Photo 4.
Cartonnage of the
mummy of priestess
Aset-iri-khet-es.
Property of the
Archaeological
Museum, Kraków.
Cartonnage after
conservation (phot.
T. Kalarus)

Photo 5.
Cartonnage of the
mummy of priestess
Aset-iri-khet-es.
Property of the
Archaeological
Museum, Kraków.
Head dress with gilded
face mask after
conservation (phot.
T. Kalarus)

Joanna Trąbska
Barbara Trybalska

Aset-iri-khet-es' mummy mask: pigments, their preparation and corrosion phenomena

The investigation of pigments applied on the mummy mask of Aset-iri-khet-es was undertaken to identify the substances used as pigments, to reconstruct preparation and application techniques, and to observe corrosion phenomena. Samples were taken from the blue, green, yellow and red paint layers. The following compounds were discovered: Egyptian blue, Egyptian green, green natural (?) copper compounds (sulphates, chlorides, phosphates), orpiment in two fraction groups, and red paint of mixed natural and mineral (haematite) origin. Egyptian blue and green were found to corrode into morphologically varied green basic-copper chlorides.

Introduction

Pigment definition

According to Doerner [1975], a pigment is a powdered substance that is not soluble in binders, while a dye is a similar substance that is soluble. Doerner discerns two groups of pigments: organic and inorganic. Inorganic pigments are mineral paints (which he fails to define, JT, BT). Organic pigments are derived from plant or animal substances, nowadays usually of synthetic origin. "Earth colors" refer to mineral paint occurring in nature.

Mora et al. [1983] describe five groups of coloring agents:
– natural pigments derived from ores: oxides, sulphates, sulphides, carbonates and others,
– synthetic mineral pigments,
– natural organic pigments obtained from animals or plants,
– synthetic organic dyes belonging to the aniline, chinonine, phenol or other groups,

– mixed pigments, for example, organic substances precipitated on an inorganic underlayer.

The pigments of Ancient Egypt

Egyptian craftsmanship has been widely described in the Theban papyri [Stawicki 1987] and in a fundamental work by Lucas and Harris [1962]. Both include detailed information on the application of various organic and mineral dyes and pigments. A more recent study by Blom-Böer [1994] presents a rich spectrum of pigments complete with information on chronology and occurrence (Table 1).

Table 1.
Pigments identified in Ancient Egypt after Blom-Böer [1994]

[1] Synonyms include: Thenard blue or Amarna blue [Blom-Böer 1994]

Color	Pigment	Ptolemaic period
Blue	Azurite, Egyptian blue, cobalt blue[1]	Egyptian blue
Green	Malachite, chrysocolla, verdigris, Egyptian green, copper glass, basic copper chlorides, mixtures of yellow and blue pigments	Egyptian green, basic copper chlorides (Early Ptolemaic period)
Yellow	Ochres, jarosite, orpiment, organic yellow	Ochres
Orange, Red	Ochres, ochres with madder, haematite, realgar, lead red oxides	Ochres
Brown, Beige	Ochres, mixtures of ochres and gypsum	(Early Ptolemaic period)
White	Gypsum, anhydrite, calcium carbonate, dolomite, huntite, lead white	Calcium carbonate (Early Ptolemaic period)
Grey	Mixture of black and white pigments (e.g. gypsum), pale yellow ochres with bone black, lamp black	
Black	Bone black, lamp black, pyrolusite and other manganese compounds	

Egyptian blue and Egyptian green

Detailed information on Egyptian blue is included in a monographic chapter by Riederer [1997] in *Artists' Pigments*, vol. III. Egyptian blue is defined as an equivalent of cuprorivaite $CaCuSi_4O_{11}$, sometimes with wollastonite $CaSiO_3$ and quartz added. Its other names: blue frit, copper frit, *Frittenblau*, are misleading. According to glass and enamel technologists, frit and glass are **both** amorphous. Egyptian blue, having the crystalline structure of cuprorivaite, has absolutely nothing in common with frit.

Known from the 31st century B.C., it was probably the first synthetic pigment in the history of mankind. It may have been discovered accidentally as a slag component, a by-product of copper smelting. It consists of chiefly calcium carbonate, copper carbonate (or other copper compounds), quartz, sometimes natrium or potassium compounds, added as fluxes. Their proportion was usually 4 SiO_2:CaO:CuO. Substrates were heated between 850°C and 1150°C and the process itself might have been so complex that products varying in shade and composition (from mineral to glass with intermediate stages) were obtained. As the recipe is known only from Vitruvius, many experiments have been performed in modern times. It has been suggested [Jaksch et al. 1988, vide Riederer 1997] that Egyptian blue was not manufactured in a single fritting or smelting process, but that it took a number of stages to arrive at the final product. Glass was ground to powder and heated repeatedly to obtain the pigment. It may have been produced during a long and slow cooling operation [S. Siwulski, oral comment].

Blom-Böer [1994] discerned green frit (defining it only as "silicate pigment", without giving any details) and green copper glass. She pointed to the different availability of the pigments (the former was expensive) and their very different stability (the latter was susceptible to corrosion into basic copper chlorides or malachite). The question is whether this "green frit" is crystalline or not, and whether the name has been used logically. If the discernment criterion is pigment structure alone, then it may of course be accepted. Whatever the case may be, this remark should not be construed as suggesting two different pigments being manufactured during separate processes [S. Siwulski, oral comment].

Egyptian blue varies in shade from dark blue through pale blue to green, depending on grain size, technological regime, substrates proportion and specific composition. An interesting colour scheme of blue and green hues was presented by Busz and Sengle [1999]. Riederer [1997] maintains that Egyptian blue is stable in all kinds of binders and environments. It has been stated, however, that in the presence of chloride ions it corrodes into green basic copper chlorides [Schiegl et al. 1989]. Pigments obtained from glass are extremely unstable [Blom-Böer 1994] mainly due to the alcali content [S. Siwulski, oral comment].

Egyptian blue is known from sarcophagi, wall painting, painted sculptures, occasionally pottery, seldom textiles. Apart from Egypt, it has been identified in Assyria, Greece, Crete, the Roman Empire and in Italy of the Etruscan period. It is known to have occurred in Central Europe and Italy until the Middle Ages, although it was never mentioned in the manuscripts of the time [Riederer 1997].

Green copper pigments of natural origin

Malachite, also used as a cosmetic, has been identified in Egyptian art [Lucas and Harris 1962]. Blom-Böer [1994] also mentions chrysocolla and basic copper chlorides. According to her, only the former is characteristic of the Early Ptolemaic period. Natural copper pigments were mined mainly in Sinai outcrops. It is a well known phenomena to ore geologists that a certain group of minerals (copper in this case) may easily alter into another, and this barely a few centimetres away in the ore layer. The kind of mineral depends on many factors, including the presence of characteristic anions, level of pH and Eh, Gibbs free energy values, moisture and others. The result is an association of minerals with one mineral prevailing (mostly malachite or chrysocolla). Green copper minerals are extremely similar, hence an identification based only on copper ion detection is absolutely insufficient.

Note should be taken whenever chrysocolla is mentioned as a pigment. It is in fact not a mineral, but a mineral phase, amorphous to a different degree, resembling very much a glassy substance. Only IR spectroscopy examination of unpolluted grains may be considered credible [Holeczek 1990].

Basic copper chlorides of different origin – synthetic and as a product of corrosion

Basic copper chlorides occur as three polymorphs of $Cu_2(OH)_3Cl$: botallackite (monoclinic), atacamite (orthorhombic) and clinoatacamite (monoclinic). The paratacamite (rhomboedral) that some have identified should actually be renamed as clinoatacamite. It requires about 2% of zinc to stabilize its structure and its formula should be written as $Cu_3(Cu, Zn)(OH)Cl_2$ [Jambor et al. 1996]. Some other rare copper compounds, summarised by Scott [2000], have been found in objects of art. Unfortunately, basic copper chlorides are often non-stechiometric, hence their unclear and misleading properties. Their morphology observed under a scanning microscope varies from flakes and splinters to trigonal-shaped crystals and other [e.g. Hannington 1993; Butuzova 1989]. When observed under a polarizing microscope, they are of yellowish-green colour under parallel Nicol prisms, either pleochroic or not, with medium relief, and greyish interference colour. All these features suggest the basic copper chlorides group, but, as these usually occur in the form of agglomerates, it is extremely difficult to identify the proper polymorph.

The synthetic pigment and the corrosion product are both highly similar, occurring as irregular agglomerates or flakes. They differ morphologically from the natural, well-crystallized atacamite [Trąbska 1998]. Synthetic basic copper chlorides are very easy to obtain, e.g. sprinkling salty water on a copper sheet surface or hanging copper sheets, smeared with honey and salted, above the surface of dry wine or vinegar [Teofil Prezbiter 1998]. They may also be by-products of artificial malachite production [Naumova et al. 1990; Rahn-Koltermann et al. 1993]. Contemporary painters do not appreciate them as they tend do dissolve in humid conditions, freeing a chloride ion that is exceedingly aggressive.

Chloride and sulphur ion origin and their corrosive properties

In the presence of the chloride and sulphur ions, the components of a paint layer, as well as of the rendering, may corrode. Chloride ions may originate, among others, from salts in a sea breeze or found in the soil in a hot and dry climate. Copper pigments – malachite, azurite, chrysocolla and Egyptian blue and green – are unstable in such conditions and basic copper chlorides form on their surfaces, penetrating deep inside. The process may be short-lived, lasting merely a few months [Trąbska 1998]. The products are both stechiometric (clinoatacamite and atacamite) and non-stechiometric.

Chlorides are very mobile in the natural environment [Pazdro 1986], as well as in materials applied on historical objects. They are the cause of what is called "chloride disease" (among others Schiegl [1989]): chloride compounds, easily soluble, are a constant source of chloride ions, which have very strong corrosive properties, reacting easily both with pigments [Trąbska 1998] and the compounds used in the rendering layer [Kurdowski 1994]. Products that frequently expand tend to destroy the object not only chemically, but also mechanically: the stability and volumetric properties differ from that of the primary substance. This type of corrosion also leads to colour change, almost unnoticeable for the green pigment, but quite spectacular in the case of the blue one (blue-green transformation).

The sulphate ion is less aggressive. It has been proved experimentally [Trąbska 1998] that in the presence of the sulphate ion malachite and azurite change their optical properties slightly slowly becoming amorphous, a process that is detectable in XRD analyses. The kinetics of chloride and sulphate corrosion reactions may be modified, however, by many factors (including a specific cation assemblage [Kurdowski 1991].

Red

Red dyes for colouring stones and textiles may have been prepared as described below [Stawicki 1987, 126]. Alkanet could have been mixed with mulberry fruit, the kermes insect and sea lichens, after which the medium was added. Stones were reddened with alkanet mixed with turpentine oil [ibidem, 250] or alkanet diluted in oil, pigeon blood, sinopia, vinegar and the so-called stone of mica [ibidem, 246]. Glaze with red copper oxide was also used in the way described later by Theophilus [Teofil Prezbiter 1998, 44]: copper powder was heated, ground and mixed with green glass and so called Greek sapphire, next wine or urine was added. Glass was painted with the mixture and then fired. The list of substances of plant and animal origin is long. The list contains kermes obtained from the Aphis *Kermes illica (K. vermilio, Coccus illicis)*, alkanet, safflower (*Carthamus tinctoris*), madder (*Rubia tinctorum*) (a deep red shade was obtained when applied on an alumina ground), fruits of *Arbutus andrachne*, mezereon (*Daphne mezereum, D. laureola*).

In the group of mineral pigments, red clay is mentioned, including sinopia and iron rust. The latter was poured wit hot vinegar which dissolved the ferric oxides, forming a liquid that gave textiles a red-brown shade. Cinnabar is also mentioned [Stawicki 1987], as well as haematite, red ochre, realgar, and red lead oxides [Lucas, Harris 1962; Blom-Böer 1994].

Orpiment

Orpiment As_2S_3 was called *arsenikon* in Greek [Stawicki 1987]. It is a monoclinic mineral with perfect cleavage in specific crystallographic directions. The resultant scaly jointing [Bolewski, Manecki 1993] provides a glittering effect that has led to its use as gold imitation (compare Photo 1). In ancient times, both natural and synthetic orpiment was known. The latter was produced by the "dry method" of heating substrates together or the "wet method" of mixing solutions. Unfortunately, it is impossible to discern the natural from the synthetic pigment or the varieties of the latter. Grain diameter may be the sole criterion, the naturally obtained pigment being coarser as a rule. But still one cannot be uncritical: grounding the mineral led to the appearance of both coarse and fine (even 1 micrometer) particles. Orpiment is stable as a pigment, but it is known that in an ozone atmosphere or in a glue medium it may turn white due to the creation of white powdered arsenic trioxide As_2O_3. Lucas and Harris [1962] say that synthetic orpiment was far more toxic than the natural kind and this, since it was a widely recognised fact, limited its use. Generally, orpiment was popular in Egypt, especially between the 15th and 11th century B.C., although it has also been identified in the 3rd millennium B.C. It was applied in wall paintings, mummy masks, polychromed stones, coffins from the 31st to the 6th century B.C. [Riederer 1997]. It has not been identified on objects from the Ptolemaic period [Blom-Böer 1994].

Mines of orpiment known since antiquity occur in the present territory of Georgia, Iran, Iraq, Kurdistan and in the Caucasus [Bolewski, Manecki 1993].

Orpiment was applied together with other yellow pigments: massicote, sulphur, ochres, and with organic dyes. Flaky orpiment was regarded as the best, but a lump variety was also acceptable. At least several kinds were available, varying in origin and properties [Drwal-Dziurawiec 1979]. Orpiment was applied as gold imitation "on parchment, papyrus, marble and other objects" [Stawicki 1987, 77], including "copper, silver, small metal statuettes and small shields" [ibidem, 235]. Applied in chrysography, it was mixed with Arabic gum and water [ibidem, 231] or with powdered glass, egg white, white gum and saffron [ibidem, 232]. It was also mixed with copperas, realgar, mercury, tragant oil and other organic substances [ibidem, 77]. Orpiment was known also from Assyria, and not very common in Greece or Rome; it was applied widely by the Arabs and painters of India, Japan, China, Tibet, Mediaeval Europe until recent times.

Experimental methods

Preliminary observations were performed with the use of binocular lenses (Carl Zeiss Jena). A polarizing microscope for transmitting light (Carl Zeiss Jena) was applied to observe the optical features of grains, magnifying the image 100 times. A scanning microscope JEOL JSM 5400 with an X-ray microanalyser EDXS AN Link (Oxford Instruments, Link Isis 3) enabled precise observation of pigment shape, size and corrosion processes. An X-ray diffraction analysis performed on the „X"pert apparatus by Philips, with Cu radiation, identified Egyptian blue as cuprorivaite.

Results

Blue pigment

The painting layer consists of blue grains of a dark and pale shade, slightly broken with green. Grains are irregular in shape, devoid of any crystallographic features, the fracture is angular, flaky. Grain diameter varies from about 0.01 to 0.03 mm. In transmitted light under parallel Nicols, a light blue colour

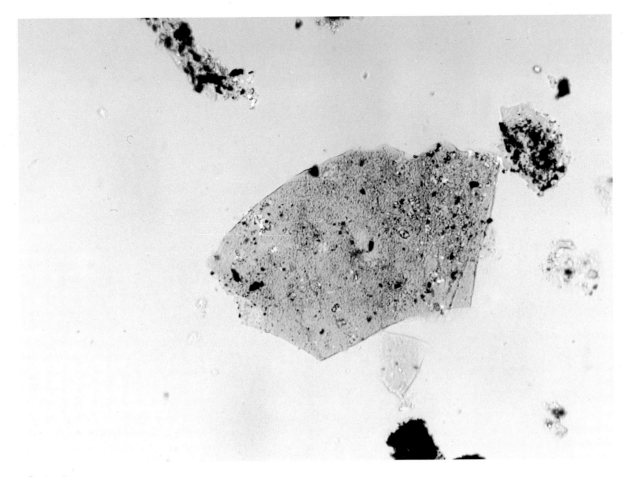

Photo 1.
Orpiment: it's flaky habit and scaly jointing provides a specific glittering effect that has led to its use as gold imitation.
A polarizing microscope, parallel Nicol prisms, magnification 600 times (phot. J. Trąbska)

without pleochroism is observed. Binder is present, but its concentration is very low. When the Nicol prisms are crossed, the grains are observed to be blue-green. Macroscopically, on the surface of the paint layer, tiny clusters (0.2 mm) of white and creamy impurities are observed, as well as tiny black spots of unknown origin. The diameter of pigment grains observed in scanning microscopy equals about 25 micrometers. The edges of grains are irregular, probably due to dissolution corrosion processes (Photo 2).

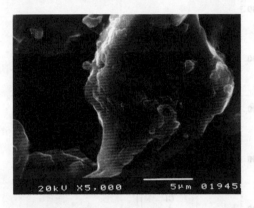

Photo 2.
Blue paint layer. Grain of Egyptian blue. Note corroded, flaky edges (phot. B. Trybalska)

Other phenomena were also observed: not only do the pigment grains have flaky and rounded edges, but also the initial crystals are of a trigonal shape (Photo 3, P1). This is significant for basic copper chlorides: clinoatacamite and atacamite, appearing in the presence of a rather high chloride-ion concentration [Trąbska 1998].

Photo 3.
Blue paint layer. Grain of Egyptian blue, undergoing chloride corrosion. Note the initial crystal phase of clinoatacamite or atacamite (P1); 1 cm = 5,7 μm (phot. B. Trybalska)

EDX chemical analysis performed at spot P1 indicates quite high chloride levels (Figure 1) contrasted with the lack of chloride in other places on the pigment surface (Figure 2).

Figure 1.
EDXS chemical analysis performed at spot P1, presented in Photo 3. Note the high level of chloride

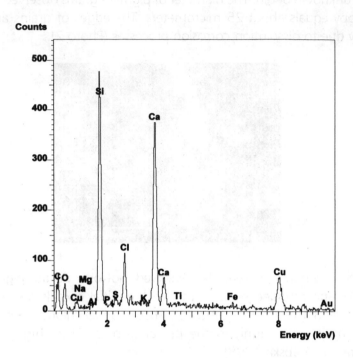

Figure 2.
EDXS chemical analysis of the pigment surface. No chlorides found here

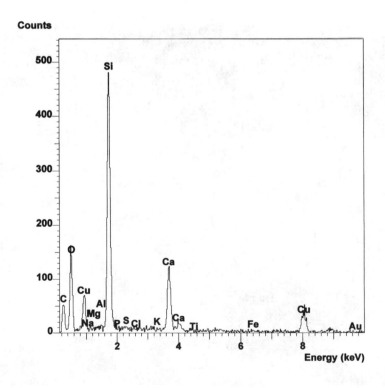

EDXS chemical analysis of a fragment of the blue paint layer shows a high concentration of silica, a lower one of calcium and the lowest of copper. Minute amounts of alumina, chloride, potassium, iron and sulphur have been noted.

The chemical composition of the examined grains, as well as the XRD phase analysis, prove the presence of Egyptian blue with the crystal structure of cuprorivaite (Figure 3).[2] Iron is a common impurity in substrates of Egyptian blue, and potassium may come from a flux: potassium bicarbonate. Sulphur may come either from intentionally added gypsum or from environmental contamination with salts containing sulphur (it may also be gypsum). Chloride occurs together with copper, calcium, silica and sulphur (Figure 4) and is dispersed on the pigment surface.

Thus, the process of chloride corrosion has been noted.

[2] Microscopically, the crystal habit of Egyptian blue, identified as cuprorivaite, is very rarely observed [Riederer 1997].

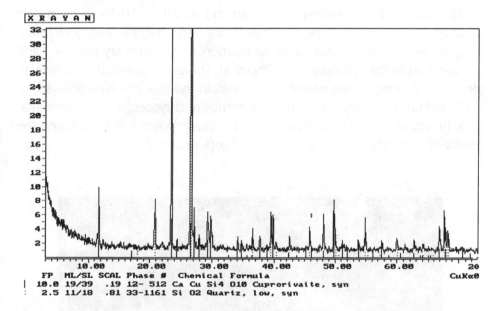

Figure 3.
Blue paint layer. XRD phase analysis of the blue pigment reveals a mixture of cuprorivaite and quartz

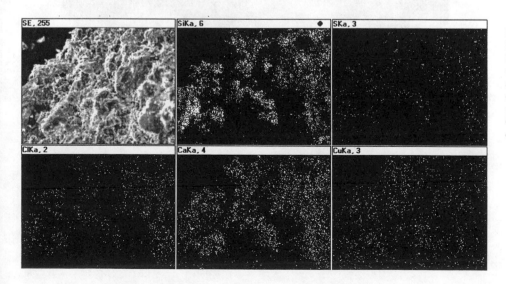

Figure 4.
Blue paint layer. Mapping shows the distribution of chloride and sulphur versus the elements in the pigments (Si, Cu, Ca). Good correlation is clearly visible

Green pigments

The green paint layer consists of very tiny pigments with an earthy lustre and grassy-green hue, locally clustered as irregular lumps. Their grainy structure is revealed at 50 times magnification. Single blue grains, as well as transparent ones, are minor admixtures. Microscopic observation reveals a weak, greenish-yellow colour, green pleochroism, flaky habit. The interference colours are low, grey.

The surface of the paint layer is locally contaminated with small spots of a resin-like substance.

Scanning microscopic observation allowed two kinds of pigments to be discerned. In the first case the paint layer has a crusty appearance and one notices, instead of single apparent grains (as in the case of Egyptian blue), flakes covering each another, of a diameter equal to 10-15 micrometers (smaller than Egyptian blue). The flakes are very irregular and their habit suggests an advanced process of dissolution of the primary pigment and precipitation of the secondary one (Photo 4). The green grains are of Egyptian green as indicated by the presence, revealed in the EDX chemical analysis, of Si, Ca and Cu. One may discuss the occurrence of chrysocolla in this particular case. In fact, no specific conclusion may be drawn when not considering the results of IR spectroscopy examination of a pure sample.

Photo 4.
Green paint layer. Egyptian green grains with flaky corrosion products (phot. B. Trybalska)

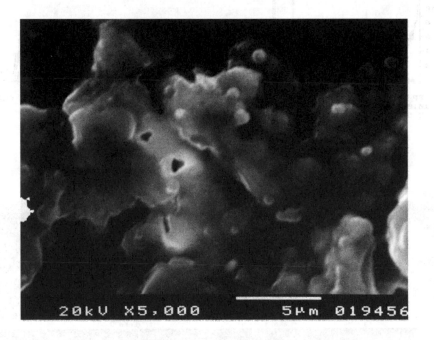

Apart from a large quantity of silica, as well as calcium and copper, quite a high concentration of chloride and sulphur together with a smaller amount of potassium is noted (Figure 5). Substances formed at the expense of Egyptian blue include basic copper chlorides, here present in abundance.

The next analysis (compare Photo 5, Figure 6) of the green paint layer brings new information about pigments. Their morphology does not resemble the previous one (compare Photo 4, Figure 5). Large grains, of about 70 micrometers, with uncorroded edges (straight and smooth) are immersed in a very fine-grained neighbourhood. The EDXS chemical analysis reveals the following data: grain 1 consists of Si and O only, grain 2 of Cu, Si, Ca, grain 3 of Cu, Ca, Cl, grain 4 of Cu, Ca, S, P, Cl, grain 5 of Si, S, Ca, Cu, Cl, grain 6 of Cu, O, C (Figure 6).

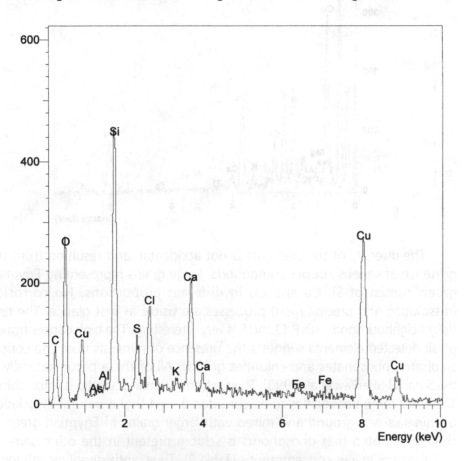

Figure 5.
EDXS chemical analysis of the surface of the pigment presented on Photo 5. Note the high level of chloride and sulphur

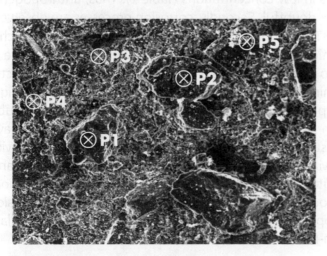

Photo 5.
Green paint layer consisting of uncorroded Egyptian green (large grains), sulphates, phosphates and chlorides of copper; 1 cm = 25 μm (phot. B. Trybalska)

Figure 6.
EDXS chemical analysis
of grain 4 from the
pigment surface
presented in Photo 5

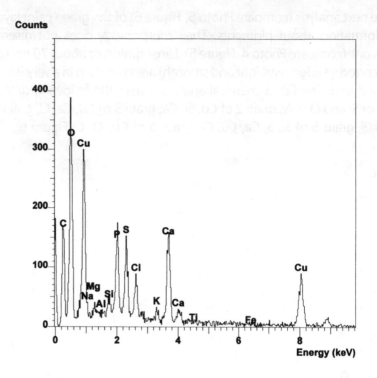

The diversity of the elements is not accidental, and resulting from the presence of various copper compounds. Large grains representing Egyptian green consist of Si, Ca and Cu in different proportions. No corrosion (dissolution and precipitation) processes are visible at first glance. The tiny, flaky neighbourhood with P, Cl and S is very interesting. The high concentration of all detected elements suggests the presence of minerals from the copper sulphates, phosphates and chlorides groups. All of these occur naturally in the Sinai [El-Sharkavi et al. 1990]. Their extremely small diameter is astonishing. There are three possibilities to be considered. First that a natural association of minerals was ground and mixed with larger grains of Egyptian green. It should be noted that phosphorus is seldom present in the other samples and it occurs in low concentrations (Table 2). Thus, anthropogenic influence here is rather doubtful. Secondly, corrosion processes are observed here as in other cases. The chemical composition of grain 5 suggests such a situation (Cl, S). Additionally, a more thorough observation of the surface of Egyptian green (Photo 6, P1) reveals the presence of flaky and round structures, where copper dominates over silica, calcium, chloride and sulphur (Figure 7). This type of morphology results from the dissolution of the initial substance and precipitation of some or all of its components. The process may occur in a number of stages. The outflux of silica (active in an alkali environment) is connected with the precipitation of non-stechiometric sulphates and chlorides.

Last but not least, the presence of flaky basic copper chlorides in the neighbourhood of large grains may result not only from corrosion, but also from the application of synthetic basic copper chlorides, popular in ancient Egypt [Blom-Böer 1994].

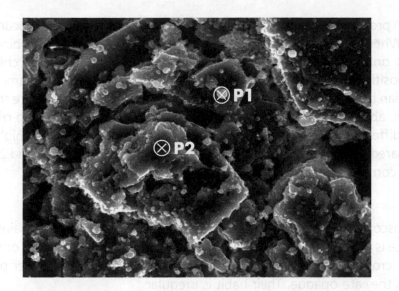

Photo 6.
Egyptian green:
magnification of a
grain presented in
Photo 5. Rounded (P1)
and flaky (P2) forms
result from chloride
corrosion active in
grain surface processes;
1 cm = 5 μm
(phot. B. Trybalska)

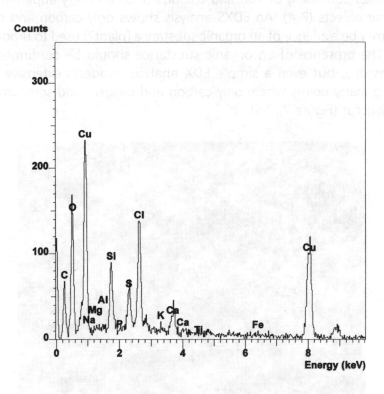

Figure 7.
EDX chemical analysis
of rounded forms (P1).
Note the very low silica
content

A probable conclusion is that all three possibilities may occur concurrently.

When observing Egyptian blue and green, even with the use of binocular lenses only, the difference between their morphology, diameter, chemical composition and corrosion intensity is easily observable. The diameter of Egyptian blue grains is about 25 micrometers and the green grains are smaller, that is, about 10 micrometers (compare Photos 2 and 4). The ratio of CaO/CuO differs: in blue grains the amount of calcium is significantly higher, as compared to the green ones, than that of copper (e.g. Figures 1 and 2). The latter corrode far more intensively.

Red

Macroscopically, no pigment grains are visible. The lustre of the paint-layer surface is fatty. Tiny (0.1 mm) blisters occur locally. Microscopically, observed under crossed Nicol prisms, the pigment grains are dark red, under parallel Nicols they are opaque. Their habit is irregular.

In scanning microscopy, tiny (about 10 micrometers) particles of Ca, Si, Cl (considerable) and Al, P, Mg, S, Fe are visible (Photo 7, P 1). There are also small clusters of not well crystallised gypsum (or another calcium sulphate; P 2), small flakes consisting of iron and chloride (P 3) and very apparent, large, columnar objects (P 4). An EDXS analysis shows only carbon and oxygen, which may be evidence of an organic substance (plant?) used to produce the paint. The presence of an organic substance should be confirmed by IR spectroscopy, but even a simple EDX analysis suggests extensive usage, showing many points where only carbon and oxygen, and sometimes also sulphur occur (Figure 7, P 5).

Photo 7.
Red paint layer. Large, columnar object represents fragments of an organic (plant?) substrate for pigment production (?). Generally, the surface consists of a mixture of clay minerals, gypsum, single occurrences of Fe compounds and organic components; 1 cm = 25 μm (phot. B. Trybalska)

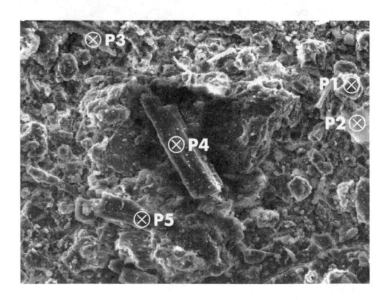

Both the morphology and the results of the chemical analyses exclude the use of red mineral pigments alone. A homogenous, locally cracked surface (Photo 8) with a fatty lustre suggests the application of a paint with predominant organic substances. The amount of iron (note the EDXS analyses) is very low (Figure 8), but in single spots it reaches a high level of concentration. Haematite and haematite with a high admixture of titanium (not ochres!)[3] were used (Figure 9).

[3] Haematite is a mineral Fe_2O_3 and ochres are always mixtures of hydroxyoxides of iron, clay minerals, quartz and other admixtures.

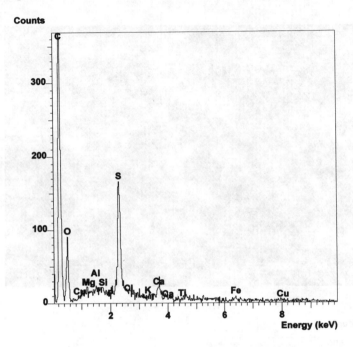

Figure 8.
EDXS chemical analysis performed at spot 5, suggests the presence of an organic substance

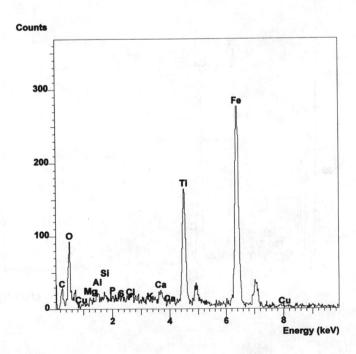

Figure 9.
EDXS chemical analysis of a haematite grain (with titanium admixture)

The red paint layer is strongly polluted with chloride compounds of external origin in considerable quantity. They are present in an organic (animal?) object on the surface of the paint layer (Photo 8, Figure 10), which consists of primarily calcium carbonate subsequently impregnated with chlorides.

The red paint consists therefore of many substrates: organic ones of both long and irregular shape, flaky concentration of aluminosilicates, calcium carbonate, haematite, gypsum, chlorides.

Photo 8.
Red paint layer. Crusty and cracked surface of the paint consists mainly of organic substances. A long object is a fragment of an organic (animal?) skeleton impregnated by chlorides;
1 cm = 5 μm
(phot. B. Trybalska)

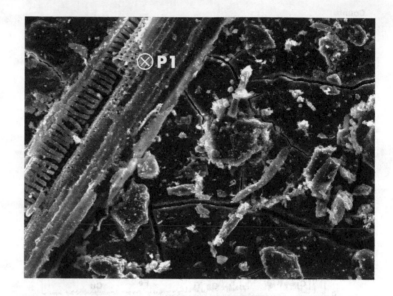

Figure 10.
EDXS chemical analysis of the spot P1. Note the very high concentration of chlorides

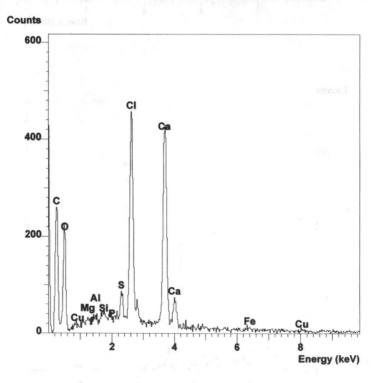

Yellow

The paint layer is very thin. Two kinds of pigments are discernible macroscopically: tiny grains of a lemon yellow, and coarser ones of orange yellow, applied with the same brush movements. The pigment lustre is fatty. Tiny quartz grains are present as an admixture. Single grains of a black substance are present on the surface of the paint layer.

The yellow pigment is As_2S_3, as concluded from the EDXS analysis. Arsenic and sulphur occur together unambigously (Figure 11). Larger grains are 50 micrometers long, whereas the smaller ones are crusty, irregular, just a few micrometers in size (Photo 9). As in the other samples, a certain amount of chloride was detected. In the rendering, calcium carbonate and quartz were used.

In conclusion, two varieties of orpiment were detected, differing in grain diameter and hue.

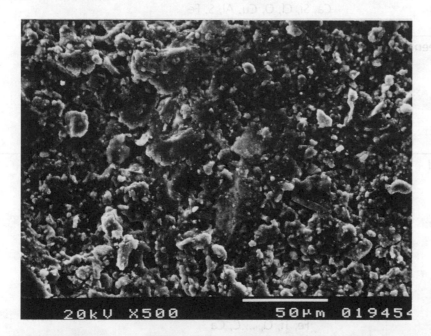

Photo 9.
Yellow paint layer.
Tiny and coarse grains
of orpiment are clearly
visible
(phot. B. Trybalska)

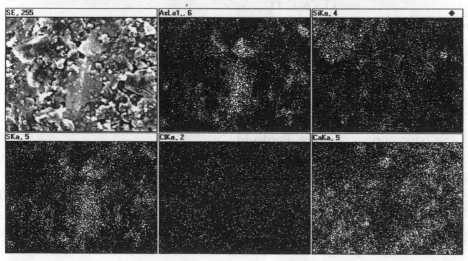

Figure 11.
Yellow paint layer.
Mapping shows the
distribution of arsenium
versus sulphur

Chloride and sulphate corrosion

Chloride and sulphate ions are always present in the EDX chemical analyses of each pigment (Table 2).

Table 2.
Summary of EDXS chemical analyses performed on samples from the Aset-iri-khet-es' mummy mask. The elements are grouped according to their relative concentration. The analyses quoted in this paper are in bold. Note the occurrence of chloride and sulphate ions

Pigment	EDX analysis	Percentage of chloride and sulphur presence
Blue	Si, Ca, O, Cu, Cl, K, Fe Si, Ca, O, Cu, C Si, Ca, Cu, O, Cl Si, O, Ca, C, Cu **Si, Ca, Cl, Cu, O, C, S** **Si, O, Ca, Cu** Cl, Ca, Cu, O, C, S, Si Ca, Cl, Cu, Si, S, O, C Ca, Si, Cl, O, Cu, Al, S, Fe Ca, Cl, O, C, Cu, Si	70% of Cl 10% of S
Green	Si, Ca, Cu, O, C, Cl Cu, Si, Ca, O, C Cu, Ca, S, O, C, Fe Cu, Ca, Si, O, C Cu, Ca, Cl, S, Cl, Fe, O, C **O, Cu, C, Ca, S, P, Cl, Si, Al, K** **Cu, O, Cl, Si, C, S, Ca, K**	70% of Cl 57% of S
Red	Cl, Ca, O, C, Si, S, Al, Fe, Mg Cl, Ca, O, Fe, C, Si, Al C, S, Ca, Cl, O **Cl, Ca, C, O, S, Si** C, O, Ca, S Si, O, Al, Ca, Mg, Fe, K, Cl Fe, Ca, Cl, O, C, Si Ca, Si, Fe, Cl, S, Al, O, K, C Ca, O, Si, Cl, C, Al, Fe, P, Mg, S S, Ca, O, C, Si, K, Al, Fe Fe, Ti, O, ...C, Ca Cl, Ca, C, O, ...S, Si	83% of Cl 50% Cl
Rendering	**Ca, O, C, ...Cl, S**	

Chloride ions occur as:
- flaky, rounded edges of pigment grains (Photo 2),
- flakes on the pigment surface (Photo 4),
- a basic copper chloride (Photo 5)
- round, tiny structures, dispersed on the pigment surface (Photos 3 and 6),
- initial trigonal crystals of clinoatacamite and atacamite (Photo 3),
- chloride compounds indiscernible from the other components of paint layers, dispersed on top of them (e.g. Figure 4),
- chloride compounds indiscernible from the other components of the rendering (e.g. Figure 12),

- impregnating calcium carbonate impurities present on the surface of the paint layer (Photo 8).

Sulphur is present in the examined samples:

- as a constituent of the pigments (e.g. orpiment, green natural pigments, Figures 6 or 11),
- dispersed on the paint layer surface (e.g. Figure 4),
- dispersed on the surface of Egyptian blue (Photo 6),
- forming irregular flakes and round-shaped forms together with chloride compounds (Photo 6),
- as a constituent of organic particles (Figure 8),
- impregnating impurities on the surfaces of paint layers together with chloride compounds (e.g. Figure 4),
- in small amounts present in the rendering (Figure 12),
- single "amorphous" grains on the surface of a pigment (Photo 7).

The concentration of sulphate contaminants is generally lower than that of chloride ones. An examination of the rendering proves that calcium sulphate is not intentionally mixed in: sulphur is only an impurity (Figure 12).

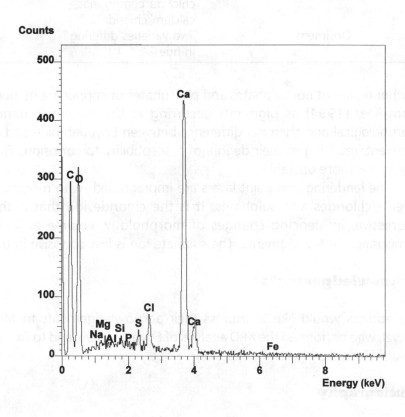

Figure 12.
EDXS chemical analysis of the rendering: the intentional use of calcium sulphates has to be excluded

Conclusions

Pigment examination results are summarised in Table 3.

Table 3.
Pigments identified on the mask of the mummy of Aset-iri-khet-es

Colour	Pigment	Other substances	Remarks
Blue	Egyptian blue: cuprorivaite	Quartz, dispersed chlorides, basic copper chlorides, aluminosilicates	Basic copper chlorides as corrosion products
Green	Egyptian green: silicate of copper and calcium	Copper and chloride compounds	copper corrosion
Green	Sulphates, phosphates and copper chlorides		Natural origin slightly more probable than one due to corrosion. Possible presence of synthetic copper chlorides
Red	Mixture of organic red and haematite	Calcium sulphate, aluminosilicates, calcium carbonate, chloride compounds, calcium chloride	
Yellow	Orpiment	Two varieties differing in hue	

Neither orpiment nor sulphates and phosphates of copper are mentioned by Blom-Böer [1994] as pigments occurring in the Ptolemaic period. The morphological and chemical difference between Egyptian blue and green is apparent, resulting in their degree of susceptibility to corrosion. The green pigment is more unstable.

The rendering and paint layers are impregnated with morphologically diverse chlorides and sulphates. It is the chloride ion that is the most aggressive, influencing changes of morphology, volume and chemical composition of the pigments. The sulphate ion is less corrosive in this case.

Acknowledgements

The authors would like to express their acknowledgements to Mr. Adam Gaweł, who performed the XRD analysis of Egyptian blue, and to Dr. Stanisław Siwulski for a very helpful discussion.

Bibliography

I. Blom-Böer, *Zusammensetzung Altägyptischer Farbpigmente und ihre Herkunfltlagerstätten,* in: *Zeit und Raum*, (OMRO) Oudheid Kundige Mede Delingen 74, 1994
A. Bolewski, A. Manecki, *Mineralogia szczegółowa*, Warszawa 1993

R. Busz, G. Sengle, *Zur Kieselkeramik-Begriffe, Werkstoffe, Verfahren*, in: R. Busz, P. Gercke (eds.), *Türkis und Azur. Quartzkeramik im Orient und Okzident*, Kassel 1999

G. J. Butuzowa, L. E. Szterenberg, B. J. Woronin, N. B. Gorkova, *Atakamit v metalonosnykh osadkakh atlanticheskogo okeana*, Doklady Akademii Nauk SSSR 309, no. 5, 1989

M. Doerner, *Materiały malarskie i ich zastosowanie*, Warszawa 1975

M. A. El-Sharkavi, M. M. El-Aref Abdel Motelib, *Syngenetic and paleocarstic copper mineralization in the Paleozoic platform sediments of West Central Sinai, Egypt*, Spec. Publs int. Ass. Sediment. 11, 1990

M. D. Hannington, *The formation of atacamite during weathering of sulphides on the modern seafloor*, Canadian Mineralogist 31, 1993

J. Holeczek, *Minerały wtórne strefy utlenienia związków polimetalicznych z okolic Miedzianki w Sudetach*, Masters Thesis, Silesian University, Katowice-Sosnowiec 1990

J. L. Jambor, J. E. Dutrizac, A. C. Roberts, J. D. Grice, J. T. Szymański, *Clinoatacamite, a new polymorph of $Cu_2(OH)_3Cl$ and its relationship to paratacamite and 'anarakite'*, Canadian Mineralogist 34, 1996

W. Kurdowski, *Chemia cementu*, 1991

W. Kurdowski, *Proces korozji zaczynów cementowych w roztworach chlorków o dużym stężeniu*, Projekt badawczy nr 7 7308 9203. WIMiC, AGH, Kraków 1994

A. Lucas, J. R. Harris, *Ancient Egyptian Materials and Industries*, London 1962

P. Mora, L. Mora, P. Philippot, *Conservation of Wall Paintings*, London 1983

M. M. Naumova, S. A. Pisareva, G. O. Nechiporenko, *Green copper pigments of old Russian frescoes*, Studies in Conservation 35, 1990

Z. Pazdro, *Hydrogeologia*, Warszawa 1986

G. Rahn-Koltermann, O. Glemser, D. Oltrogge, R. Fuchs, *Grünspan – Ein bedeutsames Pigment für das Scriptorum des Mittelalters*, Naturwissenschaftliche Rundschau 46 (6), 1993

J. Riederer, *Egyptian blue*, in: *Artists' Pigments. A Handbook of Their History and Characteristics*, ed. E. West FitzHugh, Washington 1997

S. Schiegl, K. Weiner, A. El Goresy, *Discovery of copper chloride cancer in Ancient Egyptian polychromic wall paintings and faience. A developing archaeological disaster*, Die Naturwissenschaften 79 (9), 1989

D. Scott, *A review of copper chlorides and related salts in bronze corrosion and as painting pigments*, Studies in Conservation 45, 2000

S. Stawicki, *Papirusy tebańskie. Antyczne źródło wiedzy o technikach artystycznych*, Wrocław 1987

Teofil Prezbiter, *Diversarum Artium Schedula. Średniowieczny zbiór przepisów o sztukach rozmaitych*, Tyniec-Kraków 1998

J. Trąbska, *Studium mineralogiczno-chemiczne wybranych pigmentów stosowanych w malowidłach średniowiecznych Polski*, Ph. D. Thesis, Kraków 1998

E. West FitzHugh, *Orpiment and Realgar*, in: *Artists' Pigments. A Handbook of Their History and Characteristics*, ed. E. West FitzHugh, Washington 1997

Gomaa Mohamed Mahmoud Abdel-Maksoud

Conservation of Egyptian mummies.
Part I: Experimental study on the Ancient Egyptian technique of mummification

Mummification is considered to be one of the most noticable and shining signs in the history of Ancient Egyptian civilisation. This is due to the influence on Egyptian civilisation of this innovation or this type of high science. The reason for this innovation may be the secrets which surrounded mummification processes for a long period of time, which completely confused many authors. In addition, the significance of mummification for religious beliefs caused mummification idea to grow in importance from the earliest times of the practice until its apogeum in the New Kingdom.

This paper focuses on three methods of mummification technique in Ancient Egypt, dry natron and others materials, natron solution and heat dehydration. International references in this field have shown the use of these methods.

The results showed that the mummification method using dry natron salt was a successful method. It led to a good preservation for the body. The results revealed that the mummification process did not depend only on the time, as mentioned by Herodotus, but also on many factors such as the rate of natron salts exchange and the ratio of natron volume to body volume. The results also confirm that mummification methods by natron solution and heat dehydration were inffective methods since they failed to preserve the body.

Introduction

The process of mummification in Egypt relied on the desiccation of the soft tissues to effect preservation of the body. Considerable variation in practice and efficacy occurred as mummification evolved from the 4th Dynasty (2613-

2494 B.C.) to its eventual abandonment in the christianised Egypt of the fourth century A.D. [Johnson et al. 1995]. It is believed that the injection of oils, such as cedar oil, was applied during the Middle Kingdom period. Chemical drying (using natron salt) was the most common applied method in Ancient Egypt, especially during the New Kingdom period, which is considered the best period for mummification. Moreover, the religious belief was the initial reason for the mummification process.

There are a lot of different materials used in mummification, such as natron salts, which were used for water extraction through their hygroscopic properties, which is the essential part of the mummification process. It is also mentioned that this salt in its solid state is more preferable than in its soluble form. Other materials needed for the preservation of the body are beeswax, tar, cassia (*Cinnamonum Cassia*), cinnamon (*Cinnamonum Zaeylamicum*), cedar wood oil, henna (*Lawsonia intermisll*), coriander, lichens, onion, palm-wine or date-wine, olive oil, sawdust, bitumen, myrrh, mastic and Arabic gum. The mummy bandages (made of leather, linen and papyrus) were used throughout the mummification periods [Abdel-Maksoud 1995]. There are many discussions concerning the mummification technique in ancient Egypt. Some authors reported that natron salt in solution was used, but some have confirmed that natron salt in its solid state was used while others believe that heat dehydration was also used in the mummification process. This paper aims to analyse the mummification methods (dry natron, natron solution and heat dehydration) according to international references in the field of conservation in order to follow the changes in the applied methods and determine the best mummification method for use in next step for preparing modern mummies (as samples), which will be used in experimental tests for evaluation of the conservation materials of mummies.

Materials and methods

New mummies rats
Disease free white rats were taken from laboratories of the Faculty of Science, Cairo University.

Operating table. The author prepared the mummification table, which was similar to the operating table in Ancient Egypt. This table contains a slanted section on which to place the body (rat body) and a special elliptical part with a small hole (deeper than the former) to infiltrate extraction water from the body.

Natron salts
Some natron was obtained from natron value and more was prepared from artificial sodium components using Sandison's method [Sandison 1963] (six parts of hydrated sodium carbonate, three parts of sodium chloride, one part sodium sulphate and one part sodium bicarbonate). It has been proved that natron salt was used since the fourth dynasty in Ancient Egypt.

Date-wine. This was prepared artificially by the author, since the date was soaked in water for several days and compressed in order to extract the date main liquid. The date wine contains the following main amino acids: lysine, leucine, isoleucine, thresnine, valine, phynylalanine and arginine acid. The other amino acids are as follows: aspartic, cystine, glomatic, glycine, proline, serine, citroline and glutathionic acid. It also contains fat acids as follow: louric, myristic, pentadecanoic, palmitic, margaric, stearic, oleic and linolenic acid. It was used for the washing and sterilization of the abdomen and chest cavities.

Ethyl alcohol (100%) and date-wine were used for the sterlization of vescera, formalin was used for the sterlization of the brain, and natural linen to wrap the mummy using Arabic gum as adhesive for the bandages. Beeswax with trichloroethylene was used to isolate the mummy from climatic conditions.

Permanent dry stuffing materials

Cinnamonum Zaeylanicum. It belongs to the subfamily *Lauraceae*. Its trade name is Celyon Cinnamon. It contains volitale oil (0.8–1.4%), phlobatannin, mucilage, calcium, oxalate, starch and approximetely 60–70% cinnamic aldehydes (C_9H_8O). Oils in Celyon Cinnamon contain phenols (engenol) and hydrocarbons (pinene, phellandrene and caryophyllene).

Cinnamonum Cassia. This also belongs to the subfamily *Lauraceae*. Its trade name is Chinese Cinnamonum. It has been known since approximetely 2700 B.C. It contains pure volitale oil (1–2%) and approximetely 85% cinnamic aldehyde (C_9H_8O) [George, Williams 1976; Balley 1930; James 1982; Redoute, Daffinger 1973].

Arabic gum. This is a poly succharide carbohydrate and its composition is ($C_6H_{10}O_5$)n. It also contains complex salts in its composition, and organic acids, as well as calcium, magnesium and potassium components [Abdel-Hamid 1984].

Mastic. Mastic is exuded and collected from a bushy tree *Pistacia lentiscus*. The solid resin is composed of a mixture of triterpenoids (as is shown in oleanonic acid). It contains volitale oil (2%), 20% resin materials, mastic acid and other materials [Horie 1987].

Beeswax. Beeswax is obtained from the hives of honey bees. It is a complex mixture of hydrocarbons, esters and fatty acids [Horie 1987]. Beeswax has beed used widely especially in the mummification process to cover holes of the eyes, ears and nose [Iskander 1973; Iskander 1980].

Myrrh. This is an oleo-gum-resin. It is obtained from *Commiphora molmol* and *Commiphora abyssinica*. It belongs to the subfamily *Burseraceae*. It contains volitale oil (7–17%), resin (25–40%), gum (57–61%) and impurities (3–4%). Volitale oils in myrrh contains terpenes (Sesquiterpenes), esters, cinnamic aldehydes and phenols (engenol) [Trease, Evans 1976].

Coriander. This contains volitale oil (0.5–1%), mixture oil (13%), tannin and calcium oxalate. The oil obtained from coriander contains alcohols (65–80%) [El-Gamal 1980; El-Gamal 1985].

Olibanum. This is a resin material.

Lichens. It is a symbiotic association between algae and fungus. It contains bromine, iodine and carbohydrates, which is known in lichenin and isolichenin [El-Gamal 1981].

Natron salt. This is composed from sodium salts (chloride, carbonate, bicarbonate and sodiun sulphate).

Temporary stuffing materials

These materials, including dry natron, sand crystals and linen bandages, were soaked in melted Arabic gum.

Mummification techniques

Mummification technique using natron salts and other materials. This technique was as the follow:

1. The corpse of the rat body was placed on the operating table.
2. A hole was opened in the left side of abdomen for the extraction of viscera.
3. The viscera (contents of abdomen and chest cavities) was extracted.
4. The body cavities were sterilized.
5. The body was dehydrated.
6. The body cavities were temporarily stuffed.
7. The temporary stuffing were removed and the body cavities were washed.
8. The body cavities were packed with permanent dry stuffing materials.
9. The face cavities were packed.

Mummification technique using natron solution. The contents of the abdomen and chest cavities were extracted. The body of the rat was soaked in natron solution (prepared from artificial sodium components as mentioned above).

Mummification technique using heat dehydration. The contents of the abdomen and chest cavities were extracted and the sample (body of rat) was placed in the oven at 55°C.

Results and discussion

Mummification technique using natron salts and other materials

The results showed that dry natron gave very good results in the mummification process. It was clear (Figure 1; Table 1) that there is a significant reduction in the weight of the rat body with increasing time of mummification. For example, in sample No. 1, the reduction was 28% after extraction of the viscera and at the last stage of the salt exchange was 49%.

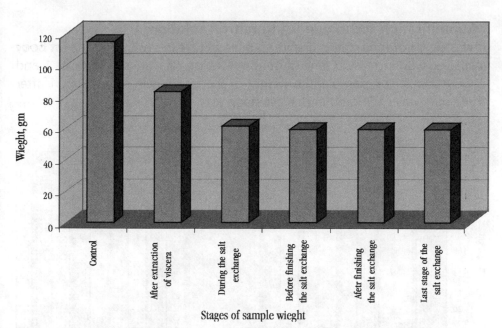

Figure 1.
Effect of mummification technique by dry natron on the weight of the rat body

Stages of sample weight	Weight gm	Date of weight	Numbers of natron salt exchange	Date of natron salt exchange
Sample No. 1				
Before extraction of the viscera	115	25-10-1992	1	25-10-1992
After extraction of the viscera	83	25-10-1992	2	28-10-1992
During the salt exchange	61	21-11-1992	3	1-11-1992
During the salt exchange	59	25-11-1992	4	7-11-1992
Before finishing the salt exchange	59	26-11-1992	5	14-11-1992
Last stage of the salt exchange	59	27-11-1992	6	25-11-1992
Sample No. 2				
Before extraction of the viscera	117	25-10-1992	1	25-10-1992
After extraction of the viscera	89	25-10-1992	2	31-10-1992
During the salt exchange	65	03-11-1992	3	3-11-1993
During the salt exchange	60	26-11-1992	4	12-11-1992
Before finishing the salt exchange	60	27-11-1992	5	19-11-1992
Last stage of the salt exchange	60	28-11-1992	6	26-11-1992
Sample No. 3				
Before extraction of the viscera	120	14-01-1993	1	14-01-1993
After extraction of the viscera	99	14-01-1993	2	18-01-1993
During the salt exchange	75	29-01-1993	3	22-01-1993
During the salt exchange	67	15-02-1993	4	29-01-1993
Before finishing the salt exchange	67	16-02-1993	5	07-02-1993
Last stage of the salt exchange	67	17-02-1993	6	15-02-1993

Table 1.
Mummification by use dry natron

Mummification technique using natron solution

It was clear from the results (Figure 2, Table 2) that the weight of the rat body increased with increasing time of mummification. All results in samples 1 and 2 were minus. For example, the weight of the rat body in sample No. 1 after three days was −16% and in the last stage was −30%.

Figure 2.
Effect of mummification technique by natron solution on the weight of the rat body

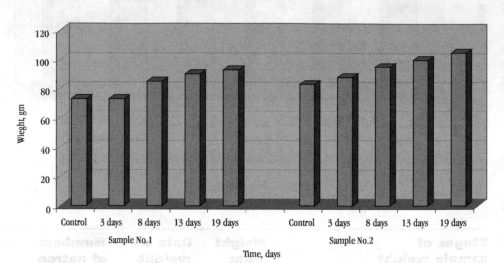

No. of sample	Weight gm	Date of weight	Numbers of natron solution exchange
1	73	04-06-1993	1
	85	07-06-1993	
	90	12-06-1993	2
	93	17-06-1993	
	95	23-06-1993	
2	83	04-06-1993	1
	88	07-06-1993	
	95	12-06-1993	2
	100	17-06-1993	
	105	23-06-1993	

Table 2.
Mummification by use natron solution

Many authors and sientifics differ according to their directions for the use of natron in the mummification process. This was thought to show that the old theory confirmed that natron was used in solution more than in its dry state. Pettigrew [1834] was one of the old school who stated that natron was used as a solution. But his opinion depended on his translation of Herodotus' text.

Smith and Dawson [1924] and David [1978] agreed with Pettigrew. They justified their opinions using the following reasons:
1. the epidermis of the mummies was absent in many cases;
2. some parts of the body were separated;
3. body hairs were often absent;
4. finger and toe nails were often found bundled.

But a new theory confirms that natron was used in its dry state. Lucas [1932 a, 1932 b] was one of the supporters of the new theory who reported that pands's translation of Herodotus' text was wrong. Lucas and others disagreed with reasons given for the old theory and they replied with the following reasons:

1. the absence of the epidermis in many mummies is not an indicator of the use of natron solution but may be due to putrefaction;
2. regarding the separation of some parts of the body, this is a result of the disarrangement of mummies by tomb thieves who transeferred some parts to another place, or to the mummification being poor in some cases [Lucas 1932 b];
3. absence of body hairs: this is due to putrefaction, which cause hairs to fall out with the epidermis; or to using a large amount of natron salts [Lucas 1932 a].

It was noted that the disadvantages of natron solution were as follows:

1. the texture of the body become very soft as a result of putrefaction;
2. it is difficult to treat the bodies without any consideration for deterioration;
3. the bodies continued to deteriorate for some time after removal of the natron solution;
4. the colour of the body changed.

Garner [1986] and Sandison [1986] proved that solution method does not give a well mummified body. They also stated that Egyptians used natron in its dry state. William [1980] confirmed that Iskander mummified groups of ducks by using dry natron method. After thirty years, these groups of ducks are in good condition, although they are exihibited in normal conditions.

On the other hand, it was clear that the mummification process did not take forty days, as was mentioned by Herodotus; but this process may finish before this time. It can take twenty-eight or less, since this process depends on many factors as follow:

1. The condition of the body prior to natron treatment.
   Since a body, which has already begun to exhibit signs of putrefaction may take a long time to achieve a suitable dry condition.
2. The composition of the salt mixture which makes up the natron.
   A good, high mixture of salt, especially sodium carbonate and bicarbonate, gives good mummification.
3. The re-use of natron for more than one body.
   If natron is used for more than one body, the result after the first use will deteriorate.
4. The ratio of natron volume to body volume.
   Under ideal conditions, the volume of natron used should be at least ten times more than body volume.
5. The duration of the natron treatment.
   It was found that the ideal treatment is depend on the climatic conditions. In Ancient Egypt, it was from 35 for human body.

Although, dry natron salts play a very important role in the mummification process, if dry natron salts are not exchanged many time during the mummification process, the decay by insects (*Dermestes vulpinus*) appeared, beginning with the brain and spreading to the whole body.

Mummification by use heat dehydration

It was clear that heat dehydration gave a reduction in the weight of the rat body (Figure 3; Table 3) but at the same time also gave a badly preserved mummified body. For example in sample No.1, the reduction after 24 hours was 20% and after 72 hours was 27%. So it was clear that heat dehydration is an exclusion process.

Figure 3.
Effect of mummification technique using heat dehydration on the weight of the rat body

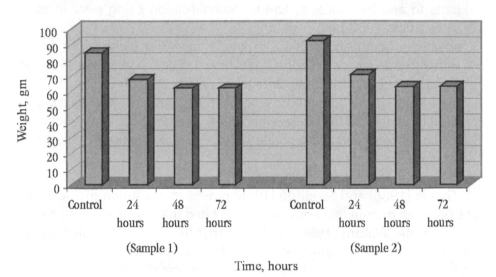

No. of sample	Dehydration period hours	Weight gm
1	Control	85
	24 hours	68
	48 hours	62
	72 hours	62
2	Control	93
	24 hours	71
	48 hours	63
	72 hours	63

Table 3.
Mummification by use heat dehydration

Dawson mentioned the use of heat dehydration in mummification because he had seen a lot of dry mummies in some tombs and he had seen traces of carbons, so he suggested that fire was used in the mummification process. But Lucas saw that the tombs might have been inhabited. Lucas also mentioned that there is no indication of the use of fire in the mummification process and he reported that this method was not used because:

1. fuel in Ancient Egypt was costly and rare;
2. it was not necessary, because general dehydration by natron was used;
3. Herodotus did not mention anything about heat (fire source) mummification.

It can be said that heat source may be used during the mummification process in order to remove any contamination, or the mummy can be exposed to heat source at the beginning of the mummification in order to sterilize the body, and the mummy will then be ready for subsequent steps using dry natron and other materials.

Conclusions

1. It was concluded that artificial natron (sodium components) was very effective for the extraction of water from the body of the rat.
2. The date-wine, which was prepared artificially, gave good results in washing and sterilization of the abdomen and chest cavities in some mummified samples.
3. The main operation in the mummification process consists in using dry natron salts, which extract water.
4. From examination of insects under a microscope, it was clear that *Dermestes vulpinus* was the most dominant insect during the mummification process.
5. Mummification by heat dehydration was ruled out, since it led to the separation of the rat skin and gave a soft body.
6. Mummification by natron solution also gave bad results, since the rat body was swollen, with separation and fall of hairs, a soft body and increase in the body weight.

References

H. Abdel-Hamid, *Scientific Procedure for Conservation of Organic Materials (Manuscripts, Woods and Textiles)*, Cairo 1984, 167

G. M. M. Abdel-Maksoud, *Experimental and applied study for treatment and conservation of mummies with application on an ancient mummy*, Master Thesis, Conservation Department, Faculty of Archaeology, Cairo University, 1995, 1-47

L. H. Balley, *The Standard Encyclopedia of Horticulture*, London 1930, 680

A. R. David, *Mysteries of the Mummies*, London 1978, 74

S. Y. El-Gamal, *Ancient Egyptian mummification*, Institute of Papyrus, Ain Shams University, 1980, 8

S. Y. El-Gamal, *Ancient Egyptian aromatics*, Institute of Papyrus, Ain Shams University, 1985, 9

S. Y. El-Gamal, *The use of microorganisms in Ancient Egypt*, Institute of Papyrus, Ain Shams University, 1981, 1

R. C. Garner, *Experimental mummification of rats*, in: *Science in Egyptology*, London 1986, 11

E. George, C. E. Williams, *Pharmacognosy*, London 1976, 440-441

C. V. Horie, *Materials for Conservation*, London 1987, 145-147

Z. Iskander, *Mummification in Ancient Egypt*, Cairo 1973, 14

Z. Iskander, *Mummification in Ancient Egypt. Development, History and Techniques*, in: *An X-Ray Atlas of the Royal Mummies*, Chicago–London 1980, 10

E. F. James, *Martindale*, London 1982, 673

C. Johnson, B. Wills, T. Peacock, G. Bott, *The conservation of an Egyptian mummy, cartonnage cover and mask*, in: *Conservation in Ancient Egyptian Collections, Archetype*, London 1995, 47

A. Lucas, *The occurrence of natron in Ancient Egypt*, Journal of Egyptian Archaeology 18 (1932a), 63

A. Lucas, *The use of natron in mummification*, Journal of Egyptian Archaeology 18 (1932b), 127

T. J. Pettigrew, *A History of Egyptian Mummies*, London, 1834, 40

A. Redoute and P. Daffinger, *Herbs and Medicinal Flowers*, New York 1973, 42

A. T. Sandison, *Human Mummification Technique in Ancient Egyptians*, in: *Science in Egyptology*, London 1986, 5-6

A. T. Sandison, *The use of natron in mummification in Ancient Egypt*, Journal of Near Eastern Studies 22 (1963), 259-267

E. G. Smith, W. R. Dawson, *Egyptian Mummies*, London 1924, 51-58

G. E. Trease, W. C. Evans, in: *Pharmacognosy*, London 1976, 314

H. P. William, *Mummies in Ancient Egypt*, in: *Mummies and Ancient Cultures*, New York 1980, 22

Gomaa Mohamed Mahmoud Abdel-Maksoud

Conservation of Egyptian mummies.
Part II: Survey study for the highest occurrence of microorganisms on Egyptian mummies

Microbial contamination is a serious problem in Egyptian mummies exposed to high relative humidity and a non ventilated environment. This paper represents an attempt to carry out a survey of the most dominant microorganisms in order to help the conservator to test it on the used mummification materials and to refer the state of mummies in some archaeological sites in Egypt to determine the state of biodeterioration of these mummies to make a plan in the future for monitoring the condition of mummies in museum stores and display. The results revealed that *Bacillus* sp., *Eriwina* sp., *Micrococus* sp., *Streptomyces* sp., *Aspergillus* sp., *Penicillum* sp., *Alternaria* sp. and *Fusarium sp.* were the most frequently occurring microorganisms on the studied samples.

Introduction

Many museums and stores are exposed to inappropriate environments that produce serious alterations in archaeological materials including mummy skin and other proteinaceous objects. The growth of microorganisms in organic materials such as mummies is basically dependent on the presence of water, although, other factors such as moisture content in combination with temperature should be taken into consideration to understand the biodeterioration mechanism [Valentin 1996]. Mummies in most stores and museums in Egypt suffer from microbiological attack by bacteria, actinomycetes and fungi, since the conditions are often unsuitable and the influences of the environment, including high relative humidity, temperature, and the harmful effects of atmospheric condition (such as sulphur dioxide etc.) are unfavourable. This study aims to isolate and identify bacteria, actinomycetes and fungi in some mummies from some archaeological sites in order to use the results in a subsequent study on the ability of these microorganisms in deterioration of used mummification materials.

Studied samples

The samples were collected from the following stores and museums:

The Museum store of the Medical Faculty of Cairo University: the samples were taken from different parts of a destroyed mummy.

The store of the Graeco-Roman Museum: the samples were taken from different mummies, which date back to the Graeco-Roman period.

The store and Museum at Com-Osheem: the samples were taken from three mummies, one of them a child.

The Agricultural Museum: the samples were taken from human and animal mummies.

Tanta Museum: the samples were taken from linen bandages and from dust around a mummy.

Media used

To isolate microorganisms from studied samples to determine the decay activities, the following growth media are used.

(1) Media for bacteria

(a) Nutrient yeast extract agar

Beef extract 3 gm, peptone 5 gm, yeast extract 1 gm, sodium chloride 5 gm, agar 20 gm and distilled water 1000 mm with pH 7.

(b) Nutrient yeast extract broth

As the last media but without agar.

(c) Tryptone glucose yeast extract agar

Tryptone 5 gm, glucose 2 gm, yeast extract 3 gm, agar 18 gm and distilled water 1000 mm with pH 7.

(2) Media for actinomysetes

(a) Jensen medium

Glucose 2 gm, casein 0.2 gm, R_2HPO_4 0.5 gm, $FeCL_3$ $6H_2O$ traces, $MgSo_4$. $7H_2O$ 0.2 gm, agar 20 gm and tap water 1000 mm with pH 6.5–6.6.

(3) Media for fungi

(a) Sabouraud's dextrose agar

Myclogical peptone 10 gm, dextrose 40 gm, agar 18 gm and distilled water 1000 mm with pH 5.2.

(b) Waksman's medium

Glucose 10 gm, peptone 5 gm, magnisum sulphite 5 gm, agar 15 gm and distilled water 1000 mm with pH 5.5.

(c) Czapek's medium

Sucrose 30 gm, Na No_3 2 gm, KH_2PO_4 1 gm, $MgSo_4$. $7H_2O$ 0.5 gm, Kcl 0.5 gm, Fe_2So_4. $7H_2O$ 0.01gm, agar 15 gm, and tap water 1000 mm with pH 5.5–6 [Abdel-Maksoud 1995].

Purification and identification

The developed microorganisms were isolated in pure cultures on the following media: Czapek-dox agar and malt extract agar [Booth 1971] for fungi. Carbon utilization medium [ibidem] for actinomycetes. Peptone agar medium for bacteria.

Bacteria and actinomycetes were identified according to Bergey's manual [Buchnan, Gibbon 1989] and the fungi isolated were identified according to Raper and Fennell [1965], Raper and Thom [1949], Barnett and Hunter [1972] and Domsch, Gams and Anderson [1980].

Results and discussion

It is well documented that mummies are particulary susceptible to biodeterioration due to their hygroscopicity. It was clear from data (Table 1) that the most dominant bacteria were *Bacillus subtilis* (18.56%), *Bacillus coagulans* (13.77%), *Micrococus agilis* (12.57%), *Bacillus brevis* and *Micrococus varians* (7.78%), *Bacillus megaterim* and *Micrococus roseus* (6.58%), *Micrococus lylae* (5.98%), *Bacillus cereus* (4.19%), *Eriwina citimaaculans* (2.99%), *Bacillus licheniformis* (2.39%), *Bacillus pumilus* and *Eriwina chryssanthemi* (1.79%). For actinomycetes (Table 2), *Streptomyces* sp. was isolated. The dominent fungi (Table 3) were *Aspergillus* sp., *Penicillum* sp., *Alternaria* sp., and *Fusarium* sp. All results showed that all the studied samples were deteriorated by microorganisms, but that the degree of biodeterioration differed from place to place. This variation was due to the conditions in the store or the museum. Conclusions from this biodeterioration pro-

Isolated bacteria	Isolating source	No. of isolated species	Percentage of isolated species (%)
Bacillus subtilis	The store of Anatomy Museum	31	18.56
Bacillus cereus	The store of Anatomy Museum	7	4.19
Bacillus megaterim	The store of Anatomy Museum	11	6.58
Bacillus coagulans	The store of the Graeco-Roman Museum	23	13.77
Bacillus licheniformis	The store of Anatomy Museum, Tanta Museum	4	2.39
Bacillus pumilus	Com-Osheem Museum	3	1.79
Bacillus brevis	The store of the Graeco-Roman Museum, Tanta Museum	13	7.78
Eriwina citimaaculans	The Agricultural Museum, Tanta Museum	5	2.99
Eriwina chryssanthemi	The Agricultural Museum	3	1.79
Micrococus agilis	Tanta Museum, The store of the Graeco-Roman Museum	21	12.57
Micrococus lylae	The store of Anatomy Museum, The Agricultural Museum	10	5.98
Micrococus luteus	Com-Osheem Museum	12	7.18
Micrococus varians	The Agricultural Museum	13	7.78
Micrococus roseus	The store of the Graeco-Roman Museum, the Agricultural Museum	11	6.58
	Total of isolates	**167**	**100.00**

Table 1.
Occurrence bacteria on Egyptian mummies

Isolated actinomycetes	Isolating source	No. of isolated species	Percentage of isolated species (%)
Streptomyces sp.	The store of Anatomy Museum	2	18.18
Streptomyces sp.	The store of the Graeco-Roman Museum		
Streptomyces sp.	The Agricultural Museum	5	45.45
	Total of isolates	**11**	**100.00**

Table 2.
Occurrence
actinomycetes on
Egyptian mummies

Isolated fungi	Isolating source	No. of isolated species	Percentage of isolated species (%)
Aspergillus niger	It was isolated from all studied samples	16	21.91
Aspergillus terreus	The store of Anatomy Museum,		
	The store of the Graeco-Roman Museum	4	5.47
Aspergillus flavus	The Agricultural Museum,		
	the store of the Graeco-Roman Museum	22	30.13
Penicillum granufatum	The Agricultural Museum, the store of Anatomy Museum	15	20.54
Penicillum rubrum	The store of the Graeco-Roman Museum	5	6.84
Penicillum chrysogenum	The store of the Graeco-Roman Museum, Com-Osheem Museum	3	4.10
Alternaria sp.	The Agricultural Museum,		
	The store of the Graeco-Roman Museum	3	4.10
Fusarium sp.	Store of Graeco-Roman Museum,		
	Tanta Museum	5	6.84
	Total of isolates	**73**	**100.00**

Table 3.
Occurrence fungi on
Egyptian mummies

cess can be as follows: the growth of microorganisms in mummies is basically dependent on the presence of water. However, other factors such as moisture content in combination with temperature should be taken into consideration in order to understand the biodeterioration mechanism. The moisture content indicates the safe humidity at which the material should be exposed. The initial development of microorganisms on an object depends on the characteristics of the surface and the hygroscopic moisture of the material. Some surfaces can easily retain water available for spores germination. So, the studied samples from museums and stores collections are susceptible to biodeterioration, since they are exposed to relative humidity (RH) of over 65%, especially in the store of the Graeco-Roman Museum (Alexandria city).

On the other hand, the effect of light in combination with other agents such as temperature, relative humidity and ventilation should be borne in mind to explain the biodeterioration process especially in the Agricultural Museum. In this museum the ventilation is not good. In fact, ventilation is essential to maintain low biological activity and microbial growth in museums and store collections.

Ventilation achieves:

1. a significant decrease in water activity;
2. a decrease in moisture content;
3. an increase in the movement of spores, which can be transported by air currents hindering the germination of microorganisms and their growth initial;
4. it avoids the condensation process produced on cold surfaces [Valentin 1996].

Pollution (especially Agricultural Museum, and store of Anatomy Museum in Cairo city including dust particles are other factors involved in biodeterioration of mummies. The adequate combination of these factors contributes to the development of fungi, bacteria and actinomycetes on Egyptian mummies.

Conculusions

1. Biodeterioration of mummies included undesirable aggressive activity of microorganisms not only on the surface of bandages but also on the bodies of mummies theirself.
2. Microbial investigation has demonstrated that mummies are more sensitive to be colonised by bacteria and fungi than actinomycetes.
3. Mummies in the store of Anatomy Museum, the store of the Graeco-Roman Museum and Agricultural Museum were more deteriorated by microorganisms than in Tanta Museum and Com-Osheem Museum.

References

G. M. M. Abdel-Maksoud, *Experimental and applied study for treatment and conservation of mummies with application on an ancient mummy*, Master Thesis, Conservation Department, Faculty of Archaeology, Cairo University, 1995, 150-155

H. L. Barnett, B. B. Hunter, *Illustrated Genera of Imperfect Fungi*, 3rd ed., Minnesota 1972

R. E. Buchnan, N. E. Gibbon, *Bergey's Manual of Determinative Bacteriology*, Baltimore 1989

C. Booth, *Methods in Microbiology*, Vols 3-4, London 1971

K. H. Domsch, W. Gams, T. H. Anderson, *Compendium of Soil Fungi*, Vols 1-2, London 1980

K. B. Raper, D. I. Fennell, *The Genus Aspergillus*, Baltimore 1965

K. B. Raper, C. Thom, *Manual of the Penicillia*, Baltimore 1949

N. Valentin, *Assessment of biodeterioration processes in organic materials. Control methods*, in: *International Conference on Conservation and Restoration of Archive and Library Materials, 22nd-29th April 1996*, Vol.1, Rome, Instituto centrale per la patologia del libro, 1996, 195

List of authors

Gomaa Mohamed Mahmoud Abdel-Maksoud
Department of Conservation
Faculty of Archaeology
Cairo University
Giza, Egypt

Barbara Aleksiejew-Wantuch
5, Zyblikiewicza St.
31-029 Kraków, Poland

Krzysztof Babraj
Department of Mediterranean Archaeology
Archaeological Museum
3, Senacka St.
31-002 Kraków, Poland

Józefa Białka
Department of Toxicology
Institute of Forensic Medicine
Collegium Medicum, Jagiellonian University
16, Grzegórzecka St.
31-531 Kraków, Poland

Jakub Czarny
The Ludwik Rydygier University School of Medical Sciences
The Forensic Medicine Institute
9, Skłodowskiej-Curie St.
85-094 Bydgoszcz, Poland

Birgit Gerisch
Max-Planck-Institut für molekulare Genetik
Ihnestr. 73
D-14195 Berlin-Dahlem, Germany

Tomasz Grzybowski
The Ludwik Rydygier University School of Medical Sciences
The Forensic Medicine Institute
9, Skłodowskiej-Curie St.
85-094 Bydgoszcz, Poland

Maria Kaczmarek
Institut of Anthropology
Adam Mickiewicz University
10, Fredry St.
61-701 Poznań, Poland

Małgorzata Kłys
Department of Toxicology
Institute of Forensic Medicine
Collegium Medicum, Jagiellonian University
16, Grzegórzecka St.
31-531 Kraków, Poland

Teresa Lech
Institute of Forensic Research
9, Westerplatte St.
31-039 Kraków, Poland

Maria Lityńska-Zając
Institute of Archaeology and Ethnology
Polish Academy of Sciences
17, Sławkowska St.
31-016 Kraków, Poland

Danuta Miścicka-Śliwka
The Ludwik Rydygier University School of Medical Sciences
The Forensic Medicine Institute,
9, Skłodowskiej-Curie St.
85-094 Bydgoszcz, Poland

Andrzej Niwiński
Institut of Archaeology
Warsaw University
26/28, Krakowskie Przedmieście St.
00-927 Warszawa, Poland

Barbara Opolska-Bogusz
Department of Toxicology
Institute of Forensic Medicine
Collegium Medicum, Jagiellonian University
16, Grzegórzecka St.
31-531 Kraków, Poland

Marian Paciorek
Department of Artwork Conservation and Restoration
Fine Arts Academy
9, Smoleńsk St.
31-108 Kraków, Poland

Barbara Próchnicka
Department of Toxicology
Institute of Forensic Medicine
Collegium Medicum, Jagiellonian University
16, Grzegórzecka St.
31-531 Kraków, Poland

Agnieszka Sutkowska
Department of Plant Breeding and Seed Science
Agricultural University of Cracow
24, Łobzowska St.
31-140 Kraków, Poland

Hanna Szymańska
Department of Mediterranean Archaeology
Archaeological Museum
3, Senacka St.
31-002 Kraków, Poland

Katarzyna Tempczyk
40, Korotyńskiego St.
02-123 Warszawa, Poland

Joanna Trąbska
Department of Conservation
Archaeological Museum
3, Senacka St.
31-002 Kraków, Poland

Barbara Trybalska
University of Mining and Metallurgy
30, Mickiewicza Ave.
30-059 Kraków, Poland

Andrzej Urbanik
Chair and Department of Radiology
Collegium Medicum
Jagiellonian University
19, Kopernika St.
31-501 Kraków, Poland

Marcin Woźniak
The Ludwik Rydygier University School of Medical Sciences
The Forensic Medicine Institute
9, Skłodowskiej-Curie St.
85-094 Bydgoszcz, Poland

Janina Zięba-Palus
Institute of Forensic Research
9, Westerplatte St.
31-039 Kraków, Poland

Polska Akademia Umiejętności
ul. Sławkowska 17, 31-016 Kraków , Poland
tel. (48 12) 424 02 12, fax (48 12) 422 54 22
e-mail: office@pau.krakow.pl